Lecture Notes in Computer Science   11143

Commenced Publication in 1973
Founding and Former Series Editors:
Gerhard Goos, Juris Hartmanis, and Jan van Leeuwen

More information about this series at http://www.springer.com/series/7410

Robert Krimmer · Melanie Volkamer
Véronique Cortier · Rajeev Goré
Manik Hapsara · Uwe Serdült
David Duenas-Cid (Eds.)

Electronic Voting

Third International Joint Conference, E-Vote-ID 2018
Bregenz, Austria, October 2–5, 2018
Proceedings

 Springer

Editors
Robert Krimmer (iD)
Tallinn University of Technology
Tallinn
Estonia

Melanie Volkamer (iD)
Karlsruhe Institute of Technology
Karlsruhe
Germany

Véronique Cortier
LORIA
Vandoeuvre-lès-Nancy Cedex
France

Rajeev Goré
Australian National University
Canberra, ACT
Australia

Manik Hapsara (iD)
University of New South Wales
Canberra, ACT
Australia

Uwe Serdült (iD)
Ritsumeikan University
Kusatsu, Shiga
Japan

David Duenas-Cid (iD)
Tallinn University of Technology
Tallinn
Estonia

ISSN 0302-9743   ISSN 1611-3349   (electronic)
Lecture Notes in Computer Science
ISBN 978-3-030-00418-7   ISBN 978-3-030-00419-4   (eBook)
https://doi.org/10.1007/978-3-030-00419-4

Library of Congress Control Number: 2018953823

LNCS Sublibrary: SL4 – Security and Cryptology

This Springer imprint is published by the registered company Springer Nature Switzerland AG
The registered company address is: Gewerbestrasse 11, 6330 Cham, Switzerland

Preface

This volume contains papers presented at E-Vote-ID 2018, the Third International Joint Conference on Electronic Voting, held during October 2–5, 2018, in Bregenz, Austria. It resulted from the merging of EVOTE and Vote-ID.

In total, more than 800 experts from over 35 countries have attended the conference series over the last 14 years. This shows that the conference continues to be one of the major events in the field of electronic voting, providing ample room for interdisciplinary and open discussion of all issues relating to electronic voting.

Also, this year, the conference consisted of:

- Security, Usability and Technical Issues Track
- Administrative, Legal, Political and Social Issues Track
- Election and Practical Experiences Track
- PhD Colloquium on the day before the conference

This year's edition, E-VOTE-ID 2018, received 45 submissions, being, each of them, reviewed by 3 to 4 program committee members, using a double blind-review process. As a result, 13 papers were accepted for this volume, representing 29% of the submitted proposals. The selected papers cover a wide range of topics connected with electronic voting, including experiences and revisions of the real uses of E-voting systems and corresponding processes in elections.

Special thanks go to the members of the international program committee for their hard work in reviewing, discussing, and shepherding papers. They ensured the high quality of these proceedings with their knowledge and experience. We would also like to thank the German Informatics Society (Gesellschaft für Informatik) with its ECOM working group for their partnership over many years.

October 2018

Robert Krimmer
Melanie Volkamer
Véronique Cortier
Rajeev Goré
Manik Hapsara
Uwe Serdült
David Duenas-Cid

Organization

Program Committee

Myrto Arapinis	The University of Edinburgh, UK
Roberto Araujo	Universidade Federal do Pará, Brazil
Jordi Barrat i Esteve	eVoting Legal Lab, Catalonia
Josh Benaloh	Microsoft, USA
David Bismark	Votato, Sweden
Nadja Braun Binder	University of Zurich, Switzerland
Christian Bull	The Norwegian Ministry of Local Government and Regional Development, Norway
Susanne Caarls	Election Consultant, Netherlands
Gianpiero Catozzi	UNDP, USA
Véronique Cortier	CNRS, Loria, France
Stephanie Delaune	IRISA, France
Ardita Driza Maurer	Zentrum für Demokratie Aarau and Zurich University, Switzerland
David Duenas-Cid	Tallinn University of Technology, Estonia
Aleksander Essex	University of Western Ontario, Canada
Joshua Franklin	NIST, USA
David Galindo	University of Birmingham, UK
Micha Germann	Katholieke Universiteit Leuven, Belgium
J. Paul Gibson	Mines-Télécom, France
Kristian Gjøsteen	Norwegian University of Science and Technology, Norway
Nicole Goodman	University of Toronto, Canada
Rajeev Goré	Australian National University, Australia
Ruediger Grimm	University of Koblenz, Germany
Rolf Haenni	Bern University of Applied Sciences, Switzerland
Thomas Haines	Queensland University of Technology, Australia
Thad Hall	MPR, USA
Manik Hapsara	The University of New South Wales, Australia
Toby James	University of East Anglia, UK
Tarmo Kalvet	Ragnar Nurkse School of Innovation and Governance at Tallinn University of Technology, Estonia
Norbert Kersting	University of Münster, Germany
Aggelos Kiayias	National and Kapodistrian University Athens, Greece
Shin Kim	Hallym University, South Korea
Reto Koenig	Bern University of Applied Sciences, Switzerland
Robert Krimmer	Ragnar Nurkse School of Innovation and Governance at Tallinn University of Technology, Estonia

Contents

Computing the Margin of Victory in Preferential Parliamentary Elections. . . .   1
Michelle Blom, Peter J. Stuckey, and Vanessa J. Teague

Ballot-Polling Risk Limiting Audits for IRV Elections.   17
Michelle Blom, Peter J. Stuckey, and Vanessa J. Teague

The Threat of SSL/TLS Stripping to Online Voting.   35
Anthony Cardillo and Aleksander Essex

Modular Formalisation and Verification of STV Algorithms   51
Milad K. Ghale, Rajeev Goré, Dirk Pattinson, and Mukesh Tiwari

Online Voting in Indigenous Communities: Lessons from Canada.   67
Nicole Goodman, Chelsea Gabel, and Brian Budd

Process Models for Universally Verifiable Elections   84
Rolf Haenni, Eric Dubuis, Reto E. Koenig, and Philipp Locher

Model Checking the SELENE E-Voting Protocol in Multi-agent Logics   100
Wojciech Jamroga, Michal Knapik, and Damian Kurpiewski

How Much Does an e-Vote Cost? Cost Comparison per Vote
in Multichannel Elections in Estonia   117
Robert Krimmer, David Duenas-Cid, Iuliia Krivonosova, Priit Vinkel,
and Arne Koitmae

Implementing an Audio Side Channel for Paper Voting.   132
Kristjan Krips, Jan Willemson, and Sebastian Värv

The E-voting Readiness Index and the Netherlands   146
Leontine Loeber

Winning the Election, but Losing the Litigation: A Prognosis of Nigerian
Judicial Attitudes Toward Evidence Produced
from 'E-Accreditation Machines'.   160
Felix Oludare Omosele

Risk-Limiting Audits by Stratified Union-Intersection Tests
of Elections (SUITE).   174
Kellie Ottoboni, Philip B. Stark, Mark Lindeman, and Neal McBurnett

Rounding Considered Harmful   189
Carsten Schürmann

Author Index   203

Contents

Computing the Margin of Victory
in Preferential Parliamentary Elections

Michelle Blom[✉], Peter J. Stuckey, and Vanessa J. Teague

School of Computing and Information Systems, The University of Melbourne,
Parkville, Australia
{michelle.blom,p.stuckey,vjteague}@unimelb.edu.au

Abstract. We show how to use automated computation of election margins to assess the number of votes that would need to change in order to alter a parliamentary outcome for single-member preferential electorates. In the context of increasing automation of Australian electoral processes, and accusations of deliberate interference in elections in Europe and the USA, this work forms the basis of a rigorous statistical audit of the parliamentary election outcome. Our example is the New South Wales Legislative Council election of 2015, but the same process could be used for any similar parliament for which data was available, such as the Australian House of Representatives.

1 Introduction

The party that wins a majority of seats in a parliamentary election may not be the party that wins a majority of votes. This has been examined extensively in the United States [7,8]. In Australian parliamentary elections, even the notion of a "popular majority" is poorly defined because Australian voters rank their candidates in order of preference. But similar results occur: sometimes in practice the Parliamentary winner is not the popular majority winner and there are even some systematic biases [2]. Nevertheless it is often assumed by the public and the media that a party that wins a comfortable overall margin will comfortably win the parliamentary election. Of course, this is not necessarily true.

In this paper we focus on computing the Parliamentary election margin: the minimal number of votes that need to be changed, in a particular election outcome, to switch the Parliamentary winner. This may be much less than the margin between the popular votes of the two major parties.

There are two ways that an Australian parliamentary election may be closer than it seems. First, there may be many seats held by a very small margin. Second, even within one seat, the margin may be smaller than it appears. Australia's preferential voting system proceeds by iteratively eliminating candidates until only two remain, then selecting the one with a larger tally of votes. A naive observer might think that the margin of victory is the number of votes that need to be switched to reverse the winner in this last step (*i.e.* half the difference in the final tallies)—we call this the *last-round margin*. The true margin may be

© Springer Nature Switzerland AG 2018
R. Krimmer et al. (Eds.): E-Vote-ID 2018, LNCS 11143, pp. 1–16, 2018.
https://doi.org/10.1007/978-3-030-00419-4_1

much smaller, however, as changing an early elimination step may cascade into a completely different elimination order. Computing the correct margin for preferential voting is, in general, a computationally difficult problem, but an efficient solution has been demonstrated [1].

In earlier work, Blom et al. [1] present an algorithm for computing the margin of victory in Instant Runoff Voting (IRV) elections (also commonly referred to as Alternative Vote elections). In an Australian state or federal Parliamentary election, an IRV election is held in each of a number of districts, electing a single candidate to a seat in the lower house. The party (or coalition of parties) that holds the majority of seats in the lower house, wins the election. Recall that Australian voters rank candidates in order of preference (for example, the ranking [a, c, b] expresses a first preference for candidate a, a second for c, and a third for b). A change to a vote replaces its ranking over candidates with an alternate ranking (for example, replacing ranking [a, c, b] with [c, b, a]). In this paper, we are interested in computing the smallest number of votes (of those cast) that need to be changed to ensure that a different party (or coalition of parties) wins the majority of seats, or that no party (or specific coalition of parties) wins a majority of seats (leading to a hung parliament). Computing the Parliamentary election margin requires a slight modification to the algorithm of [1], in that we must compute the margin of victory *with respect to a specific set of alternate winners* in each seat.

For example, to determine how many votes we would need to change to ensure that Labor wins a majority of seats (in place of the Liberal/National coalition), we would look at manipulations in which seats won by non-Labor candidates are consequently awarded to the Labor candidate.[1] A process of sorting the seats in increasing order of margin, and adding the margins in the necessary number of seats yields the desired Parliamentary election margin.

As a case study, we use data from the 2015 NSW state election to compute the margin by which the Liberal/National coalition won. The popular margin was high—the Liberal/National coalition won 46% of formal first-preference votes compared with 34% for the Labor parties and 10% for The Greens.[2] The coalition won 54 seats compared to Labor's 34. We find, however, that the number of votes necessary to switch the parliamentary outcome is less than 0.1%.

In prior work on US IRV elections, Blom et al. [1] found that the true margin is almost always the last-round margin, though exceptions did occur. This is also true of the NSW 2015 election where, for example, the Lismore seat has a last-round margin of 1173, but the true margin of victory is only 209 votes.

The source code used to compute our results is located at:

https://github.com/michelleblom/margin-irv

These techniques could be easily applied to any parliamentary outcome for which complete vote data was available. This analysis could become standard procedure for any parliamentary election with automated ballot scanning.

---

[1] The Liberal, National, and Labor parties are three Australian political parties.
[2] This is from http://pastvtr.elections.nsw.gov.au/SGE2015/la/state/formal/index.htm.

1.1 Notation

Below we give common three letter codes used to refer to parties in the 2015 New South Wales (NSW) state election.

LAB Australian Labor Party
CLP Country Labor Party
LIB Liberal Party of Australia
NAT National Party of Australia
GRN Australian Greens
IND Independent (belonging to no party).

1.2 Summary of Results

Of the 4.56 million votes cast in the 2015 New South Wales state election, we have determined that it would have taken:

- 22,746 vote changes for the Labor/Country Labor party to gain the 13 additional seats they need to win government (with 47 seats),
- 16,349 vote changes for a Labor/Greens coalition to gain the 10 additional seats they need to win government, and
- 10,398 vote changes to lose the Liberal/National coalition 8 seats and hence produce a hung parliament.

1.3 Auditing and Accuracy Testing in Elections

The margin computation tools presented in this paper can be used, whenever data[3] is available, to check automatically whether a known problem in an election was large enough to change the outcome. Similarly, when a known number of votes were received over an insecure or unscrutinisable channel, this could be used to decide whether that might have been enough to alter the outcome.

Conversely, it could be used to generate evidence that the election outcome is right.

These calculations could be used as the basis for a rigorous risk-limiting audit to confirm (or overturn) the announced election outcome. Risk limiting audits [4] take an iterative random sample of the paper ballots to check how well they reflect the announced outcome. An audit has *risk-limit* α if a mistaken outcome is guaranteed to be detected with a probability of at least $1 - \alpha$. Either the audit concludes with a certain confidence that the outcome is right, or it finds so many errors that a full manual recount is warranted. The audit process is parameterised by the margin of victory in the election. Kroll *et al.* [3] have devised audits for parliamentary outcomes but, like most US research, they focus on simple first-past-the-post elections in which the margin is obvious.

---

[3] An electronic record of the preferences expressed in each paper ballot, after scanning and digitisation.

Initially, all candidates remain standing (are not eliminated)
While there is *more than one* candidate standing
    For every candidate c standing
        Tally (count) the votes in which c is the highest-ranked
        candidate of those standing
    Eliminate the candidate with the smallest tally
The winner is the one candidate not eliminated

Fig. 1. The IRV counting algorithm: the candidate with the smallest tally is repeatedly eliminated, with the ballots in their tally redistributed to remaining candidates according to their next preference.

This is particularly important now that the Australian Parliament's Joint Standing Committee on Electoral Matters has recommended automated scanning of the ballot papers [6]. The overall Parliamentary margin could be quickly calculated using our methods. Rigorous risk-limiting audits could then be performed for each electorate, immediately after the election, in order to provide evidence that the overall election outcome was correct.

In a time where outside influencing of elections is a constant source of news, and where more and more elections systems involve electronic systems, either for voting or counting votes, it is critical that we have mechanisms in place to generate evidence of accurate election results, and indeed to check what degree of manipulation must have taken place for the election result to have been altered.

2 Background

The lower houses of parliaments in the Australian federal and state elections are the result of a number of independent Instant Runoff Voting (IRV) elections for a set of single-member electorates (seats). Each seat has a number of candidates, and each vote consists of an ordered list of the candidates for that seat.[4]

The tallying of votes in an IRV election proceeds by a series of rounds in which the candidate with the lowest number of votes is eliminated (see Fig. 1) with the last remaining candidate declared the winner. All votes in an eliminated candidate's tally are distributed to the next most-preferred (remaining) candidate in their ranking.

Let $\mathcal{C}$ be the set of candidates in an IRV election $\mathcal{B}$. We refer to sequences of candidates π in list notation (e.g., $\pi = [c_1, c_2, c_3, c_4]$), and use such sequences to represent both votes and elimination orders. We will often treat a sequence as the set of elements it contains. An election $\mathcal{B}$ is defined as a multiset[5] of votes, each vote $b \in \mathcal{B}$ a sequence of candidates in $\mathcal{C}$, with no duplicates, listed in order of preference (most preferred to least preferred). Let $first(\pi)$ denote the first candidate appearing in sequence π (e.g., $first([c_2, c_3]) = c_2$). In each round of

---

[4] Most Australian elections require all preferences to be filled in, but some allow partial lists or several equal-last candidates. Our analysis extends to all these cases.

[5] A multiset allows for the inclusion of duplicate items.

vote counting, there are a current set of eliminated candidates $\mathcal{E}$ and a current set of candidates still standing $\mathcal{S} = \mathcal{C} \setminus \mathcal{E}$. The winner c_w of the election is the last standing candidate.

Each candidate $c \in \mathcal{C}$ has a *tally* of votes. Votes are added to this tally upon the elimination of a candidate $c' \in \mathcal{C} \setminus \{c\}$, and are redistributed from this tally upon the elimination of c.

Definition 1. Tally $t_{\mathcal{S}}(c)$: *Given candidates $\mathcal{S} \subseteq \mathcal{C}$ are still standing in an election $\mathcal{B}$, the tally for candidate $c \in \mathcal{C}$, denoted $t_{\mathcal{S}}(c)$, is defined as the number of votes $b \in \mathcal{B}$ for which c is the most-preferred candidate of those remaining. Let $p_{\mathcal{S}}(b)$ denote the sequence of candidates mentioned in b that are also in $\mathcal{S}$.*

$$t_{\mathcal{S}}(c) = \mid [b \mid b \in \mathcal{B}, c = \text{first}(p_{\mathcal{S}}(b))] \mid \tag{1}$$

Definition 2. Margin of Victory (MOV): *The MOV in an election with candidates $\mathcal{C}$ and winner $c_w \in \mathcal{C}$, is the smallest number of votes whose ranking must be modified (by an adversary) so that a candidate $c' \in \mathcal{C} \setminus \{c_w\}$ is elected.*

Often the last round margin (LRM) is used as a proxy for the margin of victory.

Definition 3. Last Round Margin (LRM): *The LRM of an election, in which two candidates $\mathcal{S} = \{c, c'\}$ remain with $t_{\mathcal{S}}(c)$ and $t_{\mathcal{S}}(c')$ votes in their tallies, is equal to half the difference between the tallies of c and c' rounded up.*

$$LRM = \lceil \frac{|t_{\mathcal{S}}(c) - t_{\mathcal{S}}(c')|}{2} \rceil \tag{2}$$

In this paper, we are interested in a more restricted version of margin of victory, which is the margin of victory over a subset of the non-winning candidates.

Definition 4. Margin of Victory over Candidates $\mathcal{A}$ (MOVC): *The MOVC in an election with candidates $\mathcal{C}$ and winner $c_w \in \mathcal{C}$ over the alternate candidates $\mathcal{A} \subseteq \mathcal{C} \setminus \{c_w\}$, is the smallest number of votes whose ranking must be modified (by an adversary) so that a candidate $c' \in \mathcal{A}$ is elected.*

While the MOV calculates the number of votes required to be changed to alter the winner, the MOVC calculates the number of votes required to be changed to alter the winner *to one of a set* $\mathcal{A}$. We will require this finer information in order to calculate the smallest number of votes for a different party or coalition to win the election.

Example 1. Consider an election between candidates a, b, and c with the election profile shown in Table 1. The initial tallies of a, b, and c are 55, 41, and 40 votes, respectively, hence c is eliminated. Candidates a and b consequently have tallies of 80 and 41 votes, giving a the victory with a last round margin of 20 votes. Consider changing 1 of the $[b, c]$ votes to a $[c]$ vote. Then the initial tallies are $\{a : 55, b : 40, c : 41\}$ and b is eliminated. Candidates a and c consequently have tallies of 55 and 81 votes, and c is the winner of the election.

Clearly the MOV is 1 vote. The MOVC for $\{b\}$ is 10, which is achieved by changing 5 votes from $[a]$ to $[b, c]$ and 5 from $[a]$ to $[c]$, giving first round tallies of $\{a : 45, b : 46, c : 45\}$. An adversary can choose to eliminate a leaving b and c with tallies of 46 and 45 votes, and b winning the election.   □

Table 1. IRV example, with (a) the number of votes cast with each listed ranking over candidates a, b, c, and (b) tallies after each round of vote counting.

Ranking	Count
$[a]$	55
$[c, a]$	25
$[b, c]$	41
$[c]$	15

(a)

Candidate	Round 1	Round 2
a	55	80
b	41	41
c	40	—

(b)

2.1 Computing Margins for an IRV Election

Blom *et al.* [1] present a branch-and-bound algorithm (denoted *margin-irv*) for efficiently computing the margin of victory in an IRV election. This algorithm improves upon an existing method by Magrino *et al.* [5].

Given an IRV election with winning candidate c_w, *margin-irv* traverses a tree defining all possible *alternate* orders of candidate elimination (that result in a winning candidate other than c_w). As the algorithm explores these alternate elimination sequences, it solves a mixed integer program (MIP) to determine the minimum number of vote manipulations required to realise each elimination order. The ultimate goal is to find an elimination sequence, in which an alternate winner is elected, that requires the smallest number of vote changes to realise. Searching through the entire space of alternate elimination sequences would be too combinatorially complex, however, and so *margin-irv* incorporates rules for pruning sections of this tree from consideration. The result is an efficient algorithm for computing electoral margins.

A description of both the *margin-irv* algorithm, and the original branch-and-bound method of Magrino *et al.* [5], can be found in Blom *et al.* [1]. We summarise *margin-irv* in this section, and outline how it can be altered to compute a margin over a set of candidates $\mathcal{A}$ (the MOVC). Appendix B provides the full *margin-irv* algorithm for computing the MOVC for a single seat.

Given an IRV election with candidates $\mathcal{C}$ and winner $c_w \in \mathcal{C}$, the *margin-irv* algorithm starts by adding $|\mathcal{C}| - 1$ partial elimination sequences to the search tree, one for each of alternate winner $c'_w \in \mathcal{C} \setminus \{c_w\}$. These partial sequences form a frontier F. Each of these sequences contains a single candidate – the alternate winner in question. Following the basic structure of a branch-and-bound algorithm, we compute, for each partial sequence $\pi \in F$, a lower bound on the number of vote changes required to realise a elimination sequence that *ends* in π. These lower bounds are used to guide construction of the search tree, and are computed by both solving a MIP, and applying several rules for lower bound computation. The partial sequence π with the smallest lower bound is selected and *expanded*. For each candidate $c \in C$ that is not already present in π, we create a new sequence with c appended to the front. For example, given a set of candidates c_1, c_2, and c_3, with winning candidate c_3, the partial sequence $\pi = [c_2]$ will be expanded to create two new sequences $[c_1, c_2]$ and $[c_3, c_2]$. We evaluate each new sequence π' created by assigning it a lower bound on the number of votes required to realise any elimination order ending in π'.

While exploring and building elimination sequences, *margin-irv* maintains a running *upper bound* on the value of the true margin. This upper bound is initialised to the last round margin of the election. When a sequence π containing all candidates is constructed, our MIP computes the exact number of vote manipulations required to realise it. If this number is lower than our current upper bound, the upper bound is revised, and all orders on our frontier with a lower bound greater than or equal to it are pruned from consideration (removed from our frontier). This process continues until our frontier is empty (we have considered or pruned all possible alternate elimination sequences). The value of the running upper bound is the true margin of victory of the election.

Its easy to extend the *margin-irv* algorithm to also calculate MOVC for a set of alternate winners $\mathcal{A}$. In the first step of the algorithm, rather than adding a node for each alternate winner in $C \setminus \{c_w\}$ we add a node only for each of the alternate candidates in $\mathcal{A}$. The remainder of the algorithm is unchanged. With this modification, *margin-irv* will only explore alternate election outcomes that result in one of the candidates in $\mathcal{A}$ winning the election.

3   Calculating the Number of Votes to Change a Parliamentary Election Outcome

Given a set S of seats in a parliament, a winning coalition P is a set of parties such that the number of seats won by that coalition is at least some defined threshold T. Usually $T = \lceil \frac{|S|+1}{2} \rceil$, requiring the coalition to win more than half the seats. The NSW Legislative Assembly has 93 seats, and so 47 are required to win government.

We can use this threshold to calculate the number of vote changes required to change a parliamentary election result as follows. Assume the coalition won $W \geq T$ seats. We calculate the MOVC for each seat s won by the coalition P for the set of alternate candidates in that election *not* in coalition P. We then sort the MOVC values, and choose the $W - T + 1$ seats O with the least MOVC values. The sum of the MOVC of these seats O is the number of changes in votes required to remove the victory of the winning coalition P, and hence change the outcome of the election.

Note that if the coalition is a single party $P = \{p\}$, or more generally if no seat has two candidates from the coalition, then the MOVC values required are identical to MOV values. This is the case for the NSW Legislative Election where no seat has both a Liberal (LIB) and National (NAT) candidate. The above procedure examines how we might rob the original winning coalition P of

Table 2. The 5 seats in the 2015 NSW Legislative Assembly Parliamentary Election in which the last-round margin did not equal the true margin of victory.

Seat	$|\mathcal{C}|$	Last-round margin	True margin	Winner
Lismore	6	1173	209	NAT
Balina	7	1267	1130	GRN
Heffron	5	5835	5824	LAB
Maitland	6	5446	4012	CLP
Willoughby	6	10247	10160	LIB

Table 3. The 8 seats, won by a LIB or NAT candidate, with the lowest MOV.

Seat	$|\mathcal{C}|$	Last-round margin	True margin	Winner
East Hills	5	189	189	LIB
Lismore	6	1173	209	NAT
Upper Hunter	6	866	866	NAT
Monaro	5	1122	1122	NAT
Coogee	5	1243	1243	LIB
Tweed	5	1291	1291	NAT
Penrith	8	2576	2576	LIB
Holsworthy	6	2902	2902	LIB

its victory. However, we are interested in computing the number of vote changes required to award victory to a specific party or coalition of parties P' (such as a Labor (LAB)/Greens (GRN) coalition).

We can use a similar approach to calculate the number of vote changes required to change a parliamentary election outcome so that another coalition P' would win instead. Assume P' won $W' < T$ seats. We calculate the MOVC for each seat s not won by coalition P' with the set of alternate candidates $\mathcal{A}$ equal to the set of candidates belonging to parties in P'. We then sort the MOVC values, and choose the $W' - T$ seats O' with the least MOVC values. The sum of the MOVC of these seats O' is the number of changes in votes required to give a parliamentary victory to coalition P'.

Again if the coalition P' was always the alternate winner in the calculation of the MOV, then the MOVC and MOV calculations will coincide, and indeed if P' is a strong existing coalition it is likely that it is the alternate winner in most seats with the lowest MOVC.

4   Results

The NSW Legislative Assembly Parliamentary Election of 2015 was contested by major parties: Liberal (LIB), National (NAT), Green (GRN), Labor (LAB) and

Country Labor (CLP); as well as a number of minor parties and independents (IND). We found 5 seats in which the true margin was not the last-round margin. These seats are listed in Table 2, alongside the number of candidates up for election in each electorate ($|\mathcal{C}|$), the last-round margin for the seat, the true margin of victory for the seat, and the party whose candidate won the seat.

The LIB/NAT coalition won 54 seats to have a winning majority. In order to lose this majority, they must lose $54 - 47 + 1 = 8$ seats. Since no seat ran both a LIB and a NAT candidate, we can use the MOV values to calculate the number of votes required to lose 8 seats. The 8 LIB/NAT seats with the lowest MOV are listed in Table 3. For Lismore, the MOV differs substantially from the last-round margin. Hence, the total number of votes required for the LIB/NAT coalition to lose their majority is 10,398 (the sum of the 'True margin' values in the 4th column of Table 3).

For a LAB and CLP coalition to win the election we need them win to $47 - 34 = 13$ more seats. The 13 seats with the lowest MOVC for a change to LAB/CLP are listed in Table 4.

Table 4. The 13 seats with the lowest MOVC for a change in winner to LAB/CLP.

Seat	$|\mathcal{C}|$	Last-round margin	True margin	Winner	MOVC
East Hills	5	189	189	LIB	189
Lismore	6	1173	209	NAT	209
Upper Hunter	6	866	866	NAT	866
Monaro	5	1122	1122	NAT	1122
Balina	7	1267	1130	GRN	1130
Coogee	5	1243	1243	LIB	1243
Tweed	5	1291	1291	NAT	1291
Balmain	7	1731	1731	GRN	1731
Penrith	8	2576	2576	LIB	2576
Holsworthy	6	2902	2902	LIB	2902
Goulburn	6	2945	2945	LIB	2945
Oatley	5	3006	3006	LIB	3006
Newtown	7	3536	3536	GRN	3536

The total number of votes required to give an LAB/CLP victory is hence 22,746. In this case we can see, since the LAB/CLP is a strong alternate coalition, that all the MOVC calculations agree with the MOV calculations. Note that this is not true for all seats. For example in the NSW data Sydney is the first seat where the MOVC (=5583) for the LAB and CLP coalition is different from the MOV (=2864). This is because the runner-up was an Independent. Note that if we used MOV instead of MOVC we would incorrectly treat Sydney as one of the seats to change, and incorrectly calculate the number of votes required for an LAB/CLP coalition to win.

The full results for all seats are in Appendix A. The total numbers for changing the parliamentary outcome are computed by simply adding together the smallest margins for the necessary number of seats.

5   Conclusion

We have shown an efficient method of automated margin computation that can be used to identify the minimum number of vote changes (or errors) necessary to alter a parliamentary election outcome using single-member preferential voting. Our example was the NSW Legislative Assembly election of 2015, but the same tools and techniques could be immediately applied to any other parliament constructed in the same way for which full voting data was available, such as the Australian House of Representatives or other state lower houses.

Accurate electoral margins can form the basis of rigorous statistical auditing of paper ballot records to check the official election result. This would be valuable in any scenario, but is particularly important when an electronic (and hence unobservable) process such as automated ballot scanning is part of the count. Since these are exactly the scenarios that tend to produce detailed vote data, this work provides the basis for a count that is automated and fast (because of automated ballot scanning) and also transparent and verifiably accurate, because of rigorous auditing given an accurately computed election margin.

A   Full List of Margins for the NSW 2015 State Election

Table 5 records the last-round and true victory margins for each seat in the 2015 NSW lower house elections. In most seats, the last-round margin – the difference between the two last candidates in the elimination order – is the true margin. Exceptions to this rule are marked with an asterisk. The 8 Liberal/National coalition seats with the smallest margins are shown in bold. The total of the margins of these 8 seats gives the smallest number of vote changes required to produce a hung parliament, 10,398.

Table 6 lists the number of vote changes (denoted Δ) necessary to elect an LAB or CLP candidate. This is at least the true margin (from the previous table), but may be strictly more, for example if an independent candidate was the runner-up. The rows inside the double lines are the 10 seats with the smallest changes necessary to give the labor parties 47 seats. The combined total number of votes needed to produce this is the sum of those rows: 22746.

Table 7 records the margins for a Labor-Green coalition. In this case the total number of vote changes required to produce this outcome is 16349.

Table 5. LRM and MOV for each seat in the 2015 NSW lower house election.

Seat	$|C|$	LRM	MOV	Winner	Seat	$|C|$	LRM	MOV	Winner
Gosford	6	102	102	LAB	The Entrance	5	171	171	LAB
East Hills	5	189	**189**	**LIB**	*Lismore	6	1173	**209**	**NAT**
Strathfield	5	770	770	LAB	Granville	6	837	837	LAB
Upper Hunter	6	866	**866**	**NAT**	**Monaro**	5	1122	**1122**	**NAT**
*Balina	7	1267	1130	GRN	**Coogee**	5	1243	**1243**	**LIB**
Tweed	5	1291	**1291**	**NAT**	Prospect	5	1458	1458	LAB
Balmain	7	1731	1731	GRN	Rockdale	6	2004	2004	LAB
Port Stephens	5	2088	2088	CLP	Auburn	6	2265	2265	LAB
Penrith	8	2576	**2576**	**LIB**	Kogarah	6	2782	2782	LAB
Sydney	8	2864	2864	IND	**Holsworthy**	6	2902	**2902**	**LIB**
Goulburn	6	2945	2945	LIB	Oatley	5	3006	3006	LIB
Campbelltown	5	3096	3096	LAB	Newcastle	7	3132	3132	LAB
Wollongong	7	3367	3367	LAB	Macquarie Fields	7	3519	3519	LAB
Newtown	7	3536	3536	GRN	Heathcote	6	3560	3560	LIB
Blue Mountains	6	3614	3614	LAB	Myall Lakes	6	3627	3627	NAT
Bega	5	3663	3663	LIB	Wyong	7	3720	3720	LAB
Londonderry	5	3736	3736	LAB	Seven Hills	7	3774	3774	LIB
Summer Hill	7	3854	3854	LAB	Kiama	5	3856	3856	LIB
*Maitland	6	5446	4012	CLP	Terrigal	5	4053	4053	LIB
South Coast	5	4054	4054	LIB	Clarence	8	4069	4069	NAT
Lake Macquarie	7	4253	4253	IND	Mulgoa	5	4336	4336	LIB
Oxley	5	4591	4591	NAT	Tamworth	7	4643	4643	NAT
Maroubra	5	4717	4717	LAB	Swansea	8	4974	4974	LAB
Ryde	5	5153	5153	LIB	Barwon	6	5229	5229	NAT
Riverstone	5	5324	5324	LIB	Wagga Wagga	6	5475	5475	LIB
Parramatta	7	5509	5509	LIB	Charlestown	7	5532	5532	LAB
Bankstown	6	5542	5542	LAB	Blacktown	5	5565	5565	LAB
Coffs Harbour	5	5824	5824	NAT	*Heffron	5	5835	5824	LAB
Albury	5	5840	5840	LIB	Miranda	6	5881	5881	LIB
Mount Druitt	5	6343	6343	LAB	Canterbury	5	6610	6610	LAB
Fairfield	5	6998	6998	LAB	Epping	6	7156	7156	LIB
Bathurst	5	7267	7267	NAT	Hawkesbury	8	7311	7311	LIB
Wollondilly	6	7401	7401	LIB	Shellharbour	7	7519	7519	LAB
Cabramatta	5	7613	7613	LAB	Lane Cove	6	7740	7740	LIB
Drummoyne	6	8099	8099	LIB	Keira	5	8164	8164	LAB
Camden	5	8217	8217	LIB	Lakemba	5	8235	8235	LAB
Liverpool	5	8495	8495	LAB	North Shore	7	8517	8517	NAT
Murray	8	8574	8574	NAT	Hornsby	6	8577	8577	LIB
Dubbo	7	8680	8680	NAT	Port Macquarie	5	8715	8715	NAT
Cessnock	5	9187	9187	CLP	Cootamundra	5	9247	9247	NAT
Wallsend	5	9418	9418	LAB	Cronulla	5	9674	9674	LIB
Vaucluse	5	9783	9783	LIB	Baulkham Hills	5	10023	10023	LIB
Orange	5	10048	10048	NAT	Ku-ring-gai	5	10061	10061	LIB
*Willoughby	6	10247	10160	LIB	Wakehurst	6	10770	10770	LIB
Manly	5	10806	10806	LIB	Pittwater	5	11430	11430	LIB
Northern Tablelands	6	11969	11969	LIB	Davidson	5	12960	12960	LIB
Castle Hill	5	13160	13160	LIB					

Table 6. LRM, MOV, and the number of vote changes (Δ) required to elect an LAB or CLP candidate for each seat in the 2015 NSW lower house election.

Seat	$|\mathcal{C}|$	LRM	MOV	Winner	Δ	Seat	$|\mathcal{C}|$	LRM	MOV	Winner	Δ
Auburn	6	2265	2265	LAB	0	Bankstown	6	5542	5542	LAB	0
Blacktown	5	5565	5565	LAB	0	Blue Mountains	6	3614	3614	LAB	0
Cabramatta	5	7613	7613	LAB	0	Campbelltown	5	3096	3096	LAB	0
Canterbury	5	6610	6610	LAB	0	Cessnock	5	9187	9187	CLP	0
Charlestown	7	5532	5532	LAB	0	Fairfield	5	6998	6998	LAB	0
Gosford	6	102	102	LAB	0	Granville	6	837	837	LAB	0
Heffron	5	5835	5824	LAB	0	Keira	5	8164	8164	LAB	0
Kogarah	6	2782	2782	LAB	0	Lakemba	5	8235	8235	LAB	0
Liverpool	5	8495	8495	LAB	0	L-derry	5	3736	3736	LAB	0
Macq. Fields	7	3519	3519	LAB	0	Maitland	6	5446	4012	CLP	0
Maroubra	5	4717	4717	LAB	0	Mt. Druitt	5	6343	6343	LAB	0
Newcastle	7	3132	3132	LAB	0	P. Stephens	5	2088	2088	CLP	0
Prospect	5	1458	1458	LAB	0	Rockdale	6	2004	2004	LAB	0
Shellharbour	7	7519	7519	LAB	0	Strathfield	5	770	770	LAB	0
Summer Hill	7	3854	3854	LAB	0	Swansea	8	4974	4974	LAB	0
The Entrance	5	171	171	LAB	0	Wallsend	5	9418	9418	LAB	0
Wollongong	7	3367	3367	LAB	0	Wyong	7	3720	3720	LAB	0
East Hills	5	189	189	LIB	189	Lismore	6	1173	209	NAT	209
U. Hunter	6	866	866	NAT	866	Monaro	5	1122	1122	NAT	1122
Balina	7	1267	1130	GRN	1130	Coogee	5	1243	1243	LIB	1243
Tweed	5	1291	1291	NAT	1291	Balmain	7	1731	1731	GRN	1731
Penrith	8	2576	2576	LIB	2576	Holsworthy	6	2902	2902	LIB	2902
Goulburn	6	2945	2945	LIB	2945	Oatley	5	3006	3006	LIB	3006
Newtown	7	3536	3536	GRN	3536						
Heathcote	6	3560	3560	LIB	3560	M. Lakes	6	3627	3627	NAT	3627
Bega	5	3663	3663	LIB	3663	Seven Hills	7	3774	3774	LIB	3774
Kiama	5	3856	3856	LIB	3856	Terrigal	5	4053	4053	LIB	4053
South Coast	5	4054	4054	LIB	4054	Clarence	8	4069	4069	NAT	4069
Lake Macq.	7	4253	4253	IND	4253	Mulgoa	5	4336	4336	LIB	4336
Oxley	5	4591	4591	NAT	4591	Ryde	5	5153	5153	LIB	5153
Barwon	6	5229	5229	NAT	5229	Riverstone	6	5324	5324	LIB	5324
W-Wagga	6	5475	5475	LIB	5475	Parramatta	7	5509	5509	LIB	5509
Sydney	8	2864	2864	IND	5583	C. Harbour	5	5824	5824	NAT	5824
Albury	5	5840	5840	LIB	5840	Miranda	6	5881	5881	LIB	5881
Epping	6	7156	7156	LIB	7156	Bathurst	5	7267	7267	NAT	7267
Hawkesbury	8	7311	7311	LIB	7311	W-dilly	6	7401	7401	LIB	7401
Lane Cove	6	7740	7740	LIB	7740	D-moyne	6	8099	8099	LIB	8099
Camden	5	8217	8217	LIB	8217	Hornsby	6	8577	8577	LIB	8577
Dubbo	7	8680	8680	NAT	8680	Port Macq.	5	8715	8715	NAT	8715
North Shore	7	8517	8517	NAT	8798	C-mundra	5	9247	9247	NAT	9247
Murray	8	8574	8574	NAT	9483	Cronulla	5	9674	9674	LIB	9674
B. Hills	5	10023	10023	LIB	10023	Orange	5	10048	10048	NAT	10048
Ku-ring-gai	5	10061	10061	LIB	10061	Willoughby	6	10247	10160	LIB	10160
Vaucluse	5	9783	9783	LIB	10581	Wakehurst	6	10770	10770	LIB	10770
Tamworth	7	4643	4643	NAT	11283	N. T-lands	6	11969	11969	LIB	11969
Manly	5	10806	10806	LIB	12106	Pittwater	5	11430	11430	LIB	12181
Davidson	5	12960	12960	LIB	13065	Castle Hill	5	13160	13160	LIB	13160

Table 7. LRM, MOV, and the number of vote changes (Δ) required to elect a LAB, CLP, or GRN for each seat in the 2015 NSW lower house election.

Seat	$|C|$	LRM	MOV	Winner	Δ	Seat	$|C|$	LRM	MOV	Winner	Δ
Auburn	6	2265	2265	LAB	0	Balina	7	1267	1130	GRN	0
Balmain	7	1731	1731	GRN	0	Bankstown	6	5542	5542	LAB	0
Blacktown	5	5565	5565	LAB	0	B. Mountains	6	3614	3614	LAB	0
Cabramatta	5	7613	7613	LAB	0	C-belltown	5	3096	3096	LAB	0
Canterbury	5	6610	6610	LAB	0	Cessnock	5	9187	9187	CLP	0
Charlestown	7	5532	5532	LAB	0	Fairfield	5	6998	6998	LAB	0
Gosford	6	102	102	LAB	0	Granville	6	837	837	LAB	0
Heffron	5	5835	5824	LAB	0	Keira	5	8164	8164	LAB	0
Kogarah	6	2782	2782	LAB	0	Lakemba	5	8235	8235	LAB	0
Liverpool	5	8495	8495	LAB	0	L-derry	5	3736	3736	LAB	0
M. Fields	7	3519	3519	LAB	0	Maitland	6	5446	4012	CLP	0
Maroubra	5	4717	4717	LAB	0	Mt. Druitt	5	6343	6343	LAB	0
Newcastle	7	3132	3132	LAB	0	Newtown	7	3536	3536	GRN	0
P. Stephens	5	2088	2088	CLP	0	Prospect	5	1458	1458	LAB	0
Rockdale	6	2004	2004	LAB	0	S-harbour	7	7519	7519	LAB	0
Strathfield	5	770	770	LAB	0	S. Hill	7	3854	3854	LAB	0
Swansea	8	4974	4974	LAB	0	The Entr.	5	171	171	LAB	0
Wallsend	5	9418	9418	LAB	0	Wollongong	7	3367	3367	LAB	0
Wyong	7	3720	3720	LAB	0						
East Hills	5	189	189	LIB	189	Lismore	6	1173	209	NAT	209
U. Hunter	6	866	866	NAT	866	Monaro	5	1122	1122	NAT	1122
Coogee	5	1243	1243	LIB	1243	Tweed	5	1291	1291	NAT	1291
Penrith	8	2576	2576	LIB	2576	Holsworthy	6	2902	2902	LIB	2902
Goulburn	6	2945	2945	LIB	2945	Oatley	5	3006	3006	LIB	3006
Heathcote	6	3560	3560	LIB	3560	M. Lakes	6	3627	3627	NAT	3627
Bega	5	3663	3663	LIB	3663	Seven Hills	7	3774	3774	LIB	3774
Kiama	5	3856	3856	LIB	3856	Terrigal	5	4053	4053	LIB	4053
S. Coast	5	4054	4054	LIB	4054	Clarence	8	4069	4069	NAT	4069
Lake Macq	7	4253	4253	IND	4253	Mulgoa	5	4336	4336	LIB	4336
Oxley	5	4591	4591	NAT	4591	Ryde	5	5153	5153	LIB	5153
Barwon	6	5229	5229	NAT	5229	Riverstone	5	5324	5324	LIB	5324
W-Wagga	6	5475	5475	LIB	5475	Parramatta	7	5509	5509	LIB	5509
Sydney	8	2864	2864	IND	5583	C. Harbour	5	5824	5824	NAT	5824
Albury	5	5840	5840	LIB	5840	Miranda	6	5881	5881	LIB	5881
Epping	6	7156	7156	LIB	7156	Bathurst	5	7267	7267	NAT	7267
H-bury	8	7311	7311	LIB	7311	W-dilly	6	7401	7401	LIB	7401
Lane Cove	6	7740	7740	LIB	7740	D-moyne	6	8099	8099	LIB	8099
Camden	5	8217	8217	LIB	8217	N. Shore	7	8517	8517	NAT	8517
Hornsby	6	8577	8577	LIB	8577	Dubbo	7	8680	8680	NAT	8680
Port Macq	5	8715	8715	NAT	8715	C-mundra	5	9247	9247	NAT	9247
Murray	8	8574	8574	NAT	9483	Cronulla	5	9674	9674	LIB	9674
Vaucluse	5	9783	9783	LIB	9783	B. Hills	5	10023	10023	LIB	10023
Orange	5	10048	10048	NAT	10048	Ku-ring-gai	5	10061	10061	LIB	10061
Willoughby	6	10247	10160	LIB	10160	Wakehurst	6	10770	10770	LIB	10770
Manly	5	10806	10806	LIB	10806	Tamworth	7	4643	4643	NAT	11283
Pittwater	5	11430	11430	LIB	11430	N. T-lands	6	11969	11969	LIB	11969
Davidson	5	12960	12960	LIB	12960	Castle Hill	5	13160	13160	LIB	13160

margin-irv($\mathcal{C}, \mathcal{B}, c_w, \mathcal{A}$)

1 $F := \emptyset$

2 $U := LRM_{\mathcal{B}}$

3 **for**($c \in \mathcal{A}$)

4      $\pi' := [c]$

5      $l :=$ LOWERBOUND(π')

6   **if**($l < U$)

7          $F := F \cup \{(l, \pi')\}$

8 **while** $F \neq \emptyset$

9      $(l, \pi') := \arg \min F$

10     $F := F \setminus \{(l, \pi')\}$

11     $U :=$ expand($l, \pi', U, F, \mathcal{C}, \mathcal{B}$)

12 **return** U

expand($l, \pi', U, F, \mathcal{C}, \mathcal{B}$)

13 $l' := \max\{l,$ DISTANCETO($\pi', \mathcal{C}, \mathcal{B}$)$\}$

14 **if**($l' \geq U$)

15   **return** U

16 **for**($c \in \mathcal{C} \setminus \pi'$)

17      $\pi := [c] ++\pi'$

18   **if**($|\pi| = |\mathcal{C}|$)

19   **return** $\min\{U,$ DISTANCETO($\pi, \mathcal{C}, \mathcal{B}$)$\}$

20      $l'' = \max\{l',$ LOWERBOUND(π)$\}$

21   **if**($l'' < U$)

22          $F := F \cup \{(l'', \pi)\}$

23 **return** U

Fig. 2. MOVC computation for an IRV election $\mathcal{B}$ with candidates $\mathcal{C}$, winner $c_w \in \mathcal{C}$, and alternate winner set $\mathcal{A}$.

B   Modified *margin-irv*: Computing the MOVC

The *margin-irv* algorithm for computing the MOVC for an IRV election $\mathcal{B}$ given a set of alternate winners $\mathcal{A}$ is shown in Fig. 2. An initial upper bound on the MOVC is initialised to the last round margin ($LRM_{\mathcal{B}}$) in Step 2. For each candidate in $\mathcal{A}$, we add a partial elimination order to our frontier F. Each order π' is assigned a lower bound (computed as described by Blom *et al.* [1]) on the degree of manipulation required to realise an elimination sequence *ending* in π' – only orders with an estimated lower bound (l) that *is less than* the current MOVC upper bound (U) are added to the frontier (Steps 6 and 7). Steps 8 to 12 repeatedly select the partial order π' in F with the smallest associated lower bound for expansion. To expand an order π', we create a new order for each candidate c *not* already present in π', appending c to the start of the sequence (Step 17). If the created sequence π contains all candidates, it is a leaf node, and we evaluate the exact number of vote changes required to realise the sequence with a mixed integer linear program (MIP) denoted DISTANCETO.

Section B.1 provides the formulation of the DISTANCETO MIP, replicated from Blom *et al.* [1]. Otherwise, we compute a lower bound on the on the degree of manipulation required to realise an elimination sequence *ending* in π (l'') and add π to our frontier if this lower bound is less than our current upper bound on the MOVC (Steps 21 to 22). The algorithm terminates once there are no further partial orders to be expanded in our frontier, returning the current MOVC upper bound (U) as the computed MOVC.

B.1   The DISTANCETO MIP

The following MIP formulation, originally presented in the work of Magrino *et al.* [5], has been replicated as it appears in Blom *et al.* [1]. Let **R** denote the set of possible (partial and total) rankings R of candidates $\mathcal{C}$ that could appear on a vote, N_R the number of votes cast in the election with ranking $R \in \mathbf{R}$, and N the total number of votes cast. For each $R \in \mathbf{R}$, we define variables:

q_R integer number of votes to be changed into R;

m_R integer number of votes with ranking R in the unmodified
election to be changed into something other than R; and

y_R number of votes in the modified election with ranking R.

Given a partial or complete order π, the DISTANCETO MIP is:

$$\min \sum_{R \in \mathbf{R}} q_R$$

$$N_R + q_R - m_R = y_R \qquad\qquad \forall R \in \mathbf{R} \qquad (3)$$

$$\sum_{R \in \mathbf{R}} q_R = \sum_{R \in \mathbf{R}} m_R \qquad\qquad (4)$$

$$\sum_{R \in \mathcal{R}_{i,i}} y_R \leq \sum_{R \in \mathcal{R}_{j,i}} y_R \qquad\qquad \forall c_i, c_j \in \pi \,.\, i < j \qquad (5)$$

$$n \geq y_R \geq 0, \ N_R \geq m_R \geq 0, \ q_R \geq 0 \qquad\qquad \forall R \in \mathbf{R} \qquad (6)$$

Constraint (3) states that the number of votes with ranking $R \in \mathbf{R}$ in the new election is equal to the sum of those with this ranking in the unmodified election and those whose ranking has *changed to* R, minus the number of votes whose ranking has been *changed from* R. Constraint (5) defines a set of *special elimination constraints* which force the candidates in π to be eliminated in the stated order. $\mathcal{R}_{j,i}$ denotes the subset of rankings in $\mathbf{R}$ ($\mathcal{R}_{j,i} \subset \mathbf{R}$) in which c_j is the most preferred candidate still standing (i.e., that will count toward c_j's tally) at the start of round i (in which candidate c_i is eliminated). Constraint (4) ensures that the total number of votes cast in the election does not change as a result of the manipulation.

References

1. Blom, M., Stuckey, P.J., Teague, V., Tidhar, R.: Efficient computation of exact IRV margins. In: European Conference on AI (ECAI), pp. 480–487 (2016)
2. Jackman, S.: Measuring electoral bias: Australia, 1949–93. Br. J. Polit. Sci. **24**(3), 319–357 (1994)
3. Kroll, J.A., Halderman, J.A., Felten, E.W.: Efficiently auditing multi-level elections. Ann Arbor, 1001:48109. https://jhalderm.com/pub/papers/audit-evote14.pdf
4. Lindeman, M., Stark, P.B.: A gentle introduction to risk-limiting audits. IEEE Secur. Priv. **10**(5), 42–49 (2012)
5. Magrino, T.R., Rivest, R.L., Shen, E., Wagner, D.A.: Computing the margin of victory in IRV elections. In: USENIX Accurate Electronic Voting Technology Workshop. USENIX Association, Berkeley (2011)
6. Parliament of Australia Joint Standing Committee on Electoral Matters: Third interim report on the inquiry into the conduct of the 2016 federal election: AEC modernisation, June 2017. http://www.aph.gov.au/Parliamentary_Business/Committees/Joint/Electoral_Matters/2016Election/Third_Interim_Report

16   M. Blom et al.

7. Tufte, E.R.: The relationship between seats and votes in two-party systems. Am. Polit. Sci. Rev. **67**(2), 540–554 (1973)
8. Yang, W.C.: Democracy, minimized-given various election scenarios, what is the minimum percent of the popular vote required to win the white house? OR MS Today **35**(5), 34 (2008)

Ballot-Polling Risk Limiting Audits
for IRV Elections

Michelle Blom$^{(\boxtimes)}$, Peter J. Stuckey, and Vanessa J. Teague

School of Computing and Information Systems,
The University of Melbourne, Parkville, Australia
{michelle.blom,p.stuckey,vjteague}@unimelb.edu.au

Abstract. Risk-limiting post election audits guarantee a high probability of correcting incorrect election results, independent of why the result was incorrect. Ballot-polling audits select ballots at random and interpret those ballots as evidence for and against the actual recorded result, continuing this process until either they support the recorded result, or they fall back to a full manual recount. Ballot-polling for first-past-the-post elections is well understood, and used in some US elections. We define a number of approaches to ballot-polling risk-limiting audits for Instant Runoff Voting (IRV) elections. We show that for almost all real elections we found, we can perform a risk-limiting audit by looking at only a small fraction of the total ballots (assuming no errors).

1 Introduction

Instant Runoff Voting (IRV) is a system of preferential voting in which voters rank candidates in order of preference. IRV is used for all parliamentary lower house elections in Australia, parliamentary elections in Fiji and Papua New Guinea, presidential elections in Ireland and Bosnia/Herzogovinia, and local elections in numerous locations world-wide, including the UK and United States. Given candidates c_1, c_2, c_3, and c_4, each vote in an IRV election is a (*possibly partial*) ranking of these candidates. A vote with the ranking $[c_1, c_2, c_3]$ expresses a first preference for candidate c_1, a second preference for c_2, and a third for c_3. The tallying of votes proceeds by distributing each vote to its first ranked candidate. The candidate with the smallest number of votes is eliminated, with their votes redistributed to subsequent, less preferred candidates. Elimination proceeds in this fashion, until a single candidate w remains, who is declared the winner.

Risk Limiting Audits [6] (RLAs) provide strong statistical evidence that the reported outcome of an election is correct, or revert to a manual recount if it is wrong. The probability that the audit fails to detect a wrong outcome is bounded by a *risk limit*. An RLA with a risk limit of 1%, for example, has at most a 1% chance of failing to detect that a reported election outcome is wrong. In this paper we present several methods for undertaking ballot-polling RLAs of IRV elections, by adapting a ballot-polling RLA method (BRAVO) designed for first-past-the-post or k-winner plurality elections [7].

© Springer Nature Switzerland AG 2018
R. Krimmer et al. (Eds.): E-Vote-ID 2018, LNCS 11143, pp. 17–34, 2018.
https://doi.org/10.1007/978-3-030-00419-4_2

Blom *et al.* [3] demonstrated an efficient algorithm for exact IRV margin computation. This immediately allows for a risk-limiting *comparison audit* [6], assuming that there is infrastructure for comparing ballots with their electronic record. This would consist of simply assessing the number of discrepancies until the hypothesis that there were enough to change the outcome could be rejected. However, that might be very inefficient because it counts every error equally, including those that help the apparent winner or rearrange candidates with no hope of winning. It might be possible to extend Stark's sharper discrepancy measure [10] to IRV, but this is challenging because it may be hard to compute the implications of a particular discrepancy.

In this paper we instead consider ballot-polling audits for IRV, by applying BRAVO to auditing certain facts about an IRV election. In a k-winner plurality contest, BRAVO maintains a running statistic T_{wl} for each pair of apparent winner w and loser l. These statistics are updated as ballots are drawn uniformly at random. A ballot that shows a valid vote for winner w increases the T_{wl} statistic (by an amount dependent on the reported votes for the two candidates), while a ballot showing a valid vote for the loser l decreases it. When each statistic exceeds a threshold, dependent on the risk limit, we know that we have seen enough evidence to reject the hypothesis that l beat w.

Each round of IRV elimination could be regarded as a multiple-winner plurality election—this idea was explored in [9]. We denote this by **IRV**, annotated with the round and eliminated candidates. Adapting BRAVO directly to this is described in Sect. 5.1. This is sound, but wastes a lot of auditing work proving a much stronger result than necessary—the elimination order may be wrong though the final outcome is correct. One optimization is to eliminate batches of low-tally candidates at once when this provably doesn't affect the final outcome. These batch eliminations can also be easily audited with BRAVO—this is described in Sect. 5.2.

An even simpler fact turns out to be very powerful: suppose we wish to reject the hypothesis that w was eliminated before l. We can apply BRAVO immediately, counting every ballot with a *first preference* for w as a vote for w, which is conservative because w must have *at least* this tally at every stage. Any vote that mentions l without a higher preference for w is attributed to l, which is also conservative because l can have *at most* this tally. If BRAVO rejects the hypothesis that l can beat w, then we can reject the hypothesis that w is eliminated before l. We call this the Winner Only hypothesis, denoted **WO**(l, w). It can also be conditioned on a set of already-eliminated candidates $\mathcal{C}$—preferences for those candidates are simply ignored when auditing the w-l pair.

Winner-only audits are described in Sect. 5.3. A surprising result of this paper is that WO alone often suffices for an efficient, complete audit. In about half the real elections we simulated auditing, we found that for the announced winner w, for every loser l, hypothesis **WO**(l, w) could be efficiently rejected using BRAVO. This confirms that w won, while sidestepping almost all the complexity of IRV.

The key contribution of this paper is a good heuristic for choosing which combination of facts to audit, using BRAVO, in order to provide an efficient risk-limiting audit of an IRV election result. We present an algorithm, denoted *audit-irv*, that finds a sufficient set of facts (e.g., some version of **IRV** or **WO**(c_1, c_2) given that c_3 and c_4 have been eliminated) to prove that w won. All of these facts can be audited simultaneously using BRAVO. If one of the necessary facts is false, this will be detected, with probability of at least $1 - \alpha$, by the BRAVO audit at risk limit α.

Ideally we would like to ensure that *audit-irv* selects the set of facts that produce an optimally efficient audit, but this is very difficult. When BRAVO is assessing only a single winner, its average sample number (ASN) can be easily computed, but the expected number of samples for eliminating multiple (perhaps related) hypotheses can (as far as we know) be assessed only by simulation. *audit-irv* selects the collection of facts that minimizes the maximum ASN for each fact taken separately—this is what we mean by the "optimal" auditing program below. However, this may not actually be an optimally efficient audit, or even the optimal application of BRAVO, because it is possible that some other combination of facts can be checked together more efficiently.

Our simulations show that *audit-irv* plans a feasible IRV audit, using BRAVO, for almost all the real IRV elections we could find. Although some still require large audits, this is probably inevitable because their margins are small.

Definitions and background are in Sect. 3. Section 4 introduces the BRAVO ballot-polling RLA for first-past-the-post elections. Section 5 describes our ballot-polling approaches, then Sect. 6 simulates and evaluates them on a suite of IRV instances.

2 Related Work

There is a growing literature on the use of risk-limiting audits for auditing the outcome of varying types of election [7,9]. Risk-limiting audits have been applied to a number of plurality (first-past-the-post) elections, including four 2008 elections in California [4] and elections in over 50 Colorado counties in 2017. General auditing procedures designed to enhance electoral integrity have been outlined by [1]. The BRAVO ballot-polling risk-limiting audit of [7], designed for first-past-the-post elections, forms the basis of our IRV ballot-polling audits.

Several approaches for designing a risk-limiting comparison audit of an IRV election have been proposed [9]. Such audits retrieve paper ballots and compare them to their corresponding electronic record – an erroneous ballot is one that does not match its electronic record. The first of these methods determines whether replacing an erroneous ballot with its correct representation changes the margin of victory of the election. The second is based on auditing the elimination order, performing a plurality audit for each round of counting. The audit performed at round r checks whether the set of candidates eliminated prior to r, viewed as a single 'super candidate', loses to the set of remaining candidates (that are still standing). We consider a similar approach, in the context of a ballot-polling audit, in this paper. We show, however, that we can more efficiently audit an IRV election outcome by simply verifying that the reported winner was not defeated by any other candidate. The third method proposed by [9] samples K ballots, and determines whether the number of erroneous ballots exceeds a defined threshold, based on the margin of victory of the election.

In parliamentary elections, such as Australian state and federal elections, the overall outcome is determined by the results of a set of such elections, one for each of a set of regions or districts. In the context of multi-level elections such as these, [5] present a linear programming-based method to compute the statistical confidence with which each district-level election should be audited, given an appropriate risk-limiting auditing method, while minimising the expected number of ballots that must be checked overall. Their approach ensures that the overall outcome is audited to a given level of statistical confidence, while varying the extent to which each district-level election is audited.

For a risk-limiting audit, the margin of victory of the election provides an indication of how many ballots will need to be sampled. Automatic methods for computing electoral margins for IRV elections have been presented by [2,3,8].

3 Preliminaries

In a first-past-the-post (FPTP) election, a voter marks a single candidate on their ballot when casting their vote. The candidate who receives the most votes is declared the winner. The BRAVO risk limiting audits of [7] are designed for k-winner FPTP contests. A voter may vote for up to k of the candidates on their ballot, and the k candidates with the highest number of votes are declared winners. IRV, in contrast, is a form of preferential voting in which voters express a preference ordering over a set of candidates on their ballot. The tallying of votes in an IRV election proceeds by a series of rounds in which the candidate with the lowest number of votes is eliminated (see Fig. 1) with the last remaining candidate declared the winner. All ballots in an eliminated candidate's tally are distributed to the next most-preferred (remaining) candidate in their ranking.

> Initially, all candidates remain standing (are not eliminated)
> **While** there is *more than one* candidate standing
>   **For** every candidate c standing
>   Tally (count) the ballots in which c is the highest-ranked
>   candidate of those standing
>   Eliminate the candidate with the smallest tally
> The winner is the one candidate not eliminated

Fig. 1. An informal definition of the IRV counting algorithm.

Let $\mathcal{C}$ be the set of candidates in an IRV election $\mathcal{B}$. We refer to sequences of candidates π in list notation (e.g., $\pi = [c_1, c_2, c_3, c_4]$), and use such sequences to

Table 1. An example IRV election, stating (a) the number of ballots cast with each listed ranking over four candidates, and (b) the tallies after each round of counting.

Ranking	Count
$[c_2, c_3]$	4000
$[c_1]$	20000
$[c_3, c_4]$	9000
$[c_2, c_3, c_4]$	6000
$[c_4, c_1, c_2]$	15000
$[c_1, c_3]$	6000

(a)

Candidate	Rnd1	Rnd2	Rnd3
c_1	26000	26000	26000
c_2	10000	10000	—
c_3	9000	—	—
c_4	15000	24000	30000

(b)

represent both votes and elimination orders. An election $\mathcal{B}$ is defined as a multi-set[1] of ballots, each ballot $b \in \mathcal{B}$ a sequence of candidates in $\mathcal{C}$, with no duplicates, listed in order of preference (most preferred to least preferred). Throughout this paper we use the notation $first(\pi) = \pi(1)$ to denote the first candidate in a sequence π. In each round of vote counting, there are a current set of eliminated candidates $\mathcal{E}$ and a current set of candidates still standing $\mathcal{S} = \mathcal{C} \setminus \mathcal{E}$. The winner c_w is the last standing candidate.

Definition 1. *Projection* $p_\mathcal{S}(\pi)$: *We define the projection of a sequence π onto a set $\mathcal{S}$ as the largest subsequence of π that contains only elements of $\mathcal{S}$. (The elements keep their relative order in π). For example:*

$$P_{\{c_2,c_3\}}([c_1, c_2, c_4, c_3]) = [c_2, c_3] \text{ and } p_{\{c_2,c_3,c_4,c_5\}}([c_6, c_4, c_7, c_2, c_1]) = [c_4, c_2].$$

Each candidate $c \in \mathcal{C}$ has a *tally* of ballots. Ballots are added to this tally upon the elimination of a candidate $c' \in \mathcal{C} \setminus c$, and are redistributed upon the elimination of c.

Definition 2. *Tally* $t_\mathcal{S}(c)$: *Given candidates $\mathcal{S} \subseteq \mathcal{C}$ are still standing in an election $\mathcal{B}$, the tally for a candidate $c \in \mathcal{C}$, denoted $t_\mathcal{S}(c)$, is defined as the number of ballots $b \in \mathcal{B}$ for which c is the most-preferred candidate of those remaining. Recall that $p_\mathcal{S}(b)$ denotes the sequence of candidates mentioned in b that are also in $\mathcal{S}$.*

$$t_\mathcal{S}(c) = \mid [b \mid b \in \mathcal{B}, c = first(p_\mathcal{S}(b))] \mid \tag{1}$$

The *primary vote* of candidate $c \in \mathcal{C}$, denoted $f(c)$, is the number of votes $b \in \mathcal{B}$ for which c is ranked highest. Note that $f(c) = t_\mathcal{C}(c)$.

$$f(c) = \mid [b \mid b \in \mathcal{B}, c = first(b)] \mid \tag{2}$$

Example 1. Consider the IRV election of Table 1. The tallies of c_1, c_2, c_3, and c_4, in the 1st counting round are 26000, 10000, 9000, and 15000 votes. Candidate c_3 is eliminated, and 9000 ballots are distributed to c_4, who now has a tally of

---

[1] A multiset allows for the inclusion of duplicate items.

24000. Candidate c_2, on 10000 votes, is eliminated next with 6000 of their ballots given to c_4 (the remainder have no subsequent preferences and are exhausted). Candidates c_1 and c_4 remain with tallies of 26000 and 30000. Candidate c_1 is eliminated and c_4 elected.   □

4   Ballot-Polling Risk-Limiting Audits for FPTP

The aim of ballot-polling risk limiting audits is to be reassured that the results of the election are valid even if some counting errors occurred. To this end we will consider two versions of the statistics defined in the previous section. We use the regular definition for the *recorded* values made during the election, and add a tilde ˜ to mean the *actual* values which should have been calculated. Hence $f(c)$ is the recorded primary vote for candidate c and $\tilde{f}(c)$ is the actual primary vote for the candidate.

For now we consider a simple k-winner from n candidates FPTP election where the k candidates who have the greatest number of votes are elected. All winners are elected simultaneously and there is no transfer of votes. Given a set of $\mathcal{C}$ candidates ($|\mathcal{C}| = n$) there will be a set of $\mathcal{W}$ *winners* ($|\mathcal{W}| = k$) and $\mathcal{L}$ *losers* ($|\mathcal{L}| = n - k$).

We now present the BRAVO algorithm [7] for ballot-polling risk-limiting audits of such elections (Fig. 2(a)). BRAVO is applicable in elections where each ballot may express a vote for one or more candidates. For our proposed IRV audits, we apply BRAVO in contexts where each ballot represents a vote for a single candidate only (i.e., in any round of an IRV count, each ballot belongs to the tally of no more than one candidate). We describe the BRAVO algorithm in the context where each ballot b is equivalent to *first*(b). Then $f(c)$ is the tally of votes for each candidate $c \in \mathcal{C}$.

The ballot-polling risk-limiting audit independently tests $k(n - k)$ null hypotheses $\{\tilde{f}(w) \le \tilde{f}(l)\}$ for each winner/loser pair. A statistic for each test $\{T_{wl}\}$ is updated when a ballot is drawn for either its winner or its loser.

Given an overall risk limit α we can estimate for each hypothesis the number of ballot polls we expect will be required to reject the hypothesis assuming the election counts are perfectly accurate. Let p_c be the proportion of recorded votes for candidate c, i.e. $p_c = f(c)/|\mathcal{B}|$. Let s_{wl} be the proportion of recorded votes for the winner w of the votes for the winner and loser, $s_{wl} = p_w/(p_w + p_l)$. Clearly $s_{wl} > 0.5$. Then the *Average Sample Number (ASN)* [7], that is the expected number of samples to reject the null hypothesis $\{\tilde{p}_w \le \tilde{p}_l\}$ assuming the recorded counts are correct, is given by:

$$ASN \simeq \frac{ln(1/\alpha) + 0.5ln(2s_{wl})}{(p_w ln(2s_{wl}) + p_l ln(2 - 2s_{wl}))} \tag{3}$$

Example 2. Consider the first round of the IRV election of Example 1. The null hypotheses we need to reject are $\tilde{f}(c_1) \le \tilde{f}(c_3)$, $\tilde{f}(c_2) \le \tilde{f}(c_3)$, $\tilde{f}(c_4) \le \tilde{f}(c_3)$. We calculate $p_1 = 26000/60000$, $p_2 = 10000/60000$, $p_3 = 9000/60000$,

$p_4 = 15000/60000$ and $s_{13} = 26000/35000$, $s_{23} = 10000/19000$, and $s_{43} = 15000/24000$. The ASN for rejecting each hypothesis, assuming $\alpha = 0.05$, is 44.5, 6885, and 246 respectively.   □

bravo($\tilde{\mathcal{B}}, \mathcal{W}, \mathcal{L}, \alpha, M$)
  for($w \in \mathcal{W}, l \in \mathcal{L}$)
    $T_{wl} := 1$
    $s_{wl} := f(w)/(f(w) + f(l))$
  $H := \mathcal{W} \times \mathcal{L}$
  $m := 0$
  while($m < M \wedge H \neq \emptyset$)
    randomly draw ballot b from $\tilde{\mathcal{B}}$
    $m := m + 1$
    if($first(b) \in \mathcal{W}$)
      for($(w,l) \in H, w = first(b)$)
        $T_{wl} := T_{wl} \times 2s_{wl}$
        if($T_{wl} \geq 1/\alpha$)
          % reject the null hypothesis
          $H = H - \{(w,l)\}$
    elseif($first(b) \in \mathcal{L}$)
      for($(w,l) \in H, l = first(b)$)
        $T_{wl} := T_{wl} \times 2(1 - s_{wl})$
  if($H = \emptyset$)
    % reported results stand
    return *true*
  else % full recount required
    return *false*
          (a)

irvbravo($\tilde{\mathcal{B}}, \pi, \alpha, M$)
  $H := \emptyset$
  for($i \in 1..|\pi| - 1$)
    $l := \pi(i)$
    $C_l := \{\pi(i), \pi(i+1), \ldots, \pi(|\pi|)\}$
    for($j \in i + 1..|\pi|$)
      $w := \pi(j)$
      $T_{wl} := 1$
      $s_{wl} := t_{C_l}(w)/(t_{C_l}(w) + t_{C_l}(l))$
      $H := H \cup \{(w,l)\}$
  $m := 0$
  while($m < M \wedge H \neq \emptyset$)
    randomly draw ballot b from $\tilde{\mathcal{B}}$
    $m := m + 1$
    for($(w,l) \in H$)
      if($w = first(p_{C_l}(b))$)
        $T_{wl} := T_{wl} \times 2s_{wl}$
        if($T_{wl} \geq 1/\alpha$)
          % reject the null hypothesis
          $H = H - \{(w,l)\}$
      elseif($l = first(p_{C_l}(b))$)
        $T_{wl} := T_{wl} \times 2(1 - s_{wl})$
  if($H = \emptyset$)
    % reported results stand
    return *true*
  else % full recount required
    return *false*
          (b)

Fig. 2. (a) BRAVO algorithm for a ballot-polling RLA audit of a FPTP election with actual ballots $\tilde{\mathcal{B}}$, declared winners $\mathcal{W}$, declared losers $\mathcal{L}$, risk limit α and limit on ballots checked M, and (b) algorithm for a ballot-polling RLA of an IRV election with actual ballots $\tilde{\mathcal{B}}$, order of elimination π, risk limit α and limit on ballots checked M. In both algorithms, ballots are drawn uniformly at random from $\tilde{\mathcal{B}}$.

5 Ballot-Polling Risk-Limiting Audits for IRV

5.1 Auditing a Particular Elimination Order

The simplest approach to applying ballot-polling risk limiting auditing to IRV is to consider the IRV election as a number of simultaneous FPTP elections, one for each IRV round. This was previously suggested by Sarwate *et al.* [9], although they do not explore it algorithmically. Note that this may perform much more auditing than required, since it verifies more than just that the eventual winner is the correct winner, but that every step in the IRV election was correct (with some confidence).

Given an election $\mathcal{B}$ of n candidates $\mathcal{C}$ let the computed elimination order of the candidates be $\pi = [c_1, c_2, \ldots, c_{n-1}, c_n]$ where c_1 is the first eliminated candidate, c_2 the second, etc., and c_n the eventual winner.

Each IRV round corresponds to a FPTP election. In the ith round we have a FPTP election where $l = c_i$ is eliminated. The set of candidates of this election are $C_l = \{c_j \mid i \leq j \leq n\}$ with recorded tally $t_{C_l}(c)$ for each candidate $c \in C_l$, and loser $l = c_i$ and $n - i$ winners $C_l \setminus \{l\}$.

We can audit all these FPTP elections simultaneously, by simply considering all the null hypotheses that would violate the computed result. These are $\{\tilde{t}_{C_l}(c) \leq \tilde{t}_{C_l}(c_l) \mid 1 \leq i \leq n-1, l = c_i, c \in C_i \setminus \{l\}\}$. We represent these hypotheses by a pair (w, l) of winner $w = c$, and loser $l = c_i$. The statistic maintained for this test is T_{wl}. Note each loser only loses in one round so there is no ambiguity.

The algorithm is shown in Fig. 2(b). The set of hypotheses H are again pairs (w, l) of winner w and loser l, but they are interpreted as a hypothesis for the FPTP election corresponding to the round where l was eliminated. This means the calculation of the expected ratio of votes s_{wl} must be made using the tallies from this round. It also means we must consider every ballot to see how it is interesting for that particular hypothesis. Note that for example a ballot that is exhausted after k rounds will not play any role in determining statistics for later round hypotheses.

Example 3. Consider the IRV election shown in Example 1. The null hypotheses we need to reject are $\tilde{f}(c_1) \leq \tilde{f}(c_3)$, $\tilde{f}(c_2) \leq \tilde{f}(c_3)$, and $\tilde{f}(c_4) \leq \tilde{f}(c_3)$ from the first round election, $\tilde{t}_{\{c_1,c_2,c_4\}}(c_1) \leq \tilde{t}_{\{c_1,c_2,c_4\}}(c_2)$ and $\tilde{t}_{\{c_1,c_2,c_4\}}(c_3) \leq \tilde{t}_{\{c_1,c_2,c_4\}}(c_2)$ from the second round election and $\tilde{t}_{\{c_1,c_4\}}(c_4) \leq \tilde{t}_{\{c_1,c_4\}}(c_1)$ from the final round. Assuming $\alpha = 0.05$ the ASNs for the first round are the same as calculated in Example 2. The ASNs for the remaining elections are 51.8, 64.0 and 1186 respectively. □

Example 4. The weakness of this naive approach is that inconsequential earlier elimination rounds can be difficult to audit even if they are irrelevant to the winner. Consider an election with five candidates c_1, c_2, c_3, c_4, c_5 and ballots (with multiplicity) $[c_1] : 10000$, $[c_2] : 6000$, $[c_3, c_2] : 3000$, $[c_3, c_1] : 2000$, $[c_4] : 500$, $[c_5] : 499$. The elimination order is $[c_5, c_4, c_3, c_2, c_1]$. Assuming $\alpha = 0.05$ then rejecting the null hypothesis that c_5 beat c_4 in the first round gives an ASN of $13,165,239$ indicating a full hand audit is required. But it is irrelevant to the election result. □

5.2   Simultaneous Elimination

It is common in IRV elections to eliminate multiple candidates in a single round if it can be shown that the order of elimination cannot affect later rounds. Given an elimination order π we can simultaneously eliminate candidates

$E = \{\pi(i)..\pi(i+k)\}$ if the sum of tallies of these candidates is less than the tally of the next lowest candidate. Let $C = \{\pi(i), \pi(i+1), \ldots \pi(k), \pi(k+1), \ldots \pi(n)\}$ be the set of candidates standing after the first $i - 1$ have been eliminated. We can simultaneously eliminate E if:

$$t_C(c) > \sum_{c' \in E} t_C(c') \quad \forall c \in C \setminus E \tag{4}$$

This is because no matter which order the candidates in E are eliminated no candidate could ever garner a tally greater than one of the candidates in $C \setminus E$. Hence they will all be eliminated in any case. Note that since the remainder of the election only depends on the set of eliminated candidates and not their order, the simultaneous elimination can have no effect on later rounds of the election.

We can model the simultaneous elimination for auditing by considering all the simultaneously eliminated candidates E as as single loser l and rejecting hypotheses $\tilde{t}_C(c) \leq \tilde{t}_C(l)$ for each $c \in C \setminus E$. The statistic T_{wl} in this case is increased when we draw a ballot where w is the highest-ranked of remaining candidates C, and decreased when we draw a ballot where $c' \in E$ is the highest-ranked of remaining candidates C.

The elimination of all these null hypotheses is sufficient to prove that the multiple elimination is correct. This can then be combined with the audit of the rest of the elimination sequence, as described in Sect. 5.1, to test whether the election's announced winner is correct. Like the audit of a particular elimination sequence in Sect. 5.1, we are proving a stronger result than necessary, i.e. that a particular sequence of (possibly multiple) eliminations is valid, though there may be another way of getting the same candidate to win even if the multiple elimination isn't correct.

This often results in a much lower ASN, though not necessarily: sometimes the combined total of first preferences in E is very close to the next tally, so a lot of auditing is required. It may be better to audit each elimination individually in this case. It is possible to compute the ASN for each approach and choose the method that requires the least auditing, assuming the outcome is correct.

Example 5. Consider the election in Example 4. We can multiply eliminate the candidates $E = \{c_5, c_4\}$ since the sum of their tallies $499 + 500 < 5000$ which is the lowest tally of the other candidates. If we do this the difficult first round elimination auditing disappears. This shows the benefit of multiple elimination. The ASNs required for the joint elimination of E are 17.0, 36.2 and 49.1 as opposed to requiring a full hand audit.

Note that after this simultaneous elimination, the tallies for the three candidate election $\{c_1, c_2, c_3\}$ are $c_1 : 10000$, $c_2 : 6000$ and $c_3 : 5000$ and the ASNs to reject the hypotheses $\tilde{t}_C(c_1) \leq \tilde{t}_C(c_3)$ and $\tilde{t}_C(c_2) \leq \tilde{t}_C(c_3)$ are 77.6 and 1402 respectively.

Note we could also simultaneously eliminate the candidates $E = \{c_5, c_4, c_3\}$ since the sum of their tallies $499 + 500 + 5000 < 6000$ which is the lowest tally of the other candidate (that of c_2). But this will lead to a very difficult hypothesis to reject, $\tilde{t}_C(c_2) \leq \tilde{t}_C(\{c_5, c_4, c_3\})$ since the tallies are almost identical! The ASN is 158,156,493! This illustrates that multiple elimination may not always be beneficial.   □

5.3   Winner only Auditing

Up until now we consider auditing the entire IRV process to ensure that we are confident on all its outcomes. This is too strong since even if earlier eliminations happened in a different order it may not have any effect on the eventual winner.

Example 6. Consider an election with ballots $[c_1, c_2, c_3] : 10000$, $[c_2, c_1, c_3] : 6000$ and $[c_3, c_1, c_2] : 5999$. No simultaneous elimination is possible, and auditing that c_3 is eliminated before c_2 will certainly require a full hand audit. But even if c_2 were eliminated first it would not change the winner of the election.   □

An alternate approach to ballot-polling RLAs for IRV elections is to simply reject the $n-1$ null hypotheses $\{\tilde{f}(w) \leq \tilde{t}_{\{w,l\}}(l)\}$ where w is the declared winner of the IRV election, and $l \in \mathcal{C} \setminus \{w\}$. This hypothesis states that l gets more votes than w where l is given the maximal possible votes it could ever achieve before w is eliminated, and w gets only its first round votes (the minimal possible votes it could ever hold). When we reject this hypothesis we are confident that there could not be any elimination order where w is eliminated before l. If all these hypotheses are rejected then we are assured that w is the winner of the election, independent of a particular elimination order.

Example 7. Consider the election of Example 6. We must reject the hypotheses that $\{\tilde{f}(c_1) \leq \tilde{t}_{\{c_1,c_2\}}(c_2)\}$ (c_1 is eliminated before c_2) and $\{\tilde{f}(c_1) \leq \tilde{t}_{\{c_1,c_2\}}(c_3)\}$ (c_1 is eliminated before c_3). The primary votes for c_1 are 10000, while the maximum votes that c_2 can achieve before c_1 is eliminated are 6000. Simultaneously the maximum votes that c_3 can achieve before c_1 is eliminated are 5999. Auditing to reject these hypotheses is not difficult. The ASNs are 98.4 and 98.3 ballots.

Note however that if the $[c_2, c_1, c_3]$ ballots were changed to be $[c_2, c_3, c_1]$ then the maximum votes that c_3 can achieve are 12000, and the hypothesis that (c_1 is eliminated before c_3) could not be rejected. Indeed in this case just changing a single vote could result in c_3 winning the election, so this election will need a full recount.   □

There are, of course, some circumstances in which this does not work efficiently even though the margin of victory is large, for example if there are two runners-up who mostly (but not exclusively) preference each other.

Example 8. Consider an election with ballots $[c_1, c_2, c_3] : 10000$, $[c_2, c_3, c_1] : 5000$ $[c_2, c_1, c_3] : 1500$, $[c_3, c_2, c_1] : 5000$ and $[c_3, c_1, c_2] : 500$, and winner c_2. We cannot validate that c_2 won the election by a winner-only audit as we cannot reject the hypotheses that $\{\tilde{f}(c_2) \leq \tilde{t}_{\{c_2,c_1\}}(l)\}$. The winner's first preference tally is 6,500, while the total number of votes c_1 could have prior to c_2 being eliminated is 10,500.   □

5.4   A General Algorithm for Finding Efficient RLAs for IRV

This idea can be generalised to a method of choosing the set of facts that can be checked most efficiently (assuming no errors are found). We present an algorithm that achieves this by finding the easiest way to show that all election outcomes in which a candidate other than c_w won, did not arise, with a given level of statistical confidence.

Our algorithm, *audit-irv*, outlined in Fig. 3, explores the tree of alternate elimination sequences, ending in a candidate $c' \neq c_w$. Each node is a partial (or complete) elimination sequence. For each node π, we consider the set of hypotheses that (i) can be proven with an application of BRAVO and (ii) any one of which disproves the outcome that π represents. We label each node π with the hypothesis h from this set that requires the least number of anticipated ballot polls (ASN) to prove, denoted $asn(h)$. We use the notation $h(\pi)$ and $asn(\pi)$ to represent the hypothesis assigned to π and the ASN for this hypothesis, respectively. Our algorithm finds a set of hypotheses to prove, denoted *audits*, that: validates the correctness of a given election outcome, with risk limit α; and for which the largest ASN of these hypothesis is minimised.

Note that our *risk-limit* follows directly from BRAVO: if the election outcome is wrong, then one of the facts in h must be false—a BRAVO audit with risk limit α will detect this with probability of at least $1 - \alpha$. However, our estimate of *efficiency* is only heuristic: ASNs for testing a single fact can be derived analytically, but the expected number of samples required to reject multiple hypothesis at once is very hard to compute, even if there are no discrepancies. We make a best guess based on the maximum ASN for any single fact—this is what we meant by "optimal" in this section, though it may not guarantee an optimally efficient audit overall. In Sect. 6 we describe simulated sample numbers for the results of our algorithm applied to real elections (assuming no discrepancies).

Consider a partial elimination sequence $\pi = [c, \ldots, w]$ of at least two candidates, leading to an alternate winner w. This sequence represents the suffix of a complete order – an outcome in which the candidates in $\mathcal{C} \setminus \pi$ have been previously eliminated, in some order. We define a function FindBestAudit($\pi, \mathcal{C}, \mathcal{B}, \alpha$) that finds the easiest to prove hypothesis (or fact) h, with the smallest ASN, which disproves the outcome π given risk limit α. For the outcome $\pi = [c| \ldots]$, FindBestAudit considers the following hypotheses:

WO(c, c'): Hypothesis that c beats $c' \in \pi$, for some $c' \in \pi, c' \neq c$, in a winner only audit of the form described in Sect. 5.3, with winner c and loser c', thus invalidating the sequence since c cannot be eliminated before c';

WO(c'', c): Hypothesis that $c'' \in \mathcal{C} \setminus \pi$ beats c in a winner only audit with winner c'' and loser c, thus invalidating the sequence since c'' cannot be eliminated before c;

IRV$(c, c', \{c'' \mid c'' \in \pi\})$: Hypothesis that c beats some $c' \neq c \in \pi$ in a BRAVO audit with winner c and loser c', under the assumption that the only candidates remaining are those in π (i.e. the set $\{c'' \mid c'' \in \pi\}$) with other candidates eliminated with their votes distributed to later preferences, thus invalidating the sequence since then c is not eliminated at this stage in an IRV election.

audit-irv($\mathcal{C}, \mathcal{B}, c_w, \alpha$)

1    $audits \leftarrow \emptyset$

2    $F \leftarrow \emptyset$ ▷ F is a set sequences to expand (the frontier)

3    $LB \leftarrow 0$

▷ Populate F with single-candidate sequences

4   **for each**($c \in \mathcal{C} \setminus \{c_w\}$):

5        $\pi \leftarrow [c]$

6        $h \leftarrow$ FindBestAudit($\pi, \mathcal{C}, \mathcal{B}, \alpha$)

7        $hy[\pi] \leftarrow h$ ▷ Record best hypothesis for π

8        $ba[\pi] \leftarrow \pi$ ▷ Record best ancestor sequence for π

9        $F \leftarrow F \cup \{\pi\}$

▷ Repeatedly expand the sequence with largest ASN in F

10   **while**($|F| > 0$):

11       $\pi \leftarrow$ argmax$\{ASN(hy[\pi]) \mid \pi \in F\}$

12       $F \leftarrow F \setminus \{\pi\}$

13   **if**($ASN(hy[ba[\pi]]) \leq LB$):

14           $audits \leftarrow audits \cup \{hy[ba[\pi]]\}$

15           $F \leftarrow F \setminus \{\pi' \in F \mid ba[\pi]$ is a suffix of $\pi'\}$

16   **continue**

17   **for each**($c \in \mathcal{C} \setminus \pi$):

18           $\pi' \leftarrow [c] +\!\!+ \pi$

19           $h \leftarrow$ FindBestAudit($\pi', \mathcal{C}, \mathcal{B}, \alpha$)

20           $hy[\pi'] \leftarrow h$

21           $ba[\pi'] \leftarrow$ **if** $ASN(h) < ASN(hy[ba[\pi]])$ **then** π' **else** $ba[\pi]$

22   **if**($|\pi'| = |\mathcal{C}|$):

23   **if**($ASN(hy[ba[\pi']]) = \infty$):

24   **terminate** algorithm, full recount necessary

25   **else**:

26                   $audits \leftarrow audits \cup \{hy[ba[\pi']]\}$

27                   $LB \leftarrow max(LB, ASN(hy[ba[\pi']]))$

28                   $F \leftarrow F \setminus \{\pi' \in F \mid ba[\pi]$ is a suffix of $\pi'\}$

29   **continue**

30   **else**:

31               $F \leftarrow F \cup \{\pi'\}$

32   **return** $audits$ with maximum ASN equal to LB

Fig. 3. The *audit-irv* algorithm for searching for a collection of hypothesis to audit, with parallel applications of BRAVO, that validate the outcome of an IRV election with candidates $\mathcal{C}$, ballots $\mathcal{B}$, and winner c_w, with a given risk limit α.

We assume that if no hypothesis exists with ASN less than $|\mathcal{B}|$ the function returns a dummy **INF** hypothesis with $ASN(\mathbf{INF}) = +\infty$.

For an election with candidates $\mathcal{C}$ and winner c_w, *audit-irv* starts by adding $|\mathcal{C}| - 1$ partial elimination orders to an initially empty priority queue F, one for each alternate winner $c \neq c_w$ (Steps 4 to 9). The set *audits* is initially empty. For orders π containing a single candidate c, FindBestAudit considers the hypotheses $\mathbf{WO}(c'',c)$, candidate $c'' \neq c$ beats c in a winner only audit of the form described in Sect. 5.3, with winner c'' and loser c, for each $c'' \in \mathcal{C} \setminus \{c\}$. The hypothesis

h with the smallest $ASN(h)$ is recorded in $hy[\pi]$. The best ancestor for π is recorded in $ba[\pi]$, for these singletons sequences it is always the sequence itself.

We repeatedly find and remove a partial sequence π in F for expansion (Steps 11 and 12). This is the sequence with the (equal) highest ASN. If the best ancestor for this sequence has an ASN lower than the current lower bound LB (Steps 13 to 16) we simply add the corresponding hypothesis to $audits$ and remove any sequences in F which are subsumed by this ancestor (have it as a suffix), and restart the main loop.

Otherwise (Steps 17 to 31) we create a new elimination sequence π' with c appended to the start of π ($[c] ++\pi$) for each $c \in \mathcal{C} \setminus \pi$. For a new sequence π', FindBestAudit finds the hypothesis h requiring the least auditing effort to prove. We record (Step 20) this as the hypothesis for $hy[\pi'] = h$. We calculate (Step 21) the best ancestor of π' by comparing the ASN for its hypothesis with that of its ancestor.

If the sequence π' is complete, then we known one of its ancestors (including itself) must be audited. If the best of these is infinite, we terminate, a full recount is necessary. Otherwise we add the hypothesis of its best ancestor to $audits$ and remove all sequences in F which are subsumed by this ancestor. If the sequence is not complete we simply add it into the set of sequences to be expanded F.

Example 9. Consider an election with ballots $[c_1, c_2, c_3] : 5000$, $[c_1, c_3, c_2] : 5000$ $[c_2, c_3, c_1] : 5000$, $[c_2, c_1, c_3] : 1500$, $[c_3, c_2, c_1] : 5000$, $[c_3, c_1, c_2] : 500$, and $[c_4, c_1] : 5000$, and candidates c_1 to c_4. The initial tallies are: c_1: 10000; c_2: 6500; c_3: 5500; c_4: 5000. Candidates c_4, c_3, and c_2 are eliminated, in that order, with winner c_1. In a winner only audit ($\alpha = 0.05$), we cannot show that c_1 beats c_3, or that c_1 beats c_2, as c_1's first preference tally (of 10000 votes) is less than the total number of ballots that we could attribute to c_2 and c_3 (11500 and 10500, respectively). Simultaneous elimination is not applicable in this instance, as no sequences of candidates can be eliminated in a group. In an audit of the whole elimination order (as per Sect. 5.1), the loss of c_4 to c_1, c_2, and c_3 is the most challenging to audit. The ASN for this audit is 25% of all ballots.

Our *audit-irv* algorithm, however, finds a set of hypotheses that can be proven with a maximum ASN of 1% (with $\alpha = 0.05$), and that consequently rule out all elimination sequences that end in a candidate other than c_1. This audit proves the hypotheses: c_1 beats c_2 if c_3 and c_4 have been eliminated (ASN of 1%); c_1 beats c_3 if c_2 and c_4 have been eliminated (ASN 0.5%); c_1 beats c_4 in a winner only audit (ASN 0.4%); and that c_1 beats c_3 if c_4 has been eliminated (ASN 0.1%). Figure 4 shows the final state of the tree explored by *audit-irv*. We record, under each sequence, the easiest hypothesis that, if proven, *disproves* an outcome ending in that sequence (alongside its ASN). The hypotheses underneath each leaf node (excluding duplicates) form our audit. Once *audit-irv* creates the node $[c_4, c_3, c_1, c_2]$ and finds that it cannot disprove this hypothesis, all descendants of $[c_1, c_2]$ are pruned from the tree. At this stage, LB is equal to 1%, and all leaves can be disproved with an ASN $\leq LB$ and the algorithm terminates.   □

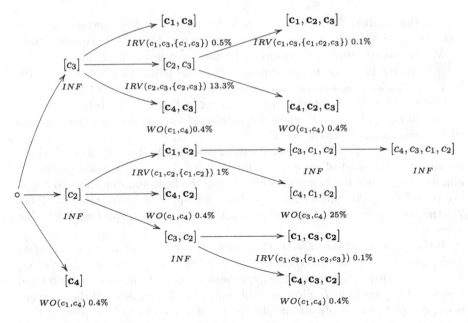

Fig. 4. Tree formed by *audit-irv* for the election of Example 9. The best hypothesis for each sequence is shown below the sequence, together with the ASN. The selected frontier is shown in bold which requires the audits: $IRV(c_1, c_3, \{c_1, c_3\})$, $IRV(c_1, c_3, \{c_1, c_2, c_3\})$, $WO(c_1, c_4)$, $IRV(c_1, c_2, \{c_1, c_2\})$.

6   Computational Results

We have simulated the audits described in Sect. 5.1 (auditing the elimination order, EO), Sect. 5.2 (auditing with simultaneous elimination, SE), and Sect. 5.3 (winner only auditing, WO), on 21 US IRV elections held between 2007 and 2014, and on the IRV elections held across 93 electorates in the 2015 state election in New South Wales (NSW), Australia. We report the average number of ballot polls (expressed as a percentage of ballots cast) required to complete each of these audits, for varying risk limits, in Table 2, alongside the ASN of each audit. Each audit is run 10 times, using 10 different random seeds to control the sequence of ballots polled, and the number of ballots polled averaged over those runs. For brevity, we include the results for only a portion of the NSW seats, with the full results provided in the full version of this paper. The margin of victory (MOV) for each election is computed using the algorithm of [3].

All experiments have been conducted on a machine with an Intel Xeon Platinum 8176 chip (2.1 GHz), and 1TB of RAM.

Table 2 shows that performing a winner only audit can be much easier than auditing the full elimination order (with or without the use of simultaneous elimination). This is the case for the 2013 Minneapolis Mayor, 2014 Oakland Mayor, and the 2010 Oakland D4 City Council elections. In some cases, winner only audits are more challenging (or not possible) as we seek to show that a

Table 2. Average ballot polls performed (as a percentage of ballots cast) over 10 simulated audits of 26 IRV elections using a series of different auditing methods (with an α of 0.01 and 0.05): auditing the elimination order (EO); auditing with simultaneous elimination (SE); and winner only auditing (WO). Also reported is each elections margin of victory (MOV). The notation ∞ indicates a percentage of ballots (or ASN) greater than 100%. CC, CE, CAD, and CAS denote City Council, County Executive, County Auditor, and County Assessor.

Election	$|C|$	$|B|$	MOV	EO α 0.01 Polls %	EO α 0.01 ASN %	EO α 0.05 Polls %	EO α 0.05 ASN %	SE α 0.01 Polls %	SE α 0.01 ASN %	SE α 0.05 Polls %	SE α 0.05 ASN %	WO α 0.01 Polls %	WO α 0.01 ASN %	WO α 0.05 Polls %	WO α 0.05 ASN %
Berkeley 2010 D7 CC	4	4,682	364 (7%)	6.7	7.2	3.9	4.7	7.5	7.2	4	4.7	8.7	22.4	4.9	14.7
Berkeley 2010 D8 CC	4	5,333	878 (16%)	∞	∞	∞	∞	2.9	4.2	2	2.8	1.3	1.8	0.8	1.2
Oakland 2010 D6 CC	4	14,040	2,603 (19%)	4.0	4.4	3	2.9	0.7	0.9	0.5	0.6	0.4	0.5	0.3	0.3
Pierce 2008 CC	4	43,661	2,007 (5%)	3.1	2.2	1.8	1.4	3.1	2.2	1.8	1.4	3.2	4.1	1.8	2.7
Pierce 2008 CAD	4	159,987	8,396 (5%)	0.3	0.5	0.2	0.3	0.3	0.5	0.2	0.3	0.5	1.2	0.3	0.8
Aspen 2009 Mayor	5	2,544	89 (4%)	62.4	71.8	52.7	46.9	62.4	71.8	54.8	46.9	∞	∞	∞	∞
Berkeley 2010 D1 CC	5	6,426	1,174 (18%)	2.4	1.7	1.6	1.1	2.4	1.7	1.6	1.1	1.1	1.1	0.8	0.7
Berkeley 2010 D4 CC	5	5,708	517 (9%)	7.5	7	6	4.7	28.7	40.7	17.8	26.6	4.9	7.3	3.8	4.8
Oakland 2012 D5 CC	5	13,482	486 (4%)	11.2	10.3	7.3	6.7	15.1	10.3	11.8	6.7	∞	∞	∞	∞
Pierce 2008 CE	5	312,771	2,027 (1%)	11.6	15.1	7.6	9.8	11.6	15.1	7.6	9.8	∞	∞	∞	∞
San Leandro 2012 D4 CC	5	28,703	2,332 (8%)	9.3	9.7	6.3	6.3	9.3	9.7	6.3	6.3	1.1	4.4	0.8	2.9
Oakland 2012 D3 CC	7	26,761	386 (1%)	∞	∞	∞	∞	∞	∞	∞	∞	∞	∞	∞	∞
Pierce 2008 CAS	7	312,771	1,111 (0.4%)	∞	∞	∞	∞	∞	∞	∞	∞	∞	∞	∞	∞
San Leandro 2010 Mayor	7	23,494	116 (0.5%)	94.6	∞	92.9	∞	∞	∞	92.9	∞	∞	∞	∞	∞
Berkeley 2012 Mayor	8	57,492	8,522 (15%)	∞	∞	77	∞	2.3	2.6	1.6	1.7	0.2	0.2	0.1	0.2
Oakland 2010 D4 CC	8	23,884	2,329 (10%)	∞	∞	76.4	∞	∞	∞	∞	∞	0.9	3.1	0.6	2
Aspen 2009 CC	11	2,544	35 (1%)	∞	∞	∞	∞	∞	∞	∞	∞	∞	∞	∞	∞
Oakland 2010 Mayor	11	122,268	1,013 (1%)	∞	∞	∞	∞	21.5	23.8	15	15.5	∞	∞	∞	∞
Oakland 2014 Mayor	11	101,431	10,201 (10%)	∞	∞	∞	8	∞	∞	∞	∞	0.8	19.8	0.5	12.9
San Francisco 2007 Mayor	18	149,465	50,837 (34%)	∞	∞	∞	∞	0.03	0.03	0.02	0.02	0.01	0.01	0.01	0.01
Minneapolis 2013 Mayor	36	79,415	6,949 (9%)	∞	∞	∞	∞	∞	∞	∞	∞	0.5	3.1	0.3	2.1
Balmain NSW 2015	7	46,952	1,731 (3.7%)	∞	∞	∞	∞	83.8	∞	65.4	82	5.2	31.6	3.7	20.6
Campbelltown NSW 2015	5	45,124	3,096 (6.9%)	13.6	12.2	8.4	8	∞	∞	∞	∞	1.3	1.7	0.9	1.1
Gosford NSW 2015	6	48,259	102 (0.2%)	∞	∞	∞	∞	∞	∞	∞	∞	∞	∞	∞	∞
Lake Macquarie NSW 2015	7	47,698	4,253 (8.9%)	27.7	22.8	14.5	15	6.9	7.8	3.2	5.1	0.7	1.6	0.5	1
Sydney NSW 2015	8	42,747	2,864 (6.7%)	∞	∞	∞	∞	3.3	4.6	2.2	3	1.6	6.9	1	4.5

candidate c (on just their first preference votes) could have beaten another c' (who is given all votes in which they appear before c or in which they appear, but c does not). Even if c does beat c' in the true outcome of the election, this audit may not be able to prove this (see Pierce 2008 County Executive, Oakland 2012 D5 City Council, and Aspen 2009 Mayor for examples). Auditing with simultaneous elimination (grouping several eliminated candidates into a single 'super' candidate) can be more efficient than auditing each individual elimination

Table 3. ASN, and average ballot polls required across 10 simulations, of audit found by *audit-irv* for 26 IRV elections, alongside best known alternative (EO, SE, or WO) given a risk limit α of 0.05. Notation ∞ indicates a percentage of ballots (or ASN) greater than 100%. 'Exp' denotes the number of node expansions performed by *audit-irv*.

Election	Best Alt.			*audit-irv* ($\alpha = 0.05$)			
	Audit	Polls %	ASN %	Polls %	ASN %	Time (s)	Exp.
Berkeley 2010 D7 CC	EO	3.9	4.7	5.4	4.7	0.003	3
Berkeley 2010 D8 CC	WO	0.8	1.2	0.9	0.9	0.01	6
Oakland 2010 D6 CC	WO	0.3	0.3	0.3	0.3	0.01	3
Pierce 2008 CC	EO,SE	1.8	1.4	1.5	1.4	0.03	3
Pierce 2008 CAD	EO,SE	0.2	0.3	0.3	0.3	0.1	3
Aspen 2009 Mayor	EO	52.7	46.9	28.1	46.9	0.01	9
Berkeley 2010 D1 CC	WO	0.8	0.7	0.6	0.6	0.01	5
Berkeley 2010 D4 CC	WO	3.8	4.8	1.6	2.7	0.01	5
Oakland 2012 D5 CC	EO	7.3	6.7	5.2	6.7	0.02	5
Pierce 2008 CE	EO,SE	7.6	9.8	13.9	9.8	0.9	10
San Leandro 2012 D4 CC	WO	0.8	2.9	0.8	0.6	0.06	8
Oakland 2012 D3 CC	–	∞	∞	**14.2**	**13.1**	**0.2**	**20**
Pierce 2008 CAS	–	∞	∞	**17**	**22.7**	**3.4**	**28**
San Leandro 2010 Mayor	EO,SE	92.9	∞	87.6	∞	0.08	8
Berkeley 2012 Mayor	WO	0.1	0.2	0.1	0.1	0.3	14
Oakland 2010 D4 CC	WO	0.6	2	0.6	0.5	0.3	15
Aspen 2009 CC	–	∞	∞	∞	∞	0.4	172
Oakland 2010 Mayor	SE	15	15.5	15.3	15.5	2.7	44
Oakland 2014 Mayor	WO	0.5	12.9	5.4	0.1	106	606
San Francisco 2007 Mayor	WO	0.01	0.01	0.01	0.01	23	130
Minneapolis 2013 Mayor	WO	0.3	2.1	0.2	0.2	10.8	43
Balmain NSW 2015	WO	3.7	20.6	3.2	1.9	0.2	8
Campbelltown NSW 2015	WO	0.9	1.1	0.8	0.7	0.1	5
Gosford NSW 2015	–	∞	∞	∞	∞	0.1	6
Lake Macquarie NSW 2015	WO	0.5	1	0.5	0.3	0.2	8
Sydney NSW 2015	SE	1	4.5	1.3	0.7	0.2	11

(see Berkeley 2010 D8 City Council, Berkeley 2012 Mayor, Oakland 2010 Mayor, San Francisco 2007 Mayor, and Sydney NSW). In some instances, however, the tally of the super candidate is quite close to that of the next eliminated candidate, resulting in a challenging audit (see Campbelltown NSW, and Berkeley 2010 D4 City Council).

Table 3 reports the maximum ASN of the audit found by *audit-irv* for each of the 26 elections examined in Table 2, alongside the ASN and average actual ballot polls required across 10 simulations of the best alternative audit (elimination order EO, simultaneous elimination SE, and winner only WO). Also reported is the runtime (in seconds) of *audit-irv* and the number nodes expanded (note that this does not include the creation of nodes forming the initial queue). Our *audit-irv* algorithm finds an audit (a collection of facts to prove by simultaneous applications of BRAVO) with an ASN that is equal to or lower than the ASN of the best alternative. The Oakland 2012 D3 City Council and Pierce 2008 County Assessor elections are particularly interesting. We are able to find a method of auditing the outcome of these elections that is significantly easier than the EO, SE, and WO methods, which suggest a full recount. The ASN is just an estimate, however, and the actual auditing effort required may deviate from this. For the Balmain NSW election, for example, the ASN of the best alternative audit (WO) is 20.6%. The average actual number of ballot polls required is 3.7% of the total, across 10 simulations of the audit. The ASN and actual audit effort required for the *audit-irv* audit in this instance is 1.9% and 3.2%, respectively. For the Oakland 2014 Mayor election, the ASN of the best alternative audit (WO) is 12.9% while the average actual auditing effort required is 0.5%. In contrast, the ASN of the audit found by *audit-irv* is 0.1% while the average actual effort required is 5.4%.

7   Conclusion

This paper provides a comprehensive, practical method of conducting risk-limiting ballot-polling audits for IRV. We use Stark's BRAVO as a black box, and show how to combine facts together to audit an IRV outcome. Most can be audited very efficiently. This algorithm dominates other approaches to auditing IRV elections. Over a collection of parliamentary seats or council races, most outcomes could be confirmed quickly with very little effort, while others would require some more careful auditing, and those with very small margins could be identified immediately and sent for a full manual recount.

References

1. Antonyan, T., et al.: State-wide elections, optical scan voting systems, and the pursuit of integrity. IEEE Trans. Inf. Forensics Secur. **4**(4), 597–610 (2009)
2. Beckert, B., Kirsten, M., Klebanov, V., Schürmann, C.: Automatic margin computation for risk-limiting audits. In: Krimmer, R. (ed.) E-Vote-ID 2016. LNCS, vol. 10141, pp. 18–35. Springer, Cham (2017). https://doi.org/10.1007/978-3-319-52240-1_2

3. Blom, M., Stuckey, P.J., Teague, V., Tidhar, R.: Efficient computation of exact IRV margins. In: European Conference on AI (ECAI), pp. 480–487 (2016)
4. Hall, J.L., et al.: Implementing risk-limiting post-election audits in California. In: Proceedings of 2009 Electronic Voting Technology Workshop/Workshop on Trustworthy Elections (EVT/WOTE 2009), August 2009, Montreal, Canada. USENIX (2009)
5. Kroll, J.A., Halderman, J.A., Felten, E.W.: Efficiently auditing multi-level elections. Ann Arbor **1001**, 48109 (2014)
6. Lindeman, M., Stark, P.B.: A gentle introduction to risk-limiting audits. IEEE Secur. Privacy **10**, 42–49 (2012)
7. Lindeman, M., Stark, P.B., Yates, V.: BRAVO: ballot-polling risk-limiting audits to verify outcomes. In: Proceedings of the 2011 Electronic Voting Technology Workshop/Workshop on Trustworthy Elections (EVT/WOTE 2011). USENIX (2012)
8. Magrino, T.R., Rivest, R.L., Shen, E., Wagner, D.A.: Computing the margin of victory in IRV elections. In: USENIX Accurate Electronic Voting Technology Workshop: Workshop on Trustworthy Elections. USENIX Association, Berkeley (2011)
9. Sarwate, A.D., Checkoway, S., Shacham, H.: Risk-limiting audits and the margin of victory in nonplurality elections. Polit. Policy **3**(3), 29–64 (2013)
10. Stark, P.B.: A sharper discrepancy measure for post-election audits. Ann. Appl. Stat. **2**(3), 982–985 (2008)

The Threat of SSL/TLS Stripping
to Online Voting

Anthony Cardillo and Aleksander Essex[✉]

Department of Electrical and Computer Engineering,
Western University, London, ON, Canada
{acardill,aessex}@uwo.ca

Abstract. In many real-world deployments of online voting, Transport Layer Security (TLS) represents the primary (and in some cases *only*) line of defense against network based man-in-the-middle attacks that can steal voter credentials and modify ballot selections. In this paper we examine online voting in the context of *TLS stripping attacks*, which exploit the situation where a voter types or clicks a URL of the form `example.com` or http://example.com. Despite the widespread availability of effective protections, we present a study of voting-related websites finding the overwhelming majority are vulnerable to TLS stripping to some degree, with most offering no explicit protection at all.

1 Introduction

Recall the last time you logged in to your social network account, an online retailer, financial institution, or even online election. You should have seen a lock icon in the address bar of your browser. Was it there? Did you check? Suppose the icon was missing. Would you notice? And if you did notice, what would you attribute it's absence to? Maybe you misunderstood the security indicators. Maybe the server was mis-configured. Or maybe you were the victim of a cyber attack that prevented your browser from initiating a secure connection using transport-layer security (TLS), enabling attackers to monitor and/or modify the content you send and receive.

TLS stripping[1] [4,15] is a network based man-in-the-middle attack which suppresses or *strips* TLS from a communication channel. The attack is made possible when a user types or clicks a non-HTTPS URL of the form `example.com` or http://example.com (as opposed to https://example.com). This instructs the browser to make an insecure request over HTTP instead of its encrypted and authenticated counterpart, HTTPS. A well configured TLS-enabled server would typically respond to such a request by directing the client to request the resource over HTTPS instead. A man-in-the-middle can intercept and suppress this response, and continue communicating with the client over HTTP. Since the

---

[1] More commonly known as *SSL Stripping*, it was originally named after the now-deprecated Secure Sockets Layer (SSL) protocol.

© Springer Nature Switzerland AG 2018
R. Krimmer et al. (Eds.): E-Vote-ID 2018, LNCS 11143, pp. 35–50, 2018.
https://doi.org/10.1007/978-3-030-00419-4_3

client requested an HTTP connection to begin with, the missing TLS redirect goes unnoticed, and the man-in-the-middle is free to observe and modify any data exchanged in the interaction.

Although TLS stripping is a significant and effective threat to online security generally, it has only briefly been considered in the context of elections [10,25]. In this paper we conducted a study of the adoption of TLS stripping mitigations by election websites. We found election websites systematically lagging in the adoption of industry best-practices. We examined an international cross-section of over 100 election, vendor, and voter registration websites and found 98% were vulnerable to TLS stripping to some degree, with 84% providing no mitigation at all. We also found a number of servers with serious TLS vulnerabilities, which we disclosed to the affected organizations.

2   Motivation

Online voting is a unique use case of the web, with a confluence of factors that increase the severity of TLS stripping attacks. The factors that warrant further study of this topic are as follows.

Critical Infrastructure. Online voting websites must conform to higher cybersecurity standards. Elections are increasingly being recognized as critical infrastructure. In 2017, for example, the U.S. Department of Homeland Security designated elections systems as critical infrastructure under the Government Facilities Sector.[2] As such, it is important to understand how online voting websites are performing relative to industry security standards.

Secret Ballot, Secret Tampering. As we discuss in Sect. 3.1, TLS represents the main (and in some cases *only*) line of defense against network based man-in-the-middle attacks. Unlike other online settings (e.g., social media, online banking, etc.), an attack stealing voter credentials or modifying ballot selections can be more difficult to detect and correct due to ballot secrecy requirements, making the impact of a man-in-the-middle attack more severe in comparison.

Communicating URLs to Voters. The transient nature of elections often makes communicating the URL of an election website to voters a weak link in a literal and figurative sense. As discussed in Sect. 3, we found numerous cases of election officials and candidates explicitly directing voters to use HTTP URLs.

Systematic Lack of Best Practice Adoption. Effective mitigations for TLS stripping have long been adopted by leading websites like Google, Amazon, Facebook, etc. If elections truly are to serve as critical infrastructure, they must provide a degree of web security that is *no worse* than current industry practices. As our findings in Sect. 4 show, however, almost every election-related website we examined is vulnerable to TLS stripping.

---

[2] https://www.dhs.gov/government-facilities-sector.

Barriers to Adoption. Unlike other vulnerabilities that can be resolved with software updates, mitigations to TLS stripping are opt-in, meaning the organization has to be aware of the attack, be aware of the mitigations, and take action to apply them. As we discuss in Sect. 5, election agencies and vendors face a variety of obstacles in this regard.

3 The Threat of TLS Stripping to Online Elections

Transport Layer Security (TLS) is a standardized group of cryptographic protocols for secure network communication [18,19], providing confidentiality, integrity and authentication of network communications at the application layer.

Attacks against TLS typically involve directly attacking components, typically by exploiting vulnerabilities in the software implementation, the cryptographic primitives, or the protocol itself. Recent examples include key-recovery attacks on export strength ciphersuites [1,23], buffer over-read vulnerabilities [8], insufficient public-key validation [7,22], and eavesdropping attacks exploiting either TLS compression (BEAST and CRIME) and padding oracles [11]. We refer the reader to the surveys of Clark and van Oorschot [4] and Sheffer et al. [20] for a systematic study of known attacks.

TLS stripping differs from these approaches. It does not exploit a concrete TLS vulnerability, but rather prevents a TLS connection from being established in the first place.

3.1 Role of TLS in Online Elections

Suppose a voter types the URL of an election website, `voting-site.com`. The server responds with the login page, and the voter enters their user id and password. The browser sends an HTTP `POST` over TLS to the login page, e.g., https://voting-site.com/login.php with the following contents:

$$\texttt{auth\_id} = \texttt{1234} \& \texttt{auth\_pwd} = \texttt{123456} \& \texttt{submit} = \texttt{Login}.$$

Most login pages do not use encryption or authentication inside of the TLS connection. Without it, or with a vulnerable implementation, a man-in-the-middle can directly recover the voter's credentials from the contents of the login `POST`. Now suppose the voter marks a vote for a candidate, Alice, and clicks on the *Cast* button. The browser makes an HTTP `POST` to the cast ballot page https://voting-site.com/cast.php with the contents:

$$\texttt{president} = \texttt{Alice} \& \texttt{election\_id} = \texttt{US\_2020} \& \texttt{submit} = \texttt{Confirm}$$

Since no other encryption or authentication exists on the *POST* contents, a man-in-the-middle can arbitrarily change the voter's selections, e.g., by setting `president=Bob`, or perhaps more simply by swapping candidate names in the ballot HTML.

Application Layer Encryption. Some online voting designers have attempted to mitigate the consequence of TLS based attacks by employing additional cryptographic protections at the application layer. For example, the iVote system in Australia[3] uses client-side Javascript to encrypt POST data. The problem remains, however, that the Javascript is delivered to the client over TLS. Teague and Halderman [12] demonstrated the ability to inject vote-stealing Javascript as a result of the use of weak cryptographic parameters [23] in the state election of New South Wales in 2014. Even without actively injecting Javascript, Culnane et al. [5] demonstrated the feasibility of passively recovering voter credentials in iVote using brute force methods.

Multi-factor Authentication. Other online voting designers mitigate TLS attacks by employing additional voter authentication factors. Online voting in the Estonian system [21], for example, is done through a special election-specific software application. The approach removes much of the user from the equation by forcing TLS and using a pre-loaded (pinned) certificate to authenticate the election server. Additionally, the Estonian system uses national Electronic ID cards to digitally sign ballots (although Nemec et al. [17] recently demonstrated a major signature forgery vulnerability in the Estonian PKI). While these additional factors add defense in depth with regard to TLS stripping attacks, both the voting application[4] and the electronic ID software[5] are still initially downloaded by the voter in a web browser over TLS.

3.2 TLS Stripping

TLS stripping (originally *SSL* stripping) was introduced Moxie Marlinspike [15] on the observation that most TLS connections occurred only when a user either clicked on an explicit HTTPS link, or when the server sent an HTTPS redirect. As he noted: "Nobody types 'https://', or even 'http://' for that matter." And when a user either types or clicks on a URL of the form example.com (or http://example.com), a TLS-enabled server typically responds by directing the client to request the resource securely over HTTPS instead. The client would then initiate a TLS handshake, after which time the interaction would continue over an encrypted and authenticated connection (See Fig. 1). A man-in-the-middle can intercept and suppress this redirect, and continue the interaction with the client over HTTP. The man-in-the-middle can then initiate and maintain its own TLS connection with the server.

Because the client requested an HTTP connection to begin with, the missing TLS redirect, and continued interaction over the insecure channel goes unnoticed, and the man-in-the-middle is free to observe or modify any messages between the client and server (See Fig. 2).

---

[3] https://ivote.nsw.gov.au.

[4] https://valimised.ee.

[5] https://www.id.ee.

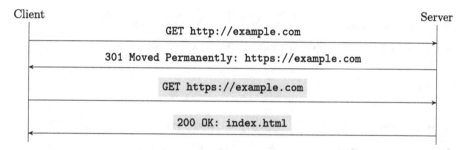

Fig. 1. Normal HTTPS redirect. When a user types or clicks an HTTP URL, a well configured TLS-enabled server would direct the client to use HTTPS instead, and the interaction would continue over a secure TLS connection (shown in grey).

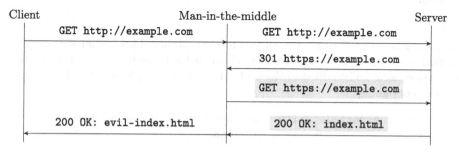

Fig. 2. TLS stripping attack. A man-in-the-middle can intercept a request made by a client over HTTP and proxy it to the server via its own separate TLS connection (shown in grey). Since the client never saw the HTTPS redirect, the man-in-the-middle is free to continue the connection over HTTP.

Detecting TLS Stripping. TLS stripping attacks cannot not be reliably detected by users in practice, as they do not generate browser errors or warnings. Instead, they require the user to notice the *absence* of security indicators such as the `https://` in the URL, and the padlock icon in the address bar [2,6]. Inconsistent and confusing security indicators add to the challenge [3]. Some browsers such as Safari and Edge do not even display the `HTTPS` indicator, and employ a subtle padlock icon (see Fig. 3). Due to limited screen resolution, many mobile browsers hide the address bar when scrolling. Even if a user consciously registers the unexpected behavior, research has suggested that voters are not likely attribute it to a malicious cause [16].

3.3 HTTP Strict Transport Security (HSTS)

When TLS stripping was first introduced, there was no mechanism to definitively declare preference for HTTPS, which led to the development of the HTTP Strict Transport Security (HSTS) standard [13]. An HSTS directive can be placed in an HTTP response header allowing a server to advertise its intention to only

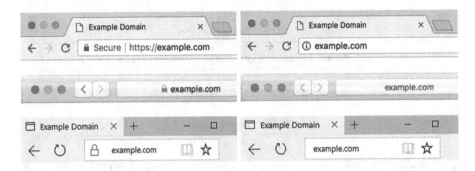

Fig. 3. Attack indicators across browsers. Secure connections (left) versus TLS stripped connections (right) in the desktop versions of Chrome (top), Safari (middle), and Edge (bottom).

communicate over HTTPS for all future connections. This includes an expiry period (expressed in seconds), and optional fields to include subdomains, and express consent to be added to the preload list. For example, an HTTP response header containing

```
Strict-Transport-Security: max-age=31536000; includeSubDomains;
                           preload;
```

would direct the browser to store the preference in cache for 1 year, for all subdomains, and would direct browser developers to add the site to the preload list. From this point forward until expiry (or until the user clears the browser's cache), the browser will make all requests to that domain (and any subdomains) over HTTPS—even if the user types or clicks an HTTP link.

Adoption of the HSTS standard has been slow but steady. At the time of writing, 16.8% of the top 150,000 TLS-enabled sites supported HSTS.[6] As of 2015, the US government instituted a policy requiring all executive (i.e., .gov) departments and agencies to use HTTPS and enable HSTS.[7]

3.4 HSTS Preload List

HSTS uses a trust-on-first-use model. To be effective in preventing a TLS stripping attack, a user must have previously visited the website in order to have received and stored the server's preference. There are, however, a number of situations where this requirement would not be met, such as when: the user has never visited the site before; the browser, operating system or device was recently upgraded or switched; the user recently cleared their browser's cache; or, the user had not visited the site for an amount of time exceeding the max-age.

---

[6] https://www.ssllabs.com/ssl-pulse.

[7] US Office of Management and Budget. Memorandum M-15-13, 2015. https://https.cio.gov.

For many websites, and especially election websites, it may not be reasonable to assume a previous visit has recently occurred. In addition, some URLs may never be visited. For example, a visit to `example.com` might redirect to https://www.example.com. Since the client never visited https://example.com, it will not receive an `includeSubDomains` directive that applies to the entire zone, and any subdomains (e.g., `sub.example.com`) will be left unprotected.

For these reasons, the Chromium security team created a list[8] of HSTS-enabled domains *preloaded* into Chrome, and each user receives this list automatically whenever Chrome is installed or updated. Visiting any domain on this list is done over HTTPS only (even on a first visit), meaning no HTTP to HTTPS redirects are ever made, and therefore no opportunity for TLS stripping exists. Other browsers like Firefox, Opera, Safari and IE/Edge use preload lists based on the Chrome list.

In 2014 the list contained only 233 non-Google domains [14], and additions were handled manually over email. At the time of writing there were 50,000 domains on the list, spanning a wide variety of sites ranging from large companies and government agencies, to small businesses and personal websites, and addition is handled by an automated submission site.[9] Although the `.gov` domains account for less then 1% of the preload list, the DotGov registrar has begun automatically preloading all newly registered `.gov` domains.

3.5 Communicating Voting Website URLs

One of the major challenges of hosting an online election is communicating authentic URLs to voters. In an effort to increase voter turnout, election officials and campaigns may employ a variety of modes of communication. A vulnerability arises, however, if the voting website does not employ HSTS preloading *and* the user types or clicks on an HTTP URL. As we will see in the following section, this first circumstance occurs in the vast majority of election websites. But how likely is a user to initially visit the voting site over HTTP? User testing is beyond the scope of this study, however we observed numerous situations in which the voter was explicitly directed to the voting site over HTTP (see Fig. 4).

For example, during the New Democratic Party of Canada's leadership election in October 2017, we observed numerous HTTP links on social media originating from the accounts of candidates, riding associations, supporters, and even the party itself. In the mailer to voters, the instructions explicitly directed voters to the website via HTTP: "How can I vote online? Type vote.ndp.ca into the address bar of your web browser."

In another example, the Ontario Labour Relations Board held an online strike vote for college teachers in November 2017. Not only was the landing page to the voting site emailed as an HTTP link to voters (`olrb-crto.isivote.com`), the site was not available over HTTPS. Only when voters selected their preferred language were they redirected to a TLS enabled site (on a different domain) to log in.

---

[8] https://www.chromium.org/hsts.
[9] https://hstspreload.org.

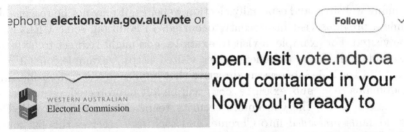

(a) Western Australia Election Commission, Poster, 2017.   (b) New Democratic Party of Canada, Twitter, 2017

Fig. 4. The weakest link. Examples from recent online elections of voters being directed to type [24] or click (https://twitter.com/NDP/status/910253791718645765) insecure HTTP URLs.

4   Study of HSTS Preload Adoption in Election-Related Websites

This section presents a study of HSTS pre-loading among websites with an election focus. We examined a number of websites, including the online voting sites of specific elections, government agencies responsible for election administration and voter registration, and the websites of companies offering online voting solutions. In total we examined 103 election sites, and chose to focus on Australia, Canada, Switzerland and the United States as countries that have a high concentration of websites pertaining to elections.

Each site was evaluated for the availability of a well-configured TLS configuration, the presence of HSTS headers with a non-trivial max-age, and membership in the HSTS preload list. We comment on any vulnerabilities in the TLS configuration for sites that scored a grade of C or lower on Qualsys SSL Test.[10]

4.1   Election Websites

Only a handful of online elections occur at any time, and many sites stay online only during the polling period. For this study, our goal was to present a diverse (not necessarily complete) sample of voting sites. We examined the TLS configuration of voting sites with active login pages during mid May 2018, and present our findings in Table 1, which revealed minimal protection against TLS stripping attacks.

Of the 10 sites examined, only two were on the preload list. The first is Helios, an end-to-end verifiable internet voting scheme (E2E-VIV) [9], which has been used to conduct elections for organizations such as the International Association of Cryptologic Researchers (IACR) and the Princeton Graduate Students' Association. We contacted the Helios maintainers in October 2017 asking them

---

[10] https://ssllabs.com/ssltest.

Table 1. Snapshot of HSTS in online voting websites

Domain	Election	TLS	HSTS	Preload
ivote-cvs.elections.wa.gov.au	Western Australia State 2017	●	○	○
esc-vote.com/acm2018	ACM General Election 2018	●	○	○
evoting.ch	Swiss Post E-Voting	●	●	●
heliosvoting.org	Helios	●	●	●
intvoting.com/OntarioPC	Ontario PC Leadership 2018	●	○	○
innskraning.island.is	Iceland Citizen E-referendum	●	○	○
ivote.nsw.gov.au	New South Wales State 2015	●	●	○
olrb-crto.isivote.com	Ontario Labour Board 2018	○	○	○
valimised.ee	Elections Estonia	●	○	○
vote.ndp.ca	NDP Canada Leadership 2017	●	○	○

to consider adding `heliosvoting.org` to the preload list. They did, and (to our knowledge) became the first online voting site on the preload list. The second is Swiss Post's E-Voting site, which has been used by the cantons of Fribourg and Neuchâtel, and will be used for the first time in upcoming elections in the cantons of Basel-Stadt, Glarus, and Thurgau. We observed inbound links to the E-Voting site originating from the canton sites. We examined these sites and found none were using HSTS or preloading, and some even did not offer TLS (see Table 2). Voters attempting to visit via `evoting.ch` via the canton websites would, therefore, still be vulnerable to TLS stripping.

Table 2. HSTS in swiss cantons using online voting

Domain	Canton	TLS	HSTS	Preload
bs.ch	Basel-Stadt	○	○	○
fr.ch	Fribourg	●	○	○
gl.ch	Glarus	◐[a,b]	○	○
ne.ch	Neuchâtel	○	○	○
tg.ch	Thurgau	◐[c]	○	○

[a] Vulnerable to POODLE (CVE-2014-3566).
[b] Uses weak/obsolete ciphersuites.
[c] Vulnerable to ROBOT (CVE-2017-13099 and others).

4.2 Online Voting Vendor Websites

We studied the corporate websites of vendors offering online voting solutions. Vendors are the implementors of online voting sites, and although their own sites are typically not directly associated with ballot casting, we would contend that they serve as an indicator of a vendor's awareness and ability to follow best practices. A selection of 27 different online voting vendors was studied (see Table 3).

At the time of inspection, 3 domains exhibited insufficient TLS protection; Dominion and Election Service Co. were improperly serving their cloud provider's certificate, which generated a browser error. Voting Place was offering SSL 3.0 which is vulnerable to CVE-2014-3566. Of the remaining domains, only 9 implemented HSTS, and no sites were found on the preload list.

4.3 Election Agencies

Critical election information such as dates and polling locations must be communicated to voters. While web-based attacks against election agencies providing such information would not impact the vote directly, it could serve to suppress votes, and undermine public trust. For example, an automated phone scam was used in Guelph, Canada in 2011 to direct voters to a fake polling location, and led to a criminal conviction,[11] which might be harder to achieve in the more anonymous setting of the web.

We decided to study the configurations of election agency websites in two countries who have used online voting at the sub-national level: Australia (see Table 4) and Canada (see Table 5). Of the 14 federal, provincial and territorial election agencies in Canada, none used HSTS or preloading, 2 had serious TLS configuration issues, and 9 did not implement TLS protection whatsoever. Elections British Columbia was found serving a self-signed certificate, which caused a browser error. We contacted them, and they promptly responded by obtaining and installing a certificate with a valid trust path. Élections Québec acknowledged receipt of our recommendations to disable weak and obsolete ciphersuites (esp. those using RC4), but had still not done so at time of writing.

Australia's election agencies fared slightly better: all 9 domains used TLS, however HSTS was found on a single domain only, and none were on the preload list.

4.4 Voter Registration Websites

Another important online election-related activity is voter registration. Some governments allow voters to sign up to vote and access information such as registration details, contact information of elected officials, voting instructions, location of ballot drop boxes and voting centers. For this component, we decided to focus on the Unites States. Most states in the US offer online voter registration.

---

[11] R. v. Sona, 2016 ONCA 452, Court of Appeals for Ontario, 2016. http://www.ontariocourts.ca/decisions/2016/2016ONCA0452.pdf.

Table 3. HSTS in online voting vendor websites

Domain	Company	TLS	HSTS	Preload
agora.vote	Agora	●	○	○
coalichain.io	Coalichain	●	○	○
cyber.ee	Cybertentica	●	●	○
democracy.earth	Democracy Earth	●	○	○
dominionvoting.com	Dominion Voting	◐[a]	○	○
eballot.com	eBallot	●	○	○
electionrunner.com	Election Runner	●	○	○
electionservicesco.com	Election Services Co.	◐[a]	○	○
www.essvote.com	ES&S	●	●	○
everyonecounts.com	Everyone Counts	●	●	○
followmyvote.com	Follow My Vote	●	●	○
id.ee	Estonian National Identiy	●	●	○
intelivote.com	Intelivote	●	●	○
polyas.com	Polyas	●	●	○
polys.me	Polys	●	●	○
scytl.com	Scytl	●	○	○
smartmatic.com	Smartmatic	●	○	○
simplesurvey.com	Simple Survey	●	○	○
simplyvoting.com	Simply Voting	●	○	○
sk.ee	SK ID Solutions	●	○	○
tivi.io	TIVI	●	○	○
voatz.com	Voatz	◐[b]	○	○
vogo.vote	Vogo	●	○	○
votebox.co	Vote Box	●	●	○
votem.com	Votem	●	○	○
votewatcher.com	Vote Watcher	◐[a]	○	○
votingplace.net	Voting Place	◐[b]	○	○

[a] Certificate common-name mismatch with cloud host.
[b] Vulnerable to POODLE (CVE-2014-3566).

Table 4. HSTS in Australian election agencies

Domain	Division	TLS	HSTS	Preload
aec.gov.au	Australia	●	○	○
elections.act.gov.au	Australian Capital Territory	●	○	○
elections.nsw.gov.au	New South Wales	●	○	○
ntec.nt.gov.au	Northern Territory	●	○	○
ecq.qld.gov.au	Queensland	●	○	○
ecsa.sa.gov.au	South Australia	●	○	○
tec.tas.gov.au	Tasmania	●	○	○
vec.vic.gov.au	Victoria	●	●	○
waec.wa.gov.au	Western Australia	●	○	○

Table 5. HSTS in Canadian election agencies

Domain	Division	TLS	HSTS	Preload
elections.ca	Canada	○	○	○
elections.ab.ca	Alberta	○	○	○
elections.bc.ca	British Columbia	◐[a]	○	○
electionsmanitoba.ca	Manitoba	○	○	○
www.electionsnb.ca	New Brunswick	○	○	○
www.elections.gov.nl.ca	Newfoundland	○	○	○
electionsnwt.ca	Northwest Territories	○	○	○
electionsnovascotia.ca	Nova Scotia	●	○	○
elections.nu.ca	Nunavut	●	○	○
elections.on.ca	Ontario	●	○	○
electionspei.ca	Prince Edward Island	○	○	○
electionsquebec.qc.ca	Quebec	◐[b]	○	○
elections.sk.ca	Saskatchewan	○	○	○
electionsyk.ca	Yukon	○	○	○

[a] Using self-signed certificate.
[b] Using weak/obsolete ciphersuites.

According to the National Conference of State Legislators,[12] 37 US states plus the District of Columbia offered online voter registration as of 2018. We examined each of these states, and the results are given in Table 6. Only Maryland, Minnesota, Ohio and South Carolina implemented HSTS, and Florida's registration site[13] was the only one found in the preload list. Interestingly, this domain failed to meet all the preload eligibility requirements (including the use of the strict-transport-security header). Furthermore, Florida's site was present in the Chrome preload list *only*, meaning Firefox, Safari and Edge users would not be protected from TLS stripping.

Our investigation also revealed that the voter registration websites for Alaska, Louisiana, Massachusetts and Oregon had TLS configurations with serious vulnerabilities. We notified the affected states of our respective findings. Massachusetts promptly responded by disabling SSL 2 and 3, and we had a conference call with the state director of elections about our findings and their efforts to address them.

5   Barriers to Adoption

With only 50,000 entries on the HSTS preload list out of hundreds of millions of websites worldwide, adoption among voting sites was expected to be low. The question is: what barriers are faced by election management bodies and vendors?

---

[12] https://ncsl.org.
[13] https://registertovoteflorida.gov.

Table 6. HSTS in US voter registration websites

Domain	State	TLS	HSTS	Preload
alabamavotes.gov	Alabama	●	○	○
voterregistration.alaska.gov	Alaska	◐[a,b,c]	○	○
servicearizona.com	Arizona	●	○	○
registertovote.ca.gov	California	●	○	○
sos.state.co.us	Colorado	●	○	○
voterregistration.ct.gov	Connecticut	●	○	○
ivote.de.gov	Delaware	●	○	○
vote4dc.com	D.C.	●	○	○
registertovoteflorida.gov	Florida	●	○	◐[f]
registertovote.sos.ga.gov	Georgia	●	○	○
olvr.hawaii.gov	Hawaii	●	○	○
apps.idahovotes.gov	Idaho	●	○	○
ova.elections.il.gov	Illinois	●	○	○
indianavoters.in.gov	Indiana	●	○	○
sos.iowa.gov	Iowa	●	○	○
www.kdor.ks.gov	Kansas	●	○	○
vrsws.sos.ky.gov	Kentucky	●	○	○
sos.la.gov	Louisiana	◐[c]	○	○
voterservices.elections.state.md.us	Maryland	●	●	○
www.sec.state.ma.us	Massachusetts	◐[c,d]	○	○
mnvotes.sos.state.mn.us	Minnesota	●	●	○
sos.mo.gov	Missouri	●	○	○
nebraska.gov	Nebraska	●	○	○
nvsos.gov	Nevada	●	○	○
portal.sos.state.nm.us	New Mexico	●	○	○
dmv.ny.gov	New York	●	○	○
olvr.sos.state.oh.us	Ohio	●	●	○
secure.sos.state.or.us	Oregon	◐[e]	○	○
www.pavoterservices.state.pa.us	Pennsylvania	●	○	○
vote.sos.ri.gov	Rhode Island	●	○	○
info.scvotes.sc.gov	South Carolina	●	●	○
ovr.govote.tn.gov	Tennessee	●	○	○
secure.utah.gov	Utah	●	○	○
olvr.sec.state.vt.us	Vermont	●	○	○
vote.virginia.gov	Virginia	●	○	○
wei.sos.wa.gov	Washington	●	○	○
ovr.sos.wv.gov	West Virginia	●	○	○
myvote.wi.gov	Wisconsin	●	○	○

[a] Vulnerable to CVE-2014-0224.
[b] Vulnerable to Logjam (CVE-2015-4000).
[c] Vulnerable to POODLE (CVE-2014-3566).
[d] Vulnerable to DROWN (CVE-2016-0800).
[e] Vulnerable to ROBOT (CVE-2017-13099 and others).
[f] In Chrome preload list *only*.

Education and Awareness. The first barrier predominately appears to be a lack of awareness of TLS stripping, its implications, and the action required to protect against it. Increasing awareness begins by identifying at-risk websites and engaging with them. Eventually we hope to encourage the Qualsys SSL Test to include HSTS preloading in their grade scoring.

Technical Barriers. Membership in the preload list nominally requires: a valid TLS configuration; HTTPS redirects on the same domain; HSTS header with a sufficient `max-age`; the `include-subdomains` field; and, the `preload` field. Meeting these requirements can be non-trivial within the given web environment. Many web application frameworks (e.g., ASP .NET, Django, etc.) support HSTS via 3rd party plugins. The Helios maintainers observed that while Django offered an HSTS module, it did not support the preload field. In other cases (e.g., Apache, Nginx), preloading is a non-standard option which can be included only through a custom user-defined configuration. Microsoft's IIS server explicitly supports a preload attribute as of version 10, however all the US voter registration sites we observed running IIS used versions 8.5 or below.

Institutional Barriers. It is the root domain (e.g., `example.com`) that must be added, even if it is only a subdomain requiring preloading. This can be problematic in large institutions with numerous subdomains where applying a blanket HSTS policy would cause functional issues to, e.g., development severs. For example, Culnane et al. [5] observed that the online voting website of the 2017 Western Australian state (`ivote-cvs.elections.wa.gov.au`) was being hosted on the New South Wales iVote server, but would require action from the Western Australian IT staff (`wa.gov.au`) to be included in the preload list.

Scalability. Finally, there are scalability considerations to the preload list itself. Many election URLs are active only during polling period, and some domains have a clear one-time use (e.g., `election2020.org`). Adding all election websites to the preload list would, over time, risk filling it with stale domains.

We contacted the maintainers of the Chrome preload list and they were clear that, for the time being at least, all election sites are recommended for HSTS preloading, and that they be added at least 3 months in advance of the polling period to ensure time to be pushed out to voters via browser updates.

6   Conclusion

If you plan to deliver election and voting services online, the best practice to prevent TLS stripping attacks is to add your domain to the HSTS preload list. All voters using an updated browser will then be directed to your site securely over HTTPS, even if someone in your organization directs them to type or click an insecure HTTP link. This paper presented a study of over one hundred websites related to online elections and found almost none are presently doing this. The reasons are varied, but predominantly seem to be a matter of a lack of awareness of this issue, and we hope this paper will aid in this regard.

Acknowledgements. Thanks to Ben Adida, Kirsten Dorey, Lucas Garron and the anonymous reviewers.

References

1. Adrian, D., et al.: Imperfect forward secrecy: how Diffie-Hellman fails in practice. In: Proceedings of the 22nd ACM SIGSAC Conference on Computer and Communications Security, pp. 5–17. ACM (2015)
2. Alsharnouby, M., Alaca, F., Chiasson, S.: Why phishing still works: user strategies for combating phishing attacks. Int. J. Hum.-Comput. Stud. **82**, 69–82 (2015)
3. Amrutkar, C., Traynor, P., Van Oorschot, P.C.: An empirical evaluation of security indicators in mobile web browsers. IEEE Trans. Mob. Comput. **14**(5), 889–903 (2015)
4. Clark, J., van Oorschot, P.C.: SoK: SSL and HTTPS: revisiting past challenges and evaluating certificate trust model enhancements. In: 2013 IEEE Symposium on Security and Privacy (SP), pp. 511-525. IEEE (2013)
5. Culnane, C., Eldridge, M., Essex, A., Teague, V.: Trust implications of DDoS protection in online elections. In: Krimmer, R., Volkamer, M., Braun Binder, N., Kersting, N., Pereira, O., Schürmann, C. (eds.) E-Vote-ID 2017. LNCS, vol. 10615, pp. 127–145. Springer, Cham (2017). https://doi.org/10.1007/978-3-319-68687-5_8
6. Dhamija, R., Tygar, J.D., Hearst, M.: Why phishing works. In: Proceedings of the SIGCHI Conference on Human Factors in Computing Systems, pp. 581–590. ACM (2006)
7. Dorey, K., Chang-Fong, N., Essex, A.: Indiscreet logs: Diffie-Hellman backdoors in TLS. In: Proceedings of the 24th Annual Network and Distributed System Security Symposium (NDSS 2017). The Internet Society (2017)
8. Durumeric, Z., et al.: The matter of heartbleed. In: Proceedings of the 2014 Conference on Internet Measurement Conference, pp. 475–488. ACM (2014)
9. Dzieduszycka-Suinat, S., et al.: The future of voting: end-to-end verifiable internet voting - specification and feasibility study. US Vote Foundation (2015)
10. Essex, A.: Detecting the detectable: unintended consequences of cryptographic election verification. IEEE Secur. Priv. **15**(3), 30–38 (2017)
11. Fogel, B., Farmer, S., Alkofahi, H., Skjellum, A., Hafiz, M.: POODLEs, more POODLEs, FREAK attacks too: how server administrators responded to three serious web vulnerabilities. In: Caballero, J., Bodden, E., Athanasopoulos, E. (eds.) ESSoS 2016. LNCS, vol. 9639, pp. 122–137. Springer, Cham (2016). https://doi.org/10.1007/978-3-319-30806-7_8
12. Halderman, J.A., Teague, V.: The New South Wales iVote system: security failures and verification flaws in a live online election. In: Haenni, R., Koenig, R.E., Wikström, D. (eds.) VOTELID 2015. LNCS, vol. 9269, pp. 35–53. Springer, Cham (2015). https://doi.org/10.1007/978-3-319-22270-7_3
13. Hodges, J., Jackson, C., Barth, A.: HTTP strict transport security (HSTS), RFC 6797 (2012)
14. Kranch, M., Bonneau, J.: Upgrading HTTPS in mid-air: an empirical study of strict transport security and key pinning. In: NDSS (2015)
15. Marlinspike, M.: More tricks for defeating SSL in practice. Black Hat USA (2009)
16. Moher, E., Clark, J., Essex, A.: Diffusion of voter responsibility: potential failings in E2E voter receipt checking. USENIX J. Election Syst. Technol. (2015)

17. Nemec, M., Sys, M., Svenda, P., Klinec, D., Matyas, V.: The return of copper-smith's attack: practical factorization of widely used RSA moduli. In: Proceedings of the 2017 ACM SIGSAC Conference on Computer and Communications Security, pp. 1631–1648. ACM (2017)

18. Rescorla, E.: The transport layer security (TLS) protocol version 1.2, RFC 5246 (2008)

19. Rescorla, E.: The transport layer security (TLS) protocol version 1.3 (draft 28) (2018)

20. Sheffer, Y., Holz, R., Saint-Andre, P.: Summarizing known attacks on transport layer security (TLS) and datagram TLS (DTLS). RFC 7457 (2015)

21. Springall, D., et al.: Security analysis of the Estonian internet voting system. In: Proceedings of the 2014 ACM SIGSAC Conference on Computer and Communications Security, pp. 703–715. ACM (2014)

22. Valenta, L., et al.: Measuring small subgroup attacks against Diffie-Hellman (eprint). In: Proceedings of the 24th Annual Network and Distributed System Security Symposium (NDSS 2017). The Internet Society (2017)

23. Valenta, L., Cohney, S., Liao, A., Fried, J., Bodduluri, S., Heninger, N.: Factoring as a service. In: Grossklags, J., Preneel, B. (eds.) FC 2016. LNCS, vol. 9603, pp. 321–338. Springer, Heidelberg (2017). https://doi.org/10.1007/978-3-662-54970-4_19

24. Western Australian Electoral Commission: 2017 State General Election Election Report (2017)

25. Zagórski, F., Carback, R.T., Chaum, D., Clark, J., Essex, A., Vora, P.L.: Remotegrity: design and use of an end-to-end verifiable remote voting system. In: Jacobson, M., Locasto, M., Mohassel, P., Safavi-Naini, R. (eds.) ACNS 2013. LNCS, vol. 7954, pp. 441–457. Springer, Heidelberg (2013). https://doi.org/10.1007/978-3-642-38980-1_28

Modular Formalisation and Verification
of STV Algorithms

Milad K. Ghale$^{(\boxtimes)}$, Rajeev Goré, Dirk Pattinson, and Mukesh Tiwari

The Australian National University, Canberra, Australia
milad.ketabghale@anu.edu.au

Abstract. We introduce a formal, modular framework that captures a large number of different instances of the Single Transferable Vote (STV) counting scheme in a uniform way. The framework requires that each instance defines the precise mechanism of counting and transferring ballots, electing and eliminating candidates. From formal proofs of basic sanity conditions for each mechanism inside the Coq theorem prover, we then synthesise code that implements the given scheme in a provably correct way and produces a universally verifiable certificate of the count. We have applied this to various variations of STV, including several used in Australian parliamentary elections and demonstrated the feasibility of our approach by means of real-world case studies.

1 Introduction

Single Transferable Vote (STV) is a family of vote counting schemes where voters express their preferences for competing candidates by ranking them on a ballot paper. STV is used in many countries including Ireland, Malta, India, Nepal, New Zealand and Australia. It is also used to elect moderators in the StackExchange discussion forum [19] and the board of trustees of the John Muir trust [11].

To count an election according to STV, one usually computes a quota dependent on the number of ballots cast (often the Droop quota [7]) and then proceeds as follows:

1. Count all first preferences on ballot papers;
2. Elect all candidates whose first preferences meet or exceed the quota;
3. Transfer surplus votes, i.e. votes of elected candidates beyond and over the quota are transferred to the next preference;
4. If all transfers are concluded and there are still vacant seats, eliminate the least preferred candidate, and transfer his/her votes to the next preference.

While the scheme appears simple and perspicuous, the above description hides lots of detail, in particular concerning precisely which ballots are to be transferred to the next preference. Indeed, many jurisdictions differ in precisely that detail and stipulate a different subset of ballots be transferred, typically at a fractional weight (the so-called *transfer value*). For example, in the Australian Capital Territory (ACT) lower house STV election scheme, only the

© Springer Nature Switzerland AG 2018
R. Krimmer et al. (Eds.): E-Vote-ID 2018, LNCS 11143, pp. 51–66, 2018.
https://doi.org/10.1007/978-3-030-00419-4_4

last parcel of an elected candidate (the ballots attributed to the candidate at the last count) of an elected candidate is transferred. In contrast, the STV variant used in the upper house of the Australian state of Victoria transfers *all* ballots (at a reduced transfer value). Similar differences also exist for the transfer of votes when a candidate is being eliminated.

On the other hand, all variants of STV share a large set of similarities. All use the same mechanism (transfer, count, elect, eliminate) to progress the count and, for example, all cease counting once all vacancies are filled. In this paper, we abstract the commonalities of all different flavours of STV into a set of minimal requirements that we (consequently) call *minimal* STV. It consists of:

- the data (structure) that captures all states of the count
- the requirements that building blocks (transfer, count, . . .) must obey.

In particular, we formally understand each single discrete state of counting as a mathematical object which comprises some data. Based on the kind of data that such an object encapsulates, we separate them into three sets: initial states (all ballots uncounted), final states (election winners are declared) and intermediate states. The latter carry seven pieces of information: the list of remaining uncounted ballots which must be dealt with; the current tally of each candidate; the pile of ballots counted in each candidate's favour; the list of elected candidates whose votes await transfer; the list of eliminated candidates whose votes await transfer; the list of elected candidates; and the list of continuing candidates. Basically, they record the current state of the tally computation.

We realise transitions between states, corresponding to acts of counting, eliminating, transferring, electing, and declaring winners, as formal rules that relate a pre-state and a post-state. These rules are what varies between different flavours of STV, so minimal STV does not define them. Instead, it postulates minimal *conditions* that each rule must satisfy. An *instance* of STV is then given by:

1. *definitions* of the rules for counting, electing, eliminating, and transferring;
2. formal *proofs* that the rules satisfy the respective conditions.

We sometimes refer, somewhat informally, to the conditions the various rules must satisfy as *sanity checks*. They are the formal counterparts of the legislation that informs counting officers which action to perform, when. Each sanity check consists of two parts: the *applicability condition* specifies under what conditions the rule can be applied while the *progress condition* specifies the effect of the rule on the state of the count. For example, the count rule is applicable if there are uncounted ballots and reduces the number of uncounted ballots.

We establish three main properties of this generic version of STV. The first is that each application of any of the generic transitions of STV reduces a complexity measure. The second is that at any non-final state of the count, at least one of the generic transitions is applicable because it satisfies its sanity check requirements. The third is that the overall minimal STV algorithm terminates.

All this is carried out inside the Coq theorem prover [3]. Using Coq's extraction mechanism [14] we can then automatically synthesise a (provably correct) program for STV counting from the termination proof. By construction, the executables are certifying programs which produce an visualised trace of computation upon each execution. The correctness of the certificate can be checked by anyone with minimal technical knowledge, independent of the way it was obtained. That is to say, we provably implement the counted-as-cast aspect [4] of universal verifiability. Finally, our experimental tests with real elections demonstrate feasibility of our approach for real world applications. Compared with other formalisations of STV, where even small changes in the details of a single rule requires adapting a global correctness proof, the outstanding features of our work is *modularity*, since sanity checks are local to each rule, and *abstraction*, since the general correctness proof is based on the local conditions for each rule. It is precisely this simplicity that allows us to capture a large number of variations of STV, including several used in Australian parliamentary elections.

2   The Generic STV Machine

We begin by describing the components of minimal STV before discussing their implementation in the Coq theorem prover, together with examples.

2.1   The Machine States and Transitions

The best way to think of minimal STV and its instances is in terms of an abstract machine. The states can be thought of as snapshots of the hand counting procedure, where there is e.g. a current tally, and a set of uncounted ballots at every stage. Tallying is then formalised as transition between these states.

There are three types of machine states: *initial, intermediate,* and *final*. An initial state contains the list of all *formal* ballots. Final states are where winners are declared. Each intermediate state consists of seven components:

1. A set of uncounted ballots, which must be counted;
2. A tally function computing the number of votes for each candidate;
3. A pile function computing which ballots are assigned to which candidate;
4. A list of already elected candidates whose votes await transfer;
5. A list of the eliminated candidates whose votes need to be dealt with;
6. A list of elected candidates; and
7. A list of continuing candidates.

We use $\mathcal{C}$ for the set of all candidates participating in an election and use c, c', and c'' for individual candidates from $\mathcal{C}$. We use $\mathsf{List}(\mathcal{C})$ for the set of all lists over $\mathcal{C}$ and use $\mathbb{Q}$ for the set of rational numbers. A ballot is an ordered pair (l, q) where $l \in \mathsf{List}(\mathcal{C})$ is the preference order and $q \in \mathbb{Q}$ is the (possibly fractional) value of this ballot. We write $\mathcal{B} = \mathsf{List}(\mathcal{C}) \times \mathbb{Q}$ for the set of all ballots, i.e. preference ordered lists of candidates, together with a transfer value. We use h and nh for lists of continuing ("hopeful") candidates, and e and ne for lists of elected candidates. A backlog is a pair $(l1, l2)$, the lists of elected and eliminated candidates, respectively, both of whose votes await transfer. We use bl, nbl for backlogs, use qu for the quota for being elected and use st for the number of vacant seats. We use t, nt for tallies and use p, np for piles. The prefix "n" always stands for "new", thus ne is the list of elected candidates in the post state, after an action has been applied.

Suppose that $ba \in \mathsf{List}(\mathcal{B})$, and $bl, h, e, w \in \mathsf{List}(\mathcal{C})$ are given. Assume t is a function from $\mathcal{C}$ into $\mathbb{Q}$, and p is a function from $\mathcal{C}$ into $\mathsf{List}(\mathcal{B})$. We use $\mathsf{initial}(ba)$ for the initial state, use $\mathsf{intermediate}(ba, t, p, bl, e, h)$ for an intermediate state, and use $\mathsf{final}(w)$ for a final one. Having established terminology and necessary representations, we can mathematically define the states of the generic STV machine.

Definition 1 (machine states). *Suppose ba is the initial list of ballots to be counted, and l is the list of all candidates competing in the election. The set S of states of the generic STV is the union of all possible intermediate and final states that can be constructed from ba and l, together with the initial state $\mathsf{initial}(ba)$.*

We now describe the mechanisms to progress an STV count, such as electing all candidates that have reached quota. These steps, formalised as *rules*, are the essence of each particular instance of STV, and are one of the two cornerstones of our generic notion of STV: the other being the properties that rules must satisfy. We stipulate that each instance of STV needs to implement the following mechanisms that we formulate as rules relating a pre-state and a post-state:

---

start: to determine the *formal* ballots and valid initial states;

count: for counting the uncounted ballots;

elect: to elect one or more candidates who have reached or exceeded the quota;

transfer-elected: for transferring surplus votes of already elected candidates;

transfer-removed: to transfer the votes of the eliminated candidate;

eliminate: to eliminate the weakest candidate from the process; and

elected win: to terminate counting by declaring the already elected candidates as winners;

hopeful win: to terminate counting by declaring the list of elected and continuing candidates as winners.

For the moment, we treat the above as transition labels only, and provide semantical meaning in the next section.

Definition 2 (machine transitions). *The set $\mathcal{T}$ consisting of the labels **count, elect, transfer-elected, transfer-removed, eliminate, hopeful win,** and **elected win,** is the set of transition labels of the generic STV.*

2.2 The Small-Step Semantics

The textual description of STV is usually in terms of clauses that specify what actions are to be undertaken, under what conditions. In our formulation, this corresponds to pre- and post-conditions for the individual counting rules. The pre-condition is an *applicability constraint*: it specifies under what conditions a particular rule is applicable. The post-condition is a *reducibility constraint*: it specifies how applying a rule progresses the count. Taken together, they form the *sanity check* for an individual rule. Technically, applicability constraints ensure that the count never gets stuck i.e. there is always one applicable rule, while the reducibility constraint guarantees termination.

Reducibility. A careful examination of STV protocols shows that each rule reduces the size of at least one of the following four objects: the list of continuing candidates; the number of ballots in the pile of the most recently eliminated candidate; the backlog; and the list of uncounted ballots. Using lexicographic ordering, this allows us to define a complexity measure on the set of machine states in such a way that each rule application reduces this measure.

Local Rule Applicability. Each instance of STV must, and indeed does, impose restrictions on when rules can, and must, be applied. Most depend on the particular instance, but some are universal. For example, all STV algorithms require three constraints for the elimination rule to apply: there must be vacant seats; there must be no surplus votes awaiting transfer; and no candidate should have reached or exceeded the quota. We constrain each of the counting rules in this way to guarantee that at least one rule can always be applied.

To formulate the sanity checks for each transition, we define a lexicographic ordering on the set $\mathbb{N}^5$ and impose it on non-final states of the generic machine.

Definition 3. *Let $\{s : S \mid s \text{ not final}\}$ be the set of non-final machine states. We define a function* Measure $: S \rightarrow \mathbb{N}^5$ *as follows. We let* Measure *(initial(ba))* $= (1,0,0,0,0)$. *Suppose* $bl = (l_1, l_2)$, *for some lists l_1 and l_2, and for a given candidate c,* flat $(p\ c) = l_c$ *where for a list l of lists,* flat l *is the concatenation (flattening) of all elements of l. Then*

$$\text{Measure } (\text{state } (ba, t, p, bl, e, h)) = (0, \text{ length } h, \sum_{d \in l_2} \text{ length } l_d, \text{ length } l_1, \text{ length } ba).$$

Note that the first component of the co-domain of the measure function simply reduces measure from the initial state to any intermediate state, and the third component is the sum of the length of the ballots cast in favour of eliminated candidates that await transfer. In the following, we describe the sanity checks for **transfer** and **elect** in detail, and leave it to the reader to reconstruct those for the other rules from the formal Coq development.

Transfer-Elected Check. The *transfer-elected* rule that decribes the transfer of surplus votes of an elected candidate must satisfy two conditions. The applicability condition asserts that transfer-elected is applicable to any intermediate machine state input of the form state($[], t, p, bl, e, h$), where the list of uncounted ballots is empty, if there are vacancies to fill (length(e) < st), there are surpluses awaiting transfer, ($bl \neq []$), and no continuing candidate has reached or exceeded the quota. Under these conditions, we stipulate the existence of a post-state output which is reachable from input via a transition labelled *transfer-elected*. The reducibility condition requires that any application of *transfer-elected* reduces the length of the backlog *bl* while elected and continuing candidates remain unchanged. Mathematically, this takes the following form:

Definition 4 (transfer-elected sanity check). *A rule $R \subseteq S \times S$ satisfies the* transfer-elected sanity check *if and only if the following hold:*

applicability: for any state input $=$ state($[], t, p, bl, e, h$) *that satisfies* length(e) $<$ st *(there are still seats to fill),* bl $\neq$ [] *(there are votes to be transferred) and* $\forall c. (c \in h \rightarrow (t\ c < qu))$ *(no continuing candidate has reached the quota), there exists a post-state* output *such that* input R output.

reducibility: for any machine states input *and* output, *if* input R output *then* input *is of the form* state($[], t, p, bl, e, h$), output *is of the form* state(nba, t, np, nbl, e, h) *and* length(nbl) $<$ length(bl) *(i.e. the backlog is reduced).*

The following is immediate from the definition of measure (Definition 3):

Theorem 1. *If transition label R obeys the reducability condition of Definition 4,* input $\in S$, output $\in S$ *and* input R output, *then the* output *complexity* Measure(output) *is lexicographically smaller than the* input *complexity* Measure(input).

Elect Check. The action of electing a candidate, also formalised as a rule in our framework, is subject to the following constraints: in the pre-state input $=$ state($[], t, p, bl, e, h$), where the list of uncounted ballots is empty, some continuing candidate must have reached quota, and there must be a vacant seat. If so, there must exist a post-state output where the set of continuing candidates is smaller, there are still no uncounted ballots, and the piles and backlog for candidates may be updated. Mathematically, this takes the following form:

Definition 5 (elect sanity check). *A rule $R \subseteq S \times S$ satisfies the* elect sanity check *if and only if the following two conditions hold:*

applicability: For any state input $=$ state($[], t, p, bl, e, h$) *and any continuing candidate* $c \in h$, *if* $t(c) \geq qu$ *(c has reached quota) and* length(e) $<$ st *(there are vacancies), there exists a post-state* output *such that* input R output.

reducibility: for any states input *and* output, *if* input R output, *then* input *is of the form* state($[], t, p, bl, e, h$), output *is of the form* state($[], nt, np, nbl, ne, nh$) *and* length(nh) $<$ length(h) *and* length(ne) $>$ length(e).

Analogous to Theorem 1 we have the following:

Theorem 2. *If a transition rule R meets the reducibility condition of Definition 5, then any application of the transition R reduces the complexity measure.*

Similarly we define sanity checks corresponding to other transition labels, namely **start, count, eliminate, hopeful-win**, and **elected-win**. For all such sanity checks, we establish analogues of Theorems 1 and 2. Then by drawing on them, we obtain a corollary on the measure reduction for the generic STV machine.

Corollary 1. *Any transition R corresponding to a machine transition in $\mathcal{T}$ that satisfies the corresponding sanity check reduces the complexity measure.*

2.3 The Generic STV Machine

The sanity checks constrain the computation that may happen on a given input state if the corresponding rule is applied. A set of rules, each of which satisfies the corresponding sanity check, can therefore be seen as a small-step semantics for STV counting. We capture this mathematically as a generic machine.

Definition 6 (The generic STV machine). *Let S and T be the sets of STV states (Definition 1) and transition labels (Definition 2), respectively. The generic STV machine is $M = \langle T, (S_t)_{t \in T} \rangle$ where S_t is the sanity check condition for transition $t \in T$. An instance of M is a tuple $I = \langle T, (R_t)_{t \in T} \rangle$, where for each $t \in T$, $R_t \subseteq S \times S$ is a rule that satisfies the sanity check condition S_t.*

In the sequel, we show that each instance of the generic STV machine in fact produces an election result, present a formalisation, and several concrete instances.

2.4 Progress via the Applicability Conditions

One specific "sanity check", in fact the one that inspired the very term, is the ability to always "progress" the count. That is, one rule is applicable at every state, so that the count will always progress, and there are no "dead ends", i.e. states of the count that are not final but to which no rule is applicable. As an example, no rule other than count may apply if there are uncounted ballots (and indeed count must be applicable in this situation), or that all elected candidates shall be declared winners if the number of candidates marked elected equals the number of seats to be filled. The key insight is that if the sanity check conditions (and hence the applicability conditions) are satisfied, we can always progress the count by applying a rule. In a nutshell, the following steps are repeated in order:

- the start rule applies (only) at initial states;
- cease scrutiny if all vacancies are filled by elected candidates;
- cease scrutiny if all vacancies are filled by elected and continuing candidates;
- uncounted ballots shall be counted;
- candidates that reach or exceed the quota shall be elected;
- the surplus of elected candidates shall be transferred;
- the ballots of eliminated candidates shall be transferred;
- the weakest candidate shall be eliminated.

We realise this order of rule applications in the proof of the rule applicability theorem. We draw upon the local rule applicability property, present in the sanity checks satisfied by the generic STV model, to guide the theorem prover Coq to the proof, according to the pseudo-algorithm above. Hence we formally verify the expectation of STV protocols on the invariant order of transition applications.

Theorem 3 (Rule Applicability). *Let $I = \langle T, (R_t)_{t \in T} \rangle$ be an instance of the generic STV machine. For every non-final state* input, *there is a transition label $t \in T$ and a new state* output *such that* input R_t output.

Corollary 1 shows that every applicable transition R_t, for $t \in \mathcal{T}$, reduces the complexity measure. Theorem 3 shows that for any non-final machine state, a transition from the set $\mathcal{T}$ is applicable. Jointly, they give a termination property that, in the terminology of programming semantics, asserts that every execution of the generic STV model has a meaning which is the sequence of computations taken to eventually terminate, and that each execution produces an output which is the value of that execution.

Theorem 4 (Termination). *Each execution of every instance of the generic STV machine on any initial state* input *terminates at a final state* output, *and constructs the sequence of computations taken from* input *to reach to* output.

3   Formalisation of the Generic Machine in Coq

We have formalised each notion introduced in the previous section in the theorem prover Coq. Our formalisation consists of a base layer, with instances defined in separate modules. The base layer contains the generic inductive types, definitions of sanity checks, parametric transition labels, specification of the STV machine, functions which are used to formulate the generic STV machine, and theorems proved about the generic STV model. It also includes functions which are commonly called by the modules to carry computation for instances of STV. Instances consist of four parts:

1. instantiations of the generic counting conditions defined in the base, with concrete instances of counting rules of a particular STV schemes
2. proofs which establish sanity checks for the instantiated transition rules
3. possibly auxilary fuctions specific to the particular instance of STV
4. an instantiation of the termination theorem which allows us to synthesise a provably correct, and certifiable, vote counting implementation.

We now briefly discuss the framework base and explain some design decisions. In the next section, we give modular formalisations of three STV algorithms.

   We encode machine states as an inductive type (Fig. 1) with three constructors: `initial`, `state`, and `final`. The constructor `state` has six value fields which parametrise the list of uncounted ballots, a list of tallies, a pile function, and lists of backlogs, elected and continuing candidates, respectively.

Tie Breaking. To formalise some tie breaking methods used in some STV schemes, we encode tallies into a chronological list so we can trace the number of votes which each candidate received in previous rounds. This allows us to realise one popular tie breaking procedure. In this method, whenever two or more candidates have the least votes, we go backwards stepwise, if need be, to previous states of the machine which we have computed in the same execution, until we reach a state where one candidate has less votes than the tied candidates. Then we update the current state of the counting by eliminating this candidate.

Last Parcel. Some STV schemes, such as lower house ACT and Tasmania STV, employ a notion called last parcel, and transfer only ballots included in

```
Inductive STV_States :=
  | initial: list ballot -> STV_States
  | state:   list ballot
        * list (cand -> Q)
        * (cand -> list (list ballot))
        * (list cand) * (list cand)
        * {elected: list cand | length elected <= st}
        * {hopeful: list cand | NoDup hopeful} -> STV_States
  | winners: list cand -> STV_States.
```

Fig. 1. inductive definition of STV machine states

this parcel according to next preferences. Moreover, they compute the fractional transfer value based on the length of the last parcel. In short, the last parcel of a candidate is the set of votes they received which made them reach or exceed the quota to become elected. As a result, we choose to formalise the pile function to assign a list of lists of ballots to every candidate: the element of this list are the ballots that have been counted in favour of the candidate at the successive counts. This allows us to identify precisely the set of ballots that comprise the last parcel of any elected candidate. Consequently, we are able to tailor both the generic transfer and elect rule and instantiations of them in such a way to modularly formalise several STV schemes where last parcel is being used.

Parameters. We formalise the notions of candidates, the quota, and transition labels parametrically. The parameters are later specified in the modules for each particular STV. For example, each transition label is associated with a relation, that is, a function of type `STV_States -> STV_States -> Prop`.

Sanity Checks. Corresponding to each generic transition label, there is a formal definition of the sanity checking. Sanity checks are constraints which are expected of every instance of STV to successfully pass in order to be classified as an STV scheme. Here we illustrate the encoding of the sanity checks for the elect transition. Items (1) and (2) in the Fig. 2 respectively match with the first and

```
Definition Elect_Sanity_Check (R:STV_States -> STV_States-> Prop)
:=
1. (∀ input t p bl e h, input = state([],t,p,bl,e,h) ->
     ∃ (c: cand),
     length (proj1_sig e) +1 ≤ st
     ∧ In c (proj1_sig h) ∧ (quota ≤ (hd nty t) c) ->
     ∃ output, R input output) ∧
2. (∀ input output, R input output -> ∃ t p np bl nbl e ne h nh,
     input = state([],t,p,bl,e,h)
     ∧ length(proj1_sig e) < length(proj1_sig ne)
     ∧ length(proj1_sig nh) < length(proj1_sig h)
     ∧ output = state([],t,np,nbl,ne,nh))
```

Fig. 2. Sanity check for elect transition

the second items given in Definition 5. Note that the check loosens the constraint so that in order for elect rule to apply, we need an electable continuing candidate and electing them would not exceed the number of vacancies. This allows us to define a concrete elect transition for e.g. CADE STV [2] which elects only one candidate who has reached or exceeded the quota, rather than electing all of the electable candidates together. Moreover, we are able to formalise other instances of elect transitions which do elect all of the eligible candidates in one step.

Generic STV Record. We bundle the generic quota, transition labels and the evidence that the generic transitions satisfy the sanity checks in one record type named STV_record. For example, one field of STV_record is the requirement that the generic elect transition meets the constraints of the elect sanity check, which technically means (Elect_sanity_check (elect)) ∈ STV_record.

Finally, we formally prove all of the mathematical properties discussed under the previous section for any stv of type STV_record. In particular, we demonstrate the termination property. The termination theorem is instantiated in separate modules with particular STV_record values, such as ACT STV and CADE STV, to obtain termination property for them as well and carry provably correct computations upon program extraction into Haskell.

4   Modular Formalisation of Some STV Systems

We already have discussed some points where STV schemes diverge from one another. They mainly vary in their specification of formal votes, quota, what is the surplus of an elected candidate, how many candidates to elect out of all of those who are electable, how to update the transfer value of votes of an elected candidate, how to transfer the surpluses, or how to eliminate a candidate and then distribute their votes among other continuing candidates. We describe two of the real-world STV schemes we have formalised.

4.1   Victoria STV

The Australian state of Victoria employs a version of STV [20] for electing upper house representatives. Figure 3 depicts the instantiation of the generic **elect** transition label with our formulation of the Victoria STV elect rule. Each line cof the Victorian STV protocol which specify the elect rule. We only explain lines 5, 6, and 7 of Fig. 3.

The counting protocol of Victoria STV, defines surpuls votes to be *"the number, if any, of votes in excess of the quota of each elected candidate"*. Moreover it dictates, under Section 17, Subsection 7 Clause (a), that *"the number of surplus votes of the elected candidate is to be divided by the number of first preference votes received by the elected candidate and the resulting fraction is the transfer value"*. In lines 6 and 7, we compute the surplus vote and the fractional transfer value accordingly and multiply it by the current value of every ballot in the pile of the elected candidate c to update the pile of this candidate.

```
Definition Victoria_Elect input output : Prop :=
∃ t p np bl nbl nh h e ne,
1. input = state([],t,p,bl,e,h) ∧
2. ∃ l, length (projl_sig e) + length(l) ≤ st
3. ∧ ∀ c, In c l ->(In c (projl_sig h) ∧(quota ≤ hd nty t (c)))
4. ∧ ordered (hd nty t) l∧ Permutation l(projl_sig nh) (projl_sig h)
5. ∧ Permutation l(projl_sig e) (projl_sig ne)∧ (nbl= bl ++ l)
6. ∧ ∀ c, In c l -> (np (c) = map(map (fun b ⇒
7. (fst b, (snd b)× ((hd nty t (c))-quota)/((hd [] t)c))(p c)
8. ∧ output = state([],t,np,nbl,ne,nh)
```

Fig. 3. Victoria STV elect transition

The protocol further states under subsection (8), and (13) that *"Any continuing candidate who has received a number of votes equal to or greater than the quota on the completion of any transfer under subsection (7), or on the completion of a transfer of votes of an excluded candidate under subsection (12) or (16), is to be declared elected"*. The definition requires electing candidate(s) no matter how they have obtained enough votes. We therefore implement clauses (8) and (13) in Line 5, where we elect everyone over or equal to the quota, place them in the update list ne of elected candidates, and insist that the list l of elected candidates in this state and the old list e of elected candidates together form a permutation of ne. Insisting that the new (combined) lists of winners are a permutation of l and e combined also imply that no new candidates are introduced, no existing candidates are deleted, and there is no duplication.

Next, we describe how the updated pile of an elected candidate in Victoria_Elect is transferred by Victoria's transfer-elect transition. Figure 4 illustrates the instantiation of the generic transfer-elected rule with a concrete case used by Victoria STV. Notice that in the first conjunct of Line 4 in Fig. 3, we order the list of elected candidates according to the tally amount. When it comes to transferring elected surplus, as we see in Line 4 of Fig. 4, the biggest surplus is dealt with first which belongs to candidate c. Furthermore, Line 5 specifies that *all of this candidate's surplus is distributed* at the fractional value computed in Victoria_Elect.

```
Definition Victoria_TransferElected input output :=
∃ nba t p np bl nbl h e,
1. input = state([],t,p,bl,e,h) ∧
2. length(projl_sig e) < st ∧ output = state([],t,np,nbl,ne,nh)
3. ∧ ∀ c, In c (projl_sig h) -> ((hd nty t) c < quota)
4. ∧ ∃ l c, (bl= (c::l,[]) ∧ (nbl= (l,[])) ∧ (np(c) = [])
5. ∧ (nba= flat(fun x => x)(p c) ∧ (∀ d, d≠c -> (np c)=(p d))
```

Fig. 4. Victoria STV transfer-elected transition

4.2   Australian Capital Territory STV

Lower house elections in the Australian Capital Territory (ACT) use a version of STV [1] which stands out for some of its characteristics, including transfer of the "last parcel" of votes and the formulation of transfer value. The specification of the elect transition of ACT STV is similar to the one in Fig. 4 except for lines 6 and 7, which are replaced by the following:

$$\text{np(c)} = \text{map}\left(\text{fun b} => \frac{(\text{fst b, (snd   b)} \times ((\text{hd nty   t(c)}) - \text{quota})}{(\text{Sum   snd (last(p   c))})}\right)(\text{last (p c)})$$

Moreover, the ACT version of transfer-elected is as in Fig. 4 except that the fist conjunct in Line 5 is replaced and reads nba = last (p c). The two variations together tell us that we only transfer the last parcel of the elected candidate and the transfer value equals the surplus votes of this candidate divided by the sum of fractional values of this last parcel, rather than the tally of the elected candidate.

There are obvious issues with the transfer value formula used in the ACT STV [10]. For example, it is possible for the calculated fractional value of a surplus vote to exceed 1, which is clearly a flaw of the algorithm. As a result, the software used by the ACT election commission which implements the algorithm [18], makes explicit modifications to ensure no surplus votes exceeds 1. We adapt this corrected version in our formalisation. Nonetheless, nothing would restrict us from selecting the defective original formula of ACT STV, if we chose to.

5   Certifying Extracted Programs and Experiments

We use the built-in mechanisms of Coq to extract executable Haskell programs for each module. The automatic extraction method provides very high assurance that the executable behaves in accordance to its Coq formalisation. Correctness proofs established in the Coq therefore give functional correctness of the executables. However, each execution of the extracted program generates a run-time certificate, providing independently checkable evidence of the underlying computation.

Theorem 4 guarantees each run of the program produces a *formal* certificate, i.e. a sequence of states of the count that are linked by rules, as an element of an inductive data type. (This contrasts with what one may call an *concrete* certificate which would be a file that comprises a textual representation of the formal certificate.) Moreover, the theorem guarantees that the formal certificate is the sequence of computation performed in the execution to obtain the final result. To produce a concrete certificate from an execution of extracted Haskell program, we need to agree on textual representations for the elements of the data types concerned.

The certificate generated for each input witnesses the correctness of the count. Note that it is trivial to demonstrate that the existence of a correct certificate implies the correctness of the result, as the latter is defined precisely as being obtained through a sequence of correct rule applications. Certificate correctness

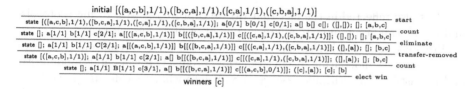

Fig. 5. Example of a certificate

can be checked by anyone, without *any* trust in the means that were used in the production of the certificate, or the underlying hardware. The fact that concrete certificates can be checked by scrutineers means that our tallying technique satisfies the count-as-recorded property of universal verifiability. Thus any election protocol designed for STV schemes which requires a proof of tallying correctness can use our tool.

Figure 5 illustrates an example of a concrete certificate, where candidates a, b, and c are competing for one seat. We discuss certification only briefly as it is described elsewhere [8]. We use exact fractions for computations to avoid the rounding issues explained in [10]. Every line shows six components, each corresponding to an abstract data representation of the intermediate states of the abstract machine: the list of uncounted ballots; the tallies of candidates; each candidate's pile; the backlog; and the lists of elected and continuing candidates.

We have evaluated the efficiency of our approach by testing the extracted module for the lower house ACT STV on some real elections held in 2008 and 2012 (Fig. 6). The Molonglo electorate of ACT is the biggest lower house electorate in Australia, both in the number of vacancies and the number of voters. The extracted program computes the result in just 22 min.

electoral	ballots	vacancies	candidates	time (sec)	certificate size (MB)	year
Brindabella	63334	5	19	116	80.6	2008
Ginninderra	60049	5	27	332	128.9	2008
Molonglo	88266	7	40	1395	336.1	2008
Brindabella	63562	5	20	205	94.3	2012
Ginninderra	66076	5	28	289	126.1	2012
Molonglo	91534	7	27	664	208.4	2012

Fig. 6. ACT legislative assembly 2008 and 2012

6   A Technical Discussion

We have introduced a framework for formalisation, verification, and provably correct computation with various STV algorithms. In the design decisions that we made, we have been balancing different aspects for designing a framework. The modular design allows for a much simpler realisation than made possibly by other frameworks (e.g. [8]) as we only need to discharge proofs at a per-rule basis which is also reflected in the fact that (a) we capture realistic voting protocols, and (b) we can accommodate a larger number of protocols with ease.

Previous work emphasises data structures and certification, and showcases this by means of monolithic specifications and proofs. Our work adds modularity, and we distil the algorithmic essence of STV into what we call *sanity checks*.

Every instance of STV satisfying the sanity checks enjoys the rule applicability and termination properties established in Theorems 3 and 4. Therefore, for an instance of STV to be verified, we simply need to establish that the sanity checks hold, rather than duplicate the whole proof process. These checks offer an abstraction on the algorithmic side which helps us avoid duplication of code. Unlike previous work, users do not need to know how the application and termination theorems have been proved in order to show termination of their particular instance. Additionally, separation into modules further improves usability. Anyone seeking a verified implementation of their preferred flavour of STV can simply use our framework and instantiate as appropriate.

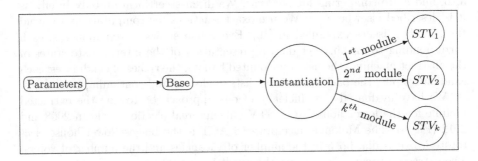

Fig. 7. System description

Figure 7 illustrates the framework architecture. The parameters component includes type level declaration of candidates, vacancies, and the quota. The base comprises the encoding of the generic STV model along with functions commonly called by the dependent modules. The instantiation component consists of instantiating types specified in the parameters file and automatically discharging of required proofs. Finally, the instantiated generic model is called into each module for discharging sanity checks and consequently extracting provably correct Hakell programs.

The ability to just instantiate is significant as many aspects are dealt with once and for all in the base layer of roughly 25000 lines of code. Each module already formalised is less than 500 lines. Therefore, an interested user has to just carry out formalisation and discharging sanity checks in about 500 lines to acquire a verified executable implementation of their favourite STV. On the other hand, accomplishing the same goal by using the previous platform, demands 25000 lines of encoding, along with overcoming numerous technicalities.

Related Work. DeYoung and Schürmann [6] formally specify an STV scheme as a linear logic [9] program and then discharge the required correctness proofs inside the logical framework Celf [17]. Celf is capable of executing the specification but their linear logic program does not scale to real-world elections.

Dawson et al. encode an ML program for STV counting into the HOL4 theorem prover [5] and prove various correctness properties of the program, including termination. HOL4 is able to execute the ML encoding within reasonable time bounds for small elections, but not for large ones. But there is a gap between the HOL4 semantics of ML and those used by ML compilers. This gap could be closed by using the proof-producing synthesis [13] of CakeML code from the HOL assertions, then using the verified CakeML compiler [12] to produce the machine code. However, this has not been done to date.

Pattinson and Schürmann [15], and Verity and Pattinson [21] formalise a simple version of STV and first-past-the-post elections in Coq and prove properties such as termination and the existence of winners. Then they extract certifying executables in Haskell which can handle real-world elections. Their crucial contribution is that their executable code produces a certificate for every run, which can be idependently verified.

Pattinson and Tiwari [16] extend this method to tackle the Schultz method. Their extracted code handles real-world election and also outputs a certificate for every run. The certificate not only witnesses how the winner was elected, but also provides concrete evidence that each losing candidate is a "loser".

7 Conclusion

We have designed a modular framework for formalisation, verification, and provably correct computation of STV algorithms. Our work is fully formalised, provides an encoding and provably correct executables for various flavours of STV.

References

1. ACT Electoral Commission: https://www.elections.act.gov.au/education/ act_electoral_commission_fact_sheets/fact_sheets_-_general_html/elections_act_ factsheet_hare-clark_electoral_system
2. Beckert, B., Goré, R., Schürmann, C.: Analysing vote counting algorithms via logic - and its application to the CADE election scheme. In: Bonacina, M.P. (ed.) CADE 2013. LNCS (LNAI), vol. 7898, pp. 135–144. Springer, Heidelberg (2013). https:// doi.org/10.1007/978-3-642-38574-2_9
3. Bertot, Y., Castéran, P., Huet, G., Paulin-Mohring, C.: Interactive Theorem Proving and Program Development: Coq'Art: The Calculus of Inductive Constructions. Springer, Heidelberg (2004). https://doi.org/10.1007/978-3-662-07964-5
4. Cortier, V., Galindo, D., Küsters, R., Müller, J., Truderung, T.: Verifiability notions for e-voting protocols. IACR Cryptology ePrint Archive 2016, 287 (2016)
5. Dawson, J.E., Goré, R., Meumann, T.: Machine-checked reasoning about complex voting schemes using higher-order logic. In: Proceedings of EVote-ID 2015, pp. 142–158 (2015)

6. DeYoung, H., Schürmann, C.: Linear logical voting protocols. In: Kiayias, A., Lipmaa, H. (eds.) Vote-ID 2011. LNCS, vol. 7187, pp. 53–70. Springer, Heidelberg (2012). https://doi.org/10.1007/978-3-642-32747-6_4

7. Droop, H.R.: On methods of electing representatives. J. Stat. Soc. Lond. **44**(2), 141–202 (1881)

8. Ghale, M.K., Goré, R., Pattinson, D.: A formally verified single transferable voting scheme with fractional values. In: Krimmer, R., Volkamer, M., Braun Binder, N., Kersting, N., Pereira, O., Schürmann, C. (eds.) E-Vote-ID 2017. LNCS, vol. 10615, pp. 163–182. Springer, Cham (2017). https://doi.org/10.1007/978-3-319-68687-5_10

9. Girard, J.: On the unity of logic. Ann. Pure Appl. Logic **59**(3), 201–217 (1993)

10. Goré, R., Lebedeva, E.: Simulating STV hand-counting by computers considered harmful: A.C.T. In: Krimmer, R., et al. (eds.) E-Vote-ID 2016. LNCS, vol. 10141, pp. 144–163. Springer, Cham (2017). https://doi.org/10.1007/978-3-319-52240-1_9

11. John Muir Trust: Apply to be a trustee. https://www.johnmuirtrust.org/assets/000/002/860/How_to_apply_to_be_a_Trustee_Jan_2018_original.pdf. Accessed 15 May 2018

12. Kumar, R., Myreen, M.O., Norrish, M., Owens, S.: CakeML: a verified implementation of ML. In: Principles of Programming Languages (POPL). ACM, January 2014

13. Magnus, M.O., Scott, O.: Proof-producing translation of higher-order logic into pure and stateful ML. J. Funct. Program. **24**(2–3), 284–315 (2014)

14. Letouzey, P.: A new extraction for CoQ. In: Geuvers, H., Wiedijk, F. (eds.) TYPES 2002. LNCS, vol. 2646, pp. 200–219. Springer, Heidelberg (2003). https://doi.org/10.1007/3-540-39185-1_12

15. Pattinson, D., Schürmann, C.: Vote counting as mathematical proof. In: Pfahringer, B., Renz, J. (eds.) AI 2015. LNCS (LNAI), vol. 9457, pp. 464–475. Springer, Cham (2015). https://doi.org/10.1007/978-3-319-26350-2_41

16. Pattinson, D., Tiwari, M.: Schulze voting as evidence carrying computation. In: Ayala-Rincón, M., Muñoz, C.A. (eds.) ITP 2017. LNCS, vol. 10499, pp. 410–426. Springer, Cham (2017). https://doi.org/10.1007/978-3-319-66107-0_26

17. Schack-Nielsen, A., Schürmann, C.: Celf - a logical framework for deductive and concurrent systems (system description). In: Proceedings of IJCAR 2008, pp. 320–326 (2008)

18. Software Improvements: Electronic and voting and counting sytems. http://www.softimp.com.au/evacs/index.html. Accessed 12 May 2015

19. StackExchange: Moderator elections (2018). https://math.stackexchange.com/election/6?tab=election. Accessed 15 May 2018

20. The Parliament of Victoria: Electoral act 2002. http://www.legislation.vic.gov.au/domino/web_notes/ldms/pubstatbook.nsf/f932b66241ecf1b7ca256e92000e23be/3264bf1de203c08aca256e5b00213ffb/%24FILE/02-023a.pdf

21. Verity, F., Pattinson, D.: Formally verified invariants of vote counting schemes. In: Proceedings of ACSW 2017, pp. 31:1–31:10 (2017)

Online Voting in Indigenous Communities: Lessons from Canada

Nicole Goodman[1]([⊠])[ID], Chelsea Gabel[2][ID], and Brian Budd[3][ID]

[1] Department of Political Science, Brock University, St. Catharines, Canada
`nicole.goodman@brocku.ca`
[2] Department of Health, Aging and Society and Indigenous Studies Program, McMaster University, Hamilton, Canada
`gabelc@mcmaster.ca`
[3] Department of Political Science, University of Guelph, Guelph, Canada
`buddb@uguelph.ca`

Abstract. Most studies of online voting examine adoption at national and subnational levels or among municipal governments. Very few examinations, however, focus on implementation in Indigenous communities. Drawing on community-engaged survey work with three First Nations in Canada – Tsuut'ina Nation, Wasauksing First Nation and Whitefish River First Nation, 27 interviews with Indigenous leaders, identified experts, online voting vendors and federal government representatives as well as a focus group, we examine why Indigenous communities in Canada are drawn to online voting, who is using it, potential impacts on participation, and good practices that can be learnt from these experiences. Our findings suggest broad support for online voting and satisfaction from Indigenous voters. Though online voters tend to be older, educated, wealthier and live off reserve, survey results indicate online ballots could engage some Indigenous electors to vote more frequently. Notably, we find that online voting is a critical tool to reach and engage off reserve citizens. Finally, we outline a number of good practices for online voting deployment that fall into four themes: (1) community knowledge and engagement (2) tools and strategies, (3) clear processes and resources, and (4) a focus on technology.

Keywords: Online voting · First Nations · Canada
Community-engaged research

1 Introduction

Online voting has been used in a number of contexts in jurisdictions around the world. Most studies examine adoption nationally [25, 29, 31], sub-nationally [28] or in the context of local governments [9, 14, 23]. Very few examinations, however, focus on online voting implementation in Indigenous communities [7, 8]. Consequently, we have a modest understanding of the effects online voting can have on Indigenous communities and the lessons that can be learnt from their experiences. Filling this lacuna is important for scholarly understandings of whether online voting can be leveraged to overcome some of the barriers to voting Indigenous peoples face, including reduced voter access and registration challenges [3]. Online voting also has

© Springer Nature Switzerland AG 2018
R. Krimmer et al. (Eds.): E-Vote-ID 2018, LNCS 11143, pp. 67–83, 2018.
https://doi.org/10.1007/978-3-030-00419-4_5

enormous practical importance as Indigenous peoples around the world pursue adoption at growing rates in countries such as Canada, the United States and New Zealand [2, 7]. Lessons from Indigenous experiences with online voting are especially valuable for remote and rural communities, where voters often face similar accessibility challenges because of limited broadband infrastructure and weaker digital literacy.

This article uses a community-based research approach with three First Nations in Canada: Tsuut'ina Nation, Wasauksing First Nation and Whitefish River First Nation. The methods include surveys with Indigenous voters, 27 semi-structured interviews with Indigenous leaders, identified experts, online voting vendors and federal government representatives, and a focus group, to understand the effects of online voting in Indigenous votes. Drawing on this rich collection of research we examine why Indigenous communities use online voting, who votes online and why, impacts on participation, and good practices that can be taken away from these experiences. Our findings indicate there is broad support for online voting and satisfaction from Indigenous voters. Though online voters tend to be older, educated, wealthier and live off reserve, survey results suggest online voting could engage some Indigenous electors to vote more frequently. Notably, we find that online voting is a critical tool to reach and engage off reserve citizens. The importance of reaching these electors is crucial given Canada's multi-level governance structure and the fact that in some cases the federal government imposes quorums that Indigenous communities must meet to pass votes. The article also presents a number of good practices to guide the implementation of online voting in Indigenous contexts.

The article proceeds in six sections. First, we summarize the relevant scholarly literature. This includes a brief historical summary of colonial governance in Canada and relevance for online voting adoption as well as a summary of literature on Indigenous adoption of digital technologies and online voting. Next, we provide a summary of First Nations we have worked with and whose experiences are reflected in this article. Fourth, we review our approach and data. Fifth, we present an overview of the survey data collected through the project and good practices that were developed from four years of community-engaged work, 27 interviews and a focus group. Finally, we conclude with a summary of results and suggest opportunities for future research.

2　Literature

Though studies explore the effects of online voting in the context of national [25, 29, 31], sub-national [28] and local governments [9, 14, 23], there is a lacuna in research examining deployment of online ballots in Indigenous communities. While projects studying Indigenous adoption of online voting are underway in New Zealand, where more than 90 iwi organisations use the technology, these findings have yet to be published. Early work with First Nations in Canada is presently the only published material that examines the impacts of online voting on participation and governance in Indigenous communities [7, 8]. This section provides historical context regarding the structures of governance in Canada and summarizes the findings of existing research.

2.1 Historical Governance Structures

The adoption of online voting by Indigenous communities in Canada is linked to a history of settler colonialism and ongoing resistance enacted by Indigenous peoples to reassert local autonomy and political self-determination. Following the passage of the Canadian constitution in 1867, steps were taken to consolidate territory by dispossessing Indigenous peoples of their traditional lands and reconstituting Indigenous governance structures under the terms set out by federal legislation [6]. These approaches to limit the territorial presence and governance capacity of Indigenous communities soon evolved into outright attempts to eliminate Indigenous peoples as distinct political and social collectives through violent and assimilative policies designed to forcefully integrate Indigenous peoples into mainstream Canadian society [30]. While Indigenous resistance to these attempts has been constant throughout Canadian history, the beginning of the 1970s marked a shift in Indigenous-State relations as Indigenous communities and politicians successfully expanded the recognition of Indigenous rights to self-determination through intergovernmental negotiations, the inclusion of Aboriginal rights in Canada's constitution and ongoing acts of organized protest at varying levels of governance [18, 22]. While Indigenous communities still face many social, political and legal challenges toward the realization of self-government and by extension self-determination, Indigenous governments have assumed a growing number of jurisdictional responsibilities while exercising greater control over the design and delivery of local policies and services. It is within this tension between settler colonialism and Indigenous resistance that we can understand and study the adoption of digital technologies by First Nations and other Indigenous bodies.

2.2 Indigenous Adoption of Digital Technologies

Digital technology and infrastructure present unique opportunities for Indigenous communities to address social and political challenges while also strengthening local governance capacity. There is a small, yet growing literature examining the adoption of digital technologies by Indigenous communities. Studies focus on the introduction of technologies in the areas of healthcare, education, social services, economic development, and cultural renewal addressing the ways in which technology can strengthen administrative capacity and overcome challenges in local service delivery [17, 24]. Others point to challenges faced by Indigenous communities in Canada interested in adopting digital technology such as digital divides. McMahon et al. [19], for example, highlight this issue by exploring the barriers remote and rural Indigenous communities face with respect to broadband infrastructure and internet services given the marketization of internet service delivery. While First Nations have proven resourceful in responding to these challenges through the development of community-based approaches to improve internet access [see 19], they continue to face structural barriers to adoption due to geographic remoteness and a lack reliable broadband infrastructure.

Despite these issues, digital technologies have become an important tool not only for the improvement of local services, but also for the pursuit of broader political goals related to self-determination. Scholars have begun to consider the implications for the adoption of digital technology for self-determination, developing concepts like "digital self-determination" [20] and "digital decolonization" [1] as a way to interpret the varied empirical examples of technological adoptions by Indigenous communities. These concepts focus on the ways in which technology can contribute to the realization of Indigenous self-determination by facilitating the decentralization of political authority and the development of governance capacity.

2.3   Indigenous Deployment of Online Voting

To date, the only published research of Indigenous use of online voting examines experiences in Canada [7, 8], albeit projects working with iwi, Te Rūnanga o Ngāti Awa and others are underway in New Zealand [2]. Research with First Nations in Canada has explored the rationales for online voting adoption, benefits to participation and governance, as well as legal, social and political challenges. All of these contributions, however, focus on examining individual First Nations and do not provide comparative assessments.

Research shows online voting fosters and strengthens community connectedness among Indigenous peoples [4, 8]. Colonial legacies have left many Indigenous persons disconnected from the political processes in their communities, especially those living off reserve lands. Online voting has been found to alleviate political alienation by generating dialogue and engagement between government and citizens, notably among youth and elders [8]. In the context of Wasauksing First Nation, Budd et al. [4] find that online voting connects off reserve members to discussions of community business and policy, and is a critical tool for enhancing participation to meet the quorums necessary for critical votes. More generally, the excitement and novelty of online voting has helped First Nations complement traditional in-person engagement strategies and strengthened administrative capacity [4]. In this way, online voting has been shown to make both direct and indirect contributions to community connectedness in First Nations.

Further, online voting makes meaningful contributions to community modernization and improve the self-governance capacity of First Nations. Interview research with First Nation officials and administrators found that First Nations are increasingly looking for ways to update processes and procedures to reflect the current realities of members' day-to-day lives. Online voting is often adopted as part of a broader suite of digital tools designed to modernize First Nation governance [4, 7]. It is also closely linked to gains in self-governance capacity in the form of improved administrative capacity and enhanced ability to develop and pass community legislation. Specifically, research finds online voting improves First Nations' administrative capacity by simplifying ballot tabulation processes and providing immediate results [7]. This improved capacity has positively influenced trust between citizens and government and increased confidence in voting results [4]. More importantly, online voting strengthens Indigenous self-government by enhancing the capacity of Indigenous communities to enact their own laws and regulations [4]. As mentioned, the ratification of community legislation requires First Nations to reach a minimum quorum of community participation. By fostering the participation of off-reserve members, online voting serves as an important tool to reach a level of participation that would otherwise would be difficult to secure through traditional voting methods alone. The ability to develop and pass legislation is an important symbolic and practical consideration in the pursuit of self-government, helping to peel back layers of colonial legislation while allowing First Nations to assume greater jurisdiction over their affairs.

Despite positive experiences, enhanced community connectedness and self-governance capacity, research also points to key challenges with Indigenous implementation of online voting. Many of these challenges stem from the lack of reliable, high-speed internet access within First Nations. Unfamiliarity with, and difficulty navigating, online voting registration procedures is also a barrier. Gabel et al. [7] point out that a two-step voting process, which requires citizens to register to vote online before accessing an internet ballot, is viewed by some as being too complicated and burdensome and discourages uptake among community members with less familiarity and experience using computers and the internet. Conflicts have also been noted between online voting and traditional Indigenous values and customs. Community members have also communicated concern that online voting and growing digitization of governance will lead to less face-to-face dialogue [4, 8]. The ability to openly discuss issues and decisions in-person is a key component of decision-making procedures within many Indigenous cultures. While these concerns have been expressed by some First Nation members, research has observed that when human connections are prioritized and online voting is integrated as complementary, rather than a replacement for traditional forms of community engagements and decision-making, satisfaction with online voting is high [4].

Finally, as noted above, the most significant impediment to online voting use is legislative in nature. While a growing number of First Nations have opted out of the provisions of the Indian Act and First Nations Elections Act by developing and ratifying their own electoral codes or self-government agreements, many continue to face legislative barriers to choosing the voting methods they will use in their elections [21].

In sum, existing research into online voting use in First Nations demonstrate its alignment with the broader political goals of building community capacity and enacting self-determination. While questions and concerns linger about the cultural appropriateness of internet ballots and working with private-sector vendors, there is an emerging relationship between online voting and self-determination. Absent in the literature on online voting use in Indigenous communities are generalizable insights into good practices that can facilitate the successfully deployment of online voting in Indigenous contexts as well as comparative analyses comparing findings across First Nations. This article addresses these gaps by reflecting on the experiences of three First Nations and providing a set of good practices for the deployment of online voting in Indigenous communities.

3 History and Context: Online Voting Developments in Indigenous Communities in Canada

Indigenous adoption of online voting is growing in Canada. Of the three groups of Indigenous peoples in Canada: First Nations, Métis and Inuit, the bulk of online voting activity has occurred in First Nations. Talthan First Nation in British Columbia was the first to use online voting in 2011 for the ratification of two agreement votes. Positive reviews of deployment spread and soon other First Nations in British Columbia carried out pilots. Huu-ay-aht First Nation adopted online voting in 2012 for its general assembly and Squamish First Nation used it to support a referendum on its membership agreement in 2013. Since then, online voting has been used in more than 80 of the 634 First Nations in Canada across six provinces: Alberta, British Columbia, Manitoba, Newfoundland, Nova Scotia, Ontario and Quebec, typically for ratification or agreement votes [21]. Use of online voting in Indigenous votes would be more frequent were it not for Canada's multi-level governance structure, whereby the Indian Act and First Nations Elections Act, legislation written by the federal government, governs elections and referendums unless a First Nation has opted out. Regulations of these acts outline the ballot methods that can be used and currently only provide for paper voting.

Table 1. Governance structure of First Nations' elections in Canada (This table is updated and adapted from an earlier paper by Goodman and Pammett [13] and reflects election governance structures as of May 11, 2018 according to federal government records The number of nations accounted for is 618, meaning there is not up to date information for 16 nations.)

Legislative framework	Number of nations
Indian Act election system	174
First Nations Elections Act	51
Custom election codes	353
Self-government agreements	40

While a majority of First Nations have taken control of their elections by passing self-government agreements or custom codes for the specific governance of elections, 225 First Nations fall under federal legislation, see Table 1, and therefore cannot use online voting for elections and referendums. These nations can, however, deploy online voting for other types of votes such as ratification votes or the passage of framework agreements such as Land Codes [21].

Interestingly, among First Nations that fall under federal legislation, online voting is often adopted in contexts where a federally mandated quorum must be met to pass community-developed legislative frameworks. For example, there is a 25% quorum to pass a Land Code agreement, which allows the nation to regain control of their lands from the federal government. In some cases about 75% of a nation's citizens can live off reserve, making meeting quorum challenging with traditional paper voting alone. As such, improving voter participation and access among those living off reserve is a key motivation for online voting adoption. Greater youth engagement, expedited ballot tabulation and other administrative efficiencies are other primary rationales [7].

Finally, online voting is typically adopted as a complementary method of voting. In some instances where internet connectivity is poor and access is limited, telephone voting is also offered to enhance voter access. A few remote and rural communities have eliminated paper voting because it was hardly used and opted for fully electronic elections.

4 Community Profiles

This article incorporates research findings from three First Nations in Canada. Two of the communities, Whitefish River First Nation and Wasauksing First Nation, are located in northern Ontario while the third community, Tsuut'ina Nation, is located in Alberta. All three have deployed online voting to ratify community-based legislation. While the legal context of these votes is beyond this article, in general, when First Nations wish to opt-out of federal legislation, they must develop and ratify legislation to replace it. As noted above, this ratification process typically involves meeting a federally mandated quorum that includes a minimum threshold of participation.

Whitefish River First Nation is an Ojibway community with a total registered population of 1336 members, 900 of whom reside off reserve. The community used online voting in 2014 to ratify Matrimonial Real Property legislation. Wasauksing First Nation is an Ojibway, Odawa and Pottawatomi community with 1341 members, 912 of which live off reserve. Wasauksing's deployment of online voting took place in 2016 and was used to ratify community-developed Land Code legislation. The third community, Tsuut'ina Nation, is the largest of the three with 2132 members with roughly half of those members residing off reserve. Tsuut'ina deployed online voting to ratify its Election Code, in a Chief and Council election, as part of a referendum on the production and sale of cannabis within the nation and for an opinion poll.

5 Approach and Data

Indigenous peoples have a history of being the most researched people in the world. This research is often undertaken without sufficient permissions being obtained or community consultations [27]. Socially-engaged research approaches, which focus on carrying out research with Indigenous peoples rather than on them are growing in popularity since they are more inclusive and often involve active community partnerships that produce knowledge outcomes which directly benefit them [21]. Research undertaken for this article takes a Community-Engaged Research (CER) approach, which falls within the spectrum of socially-engaged research approaches. CER focuses on promoting research partnerships that are based on empowerment, respect and inclusiveness, and work to balance existing power inequities between researchers and communities [15]. Adopting this framework means that partners are treated as equal members in all phases of the research process and share control over the research [16]. This approach not only ensures the production of valuable knowledge outcomes for community actors, but also enhances the depth and breadth of research questions and better informs scholarly outputs with Indigenous knowledge. It also has the added benefit of contributing to, and influencing, social change.

Since May 2014 our research project, First Nations Digital Democracy, has employed a CER approach to work collaboratively with several First Nations in Canada located in the provinces of Ontario and Alberta. Closer examinations of the findings from these communities - Tsuut'ina Nation, Wasauksing First Nation and Whitefish River First Nation – are presented in this article. Each of these First Nations used online voting during the project and partnered with us to better understand the impacts of online voting on participation and governance. The type and nature of data collected varied by community based on their unique needs and input into the research process.

Data from Wasauksing First Nation was collected from online and paper voters during a Land Code ratification vote. Online voting was available from 9:00am EST December 10, 2016 until 8:00am EST on February 25, 2017, which was the official voting day. Only paper ballots were available after 8:00am on the 25th. Once voters had cast an online ballot they were prompted to take a survey about their voting experience. Paper voters were approached at the polls by project personnel and had the option to complete exit surveys on iPads or paper. Youth and elders in the community were trained and hired to support recruitment. A total of 29 online voters took part in the survey, with 15 respondents (N = 15) completing the full survey for a response rate of 20%. Sixty-six paper voters completed a survey (N = 66), for a response rate of 66%.

The Whitefish River First Nation vote took place from March 2 to 6, 2015 as part of a ratification vote on Matrimonial Real Property. Voting from March 2 to 5 was carried out entirely online, while March 6 was paper voting only. In this community surveys were carried out with paper voters only. A total of 123 surveys were completed (N = 123), which represents a response rate of 81%. The same community-engaged approach was taken wherein youth and elders were hired to support survey recruitment on the official voting day.

Finally, Tsuut'ina Nation carried out an opinion poll during a two-day community meeting on April 17 and 18, 2018 regarding whether to allow the production and sale of cannabis on the nation and to determine which voting methods (paper, online or paper voting with electronic tabulators) should be used for elections and referendums. In an effort to build digital literacy in the community, online voting was the only available method to participate in the opinion poll. Research project members were on hand with iPads to walk citizens through the voting process and survey. A total of 139 voters (N = 139) completed the survey (out of 155 that cast a ballot in the opinion poll) for a response rate of 90%.

These samples are self-selected and quite small. While in some cases response rates are 80% or higher, contextual circumstances and attitudes in First Nations vary greatly across communities. These considerations prevent us from conducting deeper analysis and cause us to use caution in drawing conclusions about the representativeness of the results for all First Nations in Canada. That said, this data is the first of its kind and provides an understanding of attitudes toward, and satisfaction with, online voting, likelihood of use, concerns and past voting behaviour. The community-engaged research approach meant that the study was tailored to the needs of each individual First Nation, making the research design slightly different for each partnership.

The article also draws upon 27 semi-structured interviews carried out with Indigenous leaders and community actors, identified experts, online voting vendors and government agencies responsible for Indigenous affairs and elections in Canada. Interviews were conducted between December 2017 and April 2018 and were carried out as part of a project sponsored by Indigenous and Northern Affairs Canada to better understand good practices of online voting and policy recommendations for future deployment. Interview questions addressed Indigenous attitudes toward online voting, rationales for use, benefits and drawbacks of adoption, effects of online voting implementation and good practices and recommendations for future use. This research also included a focus group with four administrators from Tsuut'ina Nation conducted in March 2018. The focus group used the same guide as the interviews, but was conducted in a more interactive, focus group setting.

6 Findings

6.1 Satisfaction with and Willingness to Vote Online

Research carried out as part of the First Nations Digital Democracy Project finds broad support for the use of online voting in Indigenous elections and votes. In Wasauksing First Nations's 2017 Land Code ratification vote, for example, 30% of all ballots were cast online. The remaining 70% were cast by paper (40%) and mail-in ballot (30%). Similarly, in a 2016 Land Code vote in Metlakatla First Nation located in British Columbia, 48% of votes were cast online, 30% by mail and 21% by paper ballot at the polls. Each of these examples are cases where online voting was deployed for the first time and demonstrate that Indigenous voters are willing to make use of the voting method. In particular, the sizeable portion of votes cast remotely (by internet or mail ballot): 60% in Wasauksing and 79% in Metlakatla, highlight the importance of using remote voting methods in First Nations given the importance of engaging citizens living off reserve. Both aforementioned First Nations have sizeable off reserve popu- lations and needed to meet the 25% quorum imposed by the federal government to pass their Land Codes. In the case of Wasauksing, for example, 66% of citizens live off reserve, whereas in Metlakatla, off reserve citizens account for 89% of member- ship. Interviews with Indigenous leaders across Canada echo the importance of leveraging technology to engage off reserve citizens. Similar observations about using online voting to improve voting access for electors that do not live on territorial lands have been made in the context of Canadian municipalities with large seasonal popu- lations [13] and for expatriate voters in other countries [10].

Survey data from Wasauksing First Nation and Tsuut'ina Nation show high sat- isfaction with online voting and indicate voters would like to see it offered in the future for reasons of convenience and accessibility. Ninety-one percent of respondents in Tsuut'ina indicated that they were either 'very' or 'fairly' satisfied with the online voting process. Top reasons for using online voting included: convenience (36%), privacy (17%), wanting to try something new (17%), and accessibility (15%). Similar findings of support are present in Wasauksing First Nation. One hundred percent of online voters who completed our survey indicated they were either 'very' or 'fairly' satisfied with the voting method. Primary rationales for voting online included con- venience (41%), accessibility (24%), and wanting to try something new (12%). Such rationales for use are consistent with the reasons given by voters in Canadian municipal elections where convenience has been shown to be the main motivating factor [13].

While the above examples illustrate that voters are willing to make use of the voting method and are satisfied with it, those who prefer to vote by paper are also supportive of the policy change. Where data is available, we find that having online voting as a complementary voting method is desired by paper voters. In Wasauksing First Nation, paper voter respondents were asked whether they would consider voting online in the future. Sixty-three percent said they would consider voting by internet for a future vote. Twenty-eight percent of these respondents said they would vote online 'in all cir- cumstances', while 35% reported wanting to use it under 'special circumstances' such as in cases where being too busy, inclement weather, illness or mobility issues prevented them from attending a physical poll location. There were, however, 35% of respondents that said they would not vote online in future.

A similar survey carried out with paper voters in Whitefish River First Nation reveals comparable results. Fifty-six percent of paper voters indicated that they would vote online in the future (20% 'in all circumstances', 36% in 'special circumstances'), while 33% said they would not vote online. Though there are understandably electors who prefer to vote by paper and want to continue using that voting method, the fact that a majority of paper voters in these First Nations say that they would vote online in the future, particularly under 'special circumstances' where their participation may be limited without a remote voting option, suggests broad support for online voting.

Reasons why some paper voters may be hesitant to vote online likely have to do with concerns about internet access and online voting security. In Wasauksing First Nation a majority of paper voters said they did not have concerns about online voting (41%), however, 21% reported concerns about lack of internet access and 18% cited security as a concern. Other, less prevalent, concerns included: fraud (8%), privacy (8%), lack of computer and internet knowledge (2%) and loss of voting traditions (2%). Similarly, paper voters in Whitefish River First Nation expressed lack of a computer or access to the internet as a concern (26%), security (19%), the replacement of voting traditions (8%), privacy (6%), fraud (5%) and 'other' reasons (7%).

In both cases, concerns about lack of access to technology and the internet speaks to issues with broadband infrastructure and affordability. In some remote communities the cost of a monthly internet plan can often be 3 to 4 times the cost of a comparable plan in a suburban area. While every First Nation is different, these results suggest strong support for online voting among Indigenous voters who would use the service and those who would typically opt for a paper ballot.

6.2 Who Votes Online?

Data collected from Wasauksing First Nation allows us to compare the socio-demographic characteristics of voters who chose internet and paper ballots, and confirms that online voting seems to be especially appealing to those living off reserve. There is also evidence to suggest that online voting could motivate a modest portion of less frequent voters to take part.

Looking at the age of internet and paper voters who completed surveys in Wasauksing First Nation shows that online voters are middle-aged, with the largest group falling in the 45 to 54 age category. Online voters had a mean age of 48 years and paper voters 44 years. Although the online voter sample was small, only one person under the age of 35 who completed our survey chose to vote online. Younger voters were much more likely to cast a paper ballot. These findings are consistent with studies of online voting use by young people in municipal elections in Canada [13] and Norway [25], which suggest young voters are more likely to vote by paper given that it is often one of their first voting experiences and is seen as a symbolic and ceremonial act.

Interestingly, the oldest voters, those over the age of 55, were also more likely to vote by paper than internet. This likely has to do with older voters communicating greater concerns about lack of internet access and experience with computers. Thirty-six percent of paper voters remarked that they do not have internet access at home and a majority of this group (60%) were over the age of 55. Indigenous voters over the age of 55 were also much less likely to access the internet regularly. While online voting use in municipal elections drops off with age, it typically occurs over the age of 65. The fact that persons aged 55 years and older are much less likely to vote by internet likely has to do with the limited availability of internet and weaker digital literacy in First Nations.

Moving on to other socio-demographic characteristics, we see that online voters in Wasauksing First Nation report being more educated and having a higher household income than paper voters. Online voters are also more likely to live off reserve. Findings about online voters being more educated and having higher incomes than paper voters have also been observed in Canadian municipal examinations and suggests that the extension of online voting may be more about improving convenience for persons who were likely to vote anyway rather than attracting electors from all socio-demographic groups [11, 13]. In this context, however, higher education levels and reported income could be related to the greater education and employment opportunities located off reserve. Likewise, lower reported educational attainment and income for paper voters could be linked to living in the community. The finding about online voters being more likely to live off reserve makes sense, especially given the enhanced accessibility for these electors.

Interviews with election administrators in Wasauksing First Nation and Indigenous leaders in other nations confirm the value of online voting for off reserve citizens. As one leader remarked, "Because our community is dispersed with 85% away from our homeland, and 60% a significant distance away from the homeland, online voting helps to further include everyone, and that's quite important when it comes to thinking about it from First Nations' perspective, off reserve specifically. First Nations that are not connected to their homelands or their cultures or their peoples, have kind of created for themselves a third party, so to speak. This would allow them to include themselves in important processes, cultural processes, electronically in some way, shape or form."

Interviewees commented on citizens living in different cities, provinces and countries and the importance of engaging these members to ensure community voice is represented in the decision-making of the nation. While voting by mail is another remote voting option, many we spoke with communicated issues with delayed ballots, problems with the mail system, and electors simply not leaving enough time to mail a completed ballot as barriers that online voting can address. Online voting is clearly desired in Wasauksing First Nation and in other First Nations where a sizeable proportion of citizens typically live off reserve (places like the Mowhawk Council of the Awkwesasne which spans Ontario, Quebec and the United States and Metlakatla First Nation are other examples). In fact, in cases where a majority of citizens live off reserve, the adoption of online voting may be essential to engage residents especially in instances where quorum must be met such as in the case of Land Code and MRP ratification votes.

Table 2. Mean socio-demographic characteristics of voters in Wasauksing First Nation

Socio-demographic characteristic	Online voters	Paper voters
Age	48 years	44 years
Education	Completed technical, community college	Completed technical, community college
Annual household income	$60 000 to $79 000	$40 000 to $49 000
Marital status	Married	Married
On or off reserve	Off reserve	On reserve

6.3   Potential for Engagement

Finally, does online voting have the potential to engage Indigenous voters? The Tsuut'ina Nation survey asked respondents whether they would have taken part had online voting not been an option. A majority of participants indicated that they 'definitely' or 'probably' would have participated in the opinion poll regardless of whether online voting was used. However, 9% indicated that they 'definitely' or 'probably' would not have voted had the voting method not been available. In the Wasauksing First Nation survey, a similarly high percentage of respondents indicated that they would have voted anyway had online voting not been an option (88%), with 13% saying they 'probably' would not have. These modest percentages are consistent with studies of online voting adoption among Canadian municipal governments, which demonstrate internet voting can encourage a modest portion of less frequent voters to participate [5, 11].

Questions about voting histories were also asked, however, these were not consistent across surveys. Still, responses suggest that paper voters have more consistent voting records than those choosing to vote by internet. This may be because online voters are more likely to live off reserve and typically encounter a greater opportunity cost to attend a poll location (i.e. longer travel time). While these findings suggest positive implications for engagement, they should be taken with care given that these are self-reported measures.

Supporting the hypothesis that online voting has the potential to more consistently engage less frequent voters, paper voter respondents were asked how they would prefer to vote if unable to make it to a physical poll location. In Tsuut'ina Nation, 70% said they would vote by internet, 13% by mail, 6% by telephone, 4% would appoint a proxy to vote on their behalf and 2% would abstain from voting. In Wasauksing First Nation, by comparison, 49% said they would vote by internet, 22% by mail, 10% would appoint a proxy, 5% by telephone, 5% would abstain and 10% did not know. Of possible remote voting methods, online voting was by far the most desired way to cast a ballot in situations where electors could not make it to a polling location (i.e., being too busy, illness, inclement weather, transportation issues). The fact that a plurality of respondents in both First Nations selected online voting as their preferred voting method if unable to vote in person suggests it has the potential to enhance the participation of voters in special situations where otherwise attending a poll location may not be possible.

Taken together, survey findings indicate broad support for online voting. While paper voting is desired and is an important tradition to continue, online voting is a welcome addition to voting processes to enhance access, notably for citizens living off reserve and those residing on reserve who may encounter issues voting at a physical poll location.

6.4 Good Practices

Community-engaged work with First Nations and interviews with Indigenous leaders, practitioners and identified experts reveal a number of good practices for the implementation of online voting in Indigenous votes. Many of these are broad suggestions. However, this broad framing is suitable given that the adoption of online voting is highly contextual based on the circumstances surrounding its implementation and the unique features and needs of the community. Good practices can be grouped into four categories: (1) those relating to knowledge of the community, engagement, outreach and communication, (2) building tools and strategy, (3) clear processes and resources, and (4) a focus on technology.[1]

Broadly, under the theme of community knowledge and engagement good practices include: understanding community members – their demographics, preferences, and unique features which may make one type of voting model more successful than another – and what is needed for the particular vote (i.e., meeting a 25% quorum). Other good practices within this theme include robust education and communications about the online voting process, consultation with the community, and digital skill building, especially since this aspect was identified as an area where First Nations can be weak.

Second, building tools and strategies to support the successful deployment of online voting were communicated as good practices. This encompasses having accurate voters' lists and building email databases to reach as many members as possible. A third element involves recommending Indigenous communities take their time with online voting implementation, employing an incremental or iterative approach which involves a test and learn model wherein one or two things are tried at a time and then the approach is subsequently refined and expanded.

Third, having clear processes, resources and knowledge were identified as areas which could enhance online voting adoption. Part of this involves having a clear idea of who is in charge of the online voting aspect of Indigenous votes and outlining responsibilities of the First Nation and the technology vendor to minimize misunderstandings. Also, boosting technical knowledge is seen as critical to better enable election administrators to vet technology vendors and understand technical aspects of the vote to offer more secure voting options.

Finally, focusing on two key aspects of technology: security and access, are seen as good practices. Though no special ideas were suggested for how aspects of voting

---

[1] These are provided in a report prepared for Indigenous and Northern Affairs Canada with examples from Indigenous communities. To keep within length requirements, it was not possible to include a copy in this article.

security may be unique in the context of Indigenous votes, each First Nation citizen has a status identification card number issued by the federal government. This is a unique identifier that could, and has been used as a credential to authenticate online voters. It was recommended by computer scientists that First Nations use a hybrid model of remote online voting whereby voters print a ballot they receive electronically, mark it and mail it back to election authorities. This approach maintains a paper record while improving access, albeit not to the same extent as with true remote online voting. In addition, ensuring access to online voting for those who want to use it and learn about it, but who may not otherwise have the resources to do so, is essential for promoting voter equality.

7   Discussion and Conclusion

Overall research conducted as part of the First Nations Digital Democracy project reveals interesting findings about online voting in Indigenous communities in Canada and good practices that can be implemented to enhance deployment. Indigenous electors are willing to use online voting, voters are satisfied with it, and persons drawn to vote by paper are supportive of the policy change. Some paper voters are willing to try online voting in the future 'no matter what', whereas others (the largest proportion) say they would vote online in circumstances where they were unable to attend a polling location in person. Online voters are typically middle-aged, with slightly higher education and household income than paper voters. The youngest and oldest Indigenous voters are most inclined to vote by paper. In the case of younger voters we speculate this has to do with the fact that voting for the first time is a rite of passage and a more symbolic experience when carried out by paper, whereas for older voters concerns about access to the internet and electronic devices likely plays a large role in their willingness to not vote online.

One of the biggest takeaways from this research is that it appears online voting is an increasingly crucial tool to ensure community voice is incorporated in First Nation decision-making. This is especially true in cases where the federal government requires quorums be met for First Nations to pass their own laws and frameworks, and in instances where large portions of a community live off reserve. This is supported by our finding that online voters are more likely to live outside of the First Nation than paper voters, where travel to a polling location on reserve lands could make the voting prohibitively costly. Such findings are in line with other research which suggests voters living outside of their territories may have a disproportionate interest in voting online [10, 26].

In terms of potential improvements in engagement, further evidence is needed but our survey findings suggest that some of the people who chose online voting might not have participated otherwise. Past voting records of paper voters are also slightly more consistent than those of online voters. In this regard online voting could engage some of these electors on a more frequent basis given the greater convenience it offers. As noted, such findings are consistent with municipal studies of online voting in Canada [5, 11]. In addition, if paper voters were unable to attend a polling location, online voting would be their top choice.

Finally, our research presents a number of good practices for online voting implementation in Indigenous communities. While these lessons learned come from First Nations, much of their wisdom is transferrable to Indigenous communities in other countries as well as communities situated in rural and remote areas. Practices fall into four themed areas – those relating to knowledge of the community and outreach, building tools and taking an incremental approach, clear processes and increasing technical knowledge and resources, and addressing security and accessibility aspects of the technology.

Future studies could more deeply explore the effects of online voting on Indigenous participation, namely the degree to which it affects off reserve participation. As part of this studies could explore whether there are parallels between off reserve members' uptake of online voting and use among expatriates in other countries such as Switzerland [10]. In addition, further examination of the challenges of inadequate internet access and lack of digital skills and how these areas can be improved is needed. Finally, comparative examinations of Indigenous deployment of online voting in other countries would be a welcome addition to the literature and our knowledge of how technology affects Indigenous peoples.

Acknowledgement. The authors would like to extend sincere thanks to Tsuut'ina Nation, Wasauksing First Nation, and Whitefish River First Nation as well as the many experts who participated in interviews. We acknowledge financial support from the Social Science and Humanities Research Council of Canada, the Government of Canada, and Chelsea Gabel's Canada Research Chair in Indigenous Well- Being, Community, Engagement and Innovation.

References

1. Alcantara, C., Dick, C.: Decolonization in a digital age: cryptocurrencies and Indigenous self-determination in Canada. Can. J. Law Soc./La Revue Canadienne Droit et Société. **32**, 19–35 (2017)
2. Bargh, M.: Opportunities and complexities for Māori and mana whenua representation in local government. Polit. Sci. **68**, 143–160 (2016)
3. Belanger, Y.: You have to be involved to play a part in it: assessing Kainai attitudes about voting Canadian elections. Great Plains Q. **29**, 29–49 (2009)
4. Budd, B., Gabel, C., Goodman, N.: Technology in Indigenous communities in Canada: implications for participation and governance. In: Conference Paper, Meeting of the Canadian Political Science Association (2017)
5. Couture, J., Breux, S., Goodman, N.: La vote par Internet augmente-t-il la participation électorale? In: Loiseau, H., Waldispuehl, E. (eds.) Cyberespace et science politique: De la méthode au terrain, du virtuel au réel, pp. 123-148. Presses de l'Université du Québec, Quebec City (2017)
6. Fleras, A., Elliott, J.L.: Unequal Relations: An Introduction to Race, Ethnic and Aboriginal Dynamics in Canada. Prentice Hall, Scarborough (1999)
7. Gabel, C., Goodman, N., Bird, K., Budd, B.: Indigenous adoption of internet voting: a case study of Whitefish River First Nation. Int. Indig. Policy J. **7** (2016)
8. Gabel, C., Goodman, N., Bird, K., Budd, B.: The impact of digital technology on First Nations participation and governance. Can. J. Nativ. Stud. **36**, 107–127 (2016)

9. Germann, M., Serdült, U.: Internet voting and turnout: evidence from Switzerland. Elect. Stud. **47**, 1–12 (2017)
10. Germann, M., Serdült, U.: Internet voting for expatriates: the Swiss case. JeDEM - EJournal EDemocracy Open Gov. **6**, 197–215 (2014)
11. Goodman, N.: Internet voting in a local election in Canada. In: Grofman, B., Trechsel, A.H., Franklin, M. (eds.) The Internet and Democracy in Global Perspective, pp. 7–24. Springer, Cham (2014). https://doi.org/10.1007/978-3-319-04352-4_2
12. Goodman, N., Pammett, J.: The patchwork of internet voting in Canada. In: Electronic Voting: Verifying the Vote (EVOTE), pp 1–6. IEEE Press, New York (2014)
13. Goodman, N., Pyman, H.: Understanding the effects of internet voting on elections: results from the 2014 Ontario municipal elections. Technical Paper, Centre for e-Democracy (2016)
14. Goodman, N., Stokes, L.C.: Reducing the cost of voting: an evaluation of internet voting's effect on turnout. Br. J. Polit. Sci. 1–13 (2018). https://doi.org/10.1017/S0007123417000849
15. Green, G.: Participatory action research: lessons learned with Aboriginal grandmothers. Health Care Women Int. **22**, 471–482 (2001)
16. Israel, B., Schulz, A., Parker, E., Becker, A.: Review of community-based research: assessing partnership approaches to improve public health. Ann. Rev. Pub. Health **19**, 173–202 (1998)
17. Lockhart, E., Tenasco, A., Whiteduck, T., O'Donnell, S.: Information and communication technology for education in an Algonquin First Nation in Quebec. J. Commun. Inform. **10** (2013)
18. Maaka, R., Fleras, A.: The Politics of Indigeneity: Challenging the State in Canada and Aotearoa New Zealand. Otago University Press, Dunedin (2006)
19. McMahon, R., Gurstein, M., Beaton, B., O'Donnell, S., Whiteduck, T.: Making information technologies work at the end of the road. J. Inf. Policy **4**, 250–269 (2014)
20. McMahon, R.: Creating an enabling environment for digital self-determination. Media Dev. **2**, 11–15 (2014)
21. Midzain-Gobin, L., Goodman, N., Gabel, C., Bird, K.: Time for change? Reforming the Indian Act to allow for online voting. Policy Options Special Issue: The Indian Act: Breaking its Stubborn Grip (2017)
22. Monchalin, L.: The Colonial Problem: An Indigenous Perspective on Crime and Injustice in Canada. University of Toronto Press, Toronto (2016)
23. Norris, P.: Will new technology boost turnout? Evaluating experiments in UK local elections. In: Kersting, N., Baldersheim, H. (eds.) Electronic Voting and Democracy, pp. 193–225. Palgrave Macmillan, London (2004). https://doi.org/10.1057/9780230523531_12
24. O'Donnell, S., Beaton, B., McMahon, R., Hudson, H., Williams, D., Whiteduck, T.: First Nations Education Council: digital technology adoption in remote and northern Indigenous communities in Canada. In: Conference Paper, Meeting of the Canadian Sociological Association (2016)
25. Segaard, S., Baldersheim, H., Saglie, J.: The Norwegian trial with internet voting: results and challenges. In: Barrat, J., Esteve, I. (eds.) El voto electrónico y sus dimensiones jurídicas: entre la ingenua complacencia y el rechazo precipitado. Iustel, Madrid (2016)
26. Serdült, U., Germann, M., Mendez, F., Portenier, A., Wellig, C.: Fifteen years of internet voting in Switzerland: history, governance and use. In: 2015 2nd International Conference on eDemocracy and eGovernment, pp. 126–132. IEEE Press, New York (2015)
27. Smith, L.: Decolonizing Methodologies: Research and Indigenous Peoples. Zed Books Ltd, London (2013)
28. Solop, F.: Digital democracy comes of age: internet voting and the 2000 Arizona democratic primary election. Polit. Sci. Polit. **34**, 289–293 (2001)

29. Trechsel, A., Vassil, K.: Internet voting in Estonia. A comparative analysis of four elections since 2005. Technical Report, Council of Europe (2010)
30. Truth and Reconciliation Commission of Canada: Calls to Action (2015). http://www.trc.ca/websites/trcinstitution/File/2015/Findings/Calls_to_Action_English2.pdf
31. Vassil, K., Solvak, M., Vinkel, P., Trechsel, A., Alvarez, A.: The diffusion of internet voting. Usage patterns of internet voting in Estonia between 2005 and 2015. Gov. Inf. Q. **33**, 453–459 (2016)

Process Models for Universally Verifiable Elections

Rolf Haenni$^{(\boxtimes)}$, Eric Dubuis, Reto E. Koenig, and Philipp Locher

Bern University of Applied Sciences, 2501 Biel, Switzerland
{rolf.haenni,eric.dubuis,reto.koenig,philipp.locher}@bfh.ch

Abstract. In this paper, we analyze the process of performing the universal verification of an electronic election. We propose a general model of the election process and define the data flow into the verification process. We also define the purpose and outcome of the verification process and propose some general categories of tests to be performed during the verification. As a guideline for dealing with negative verification outcomes, we propose some general evaluation criteria for assessing the impact and consequences of the encountered problem. Finally, we generalize the proposed process models to the case of hybrid elections, in which multiple voting channels are available simultaneously. The primary target audience of this paper are people in charge of implementing and organizing verifiable elections in practice.

1 Introduction

Universal verifiability is a key concept for making electronic voting systems secure enough for using them in real political elections. It is a counter-measure against all sorts of threads from very powerful adversaries, which for example may try manipulate the election result by taking control over some of the central system components. To prevent such attacks, the system generates some public election data during the election process, which can be used to reconstruct the final election result in a publicly verifiable manner. Independent third parties (auditors) can then be invited to verify the correctness of the election result based on the cryptographic evidence included in the public election data. Provided that the verification has succeeded, one can then conclude that no such attacks have been conducted. By providing this simple functionality, universal verifiability is a very important trust-establishing measure. Its ultimate goal is to convince even the losers of an election to accept the result [7,11].

1.1 Universal Verifiability in Practice

One of the major challenges of building a universally verifiable election system is to provide verifiability simultaneously with vote secrecy. Many cryptographic protocols have been invented for that purpose. Their main problem is to define the verification process in a way that the correct election result can be reconstructed without explicitly decrypting the submitted encrypted votes. For this,

© Springer Nature Switzerland AG 2018
R. Krimmer et al. (Eds.): E-Vote-ID 2018, LNCS 11143, pp. 84–99, 2018.
https://doi.org/10.1007/978-3-030-00419-4_6

some anonymization mechanism must be applied to the submitted votes to unlink them from the voters. Techniques for solving this problem, for example mix-nets or homomorphic tallying, are well-understood today and widely applied. Practical systems using these technologies have been introduced for both academic and real-world purposes [2–6].

Based on today's generally accepted understanding that verifiability is crucial for electronic elections, countries such as Switzerland and Estonia have decided to update the requirements for their existing e-voting systems. The following quote from the *Federal Chancellery Ordinance on Electronic Voting* (VEleS) underlines this change of paradigm in Switzerland [1, p. 3]:

> *"Auditors receive proof that the result has been ascertained correctly. They must evaluate the proof in a observable procedure. To do this, they must use technical aids that are independent of and isolated from the rest of the system."*

To fulfill the extended requirements, the two remaining Swiss e-voting system providers have launched corresponding development projects. By releasing a detailed and comprehensive protocol specification together with two different proof-of-concept implementations [8,9], the CHVote project of the State of Geneva has reached an important milestone in 2017. The launch of the new system, which is currently being developed according to the specification, is planned for the 2019 parliament elections. Similar plans exist for the system offered by the Post CH Ltd, which has officially reached an intermediate expansion stage in early 2018. In both projects, the legal ordinance is clear about implementing proper verification processes along with the introduction of the next-generation systems. However, since VEleS does not further specify the details of such processes, it does not provide sufficient legal grounds for most of the conclusions and recommendations contained this paper.

1.2   Goals and Overview

Despite the recent developments in Switzerland and other places in the world, only little experience exists with respect to conducting an actual verification process for real political elections. The foremost problem is the necessity of providing suitable *technical aids* that offer the desired functionality while satisfying the requirement of being independent from the rest of the system. In some of the above-mentioned systems, such technical aids have never been developed. This leads to a paradoxical situations, where systems are promoted as (potentially) verifiable, but without offering the full package for performing an actual verification.

Another problem is the lack of a common understanding of the exact purpose of a verification and the necessary processes around it. Simple questions like what are the exact input data of a verification process and what are the possible verification results have never been defined in a precise manner. Such a high-level view of the verification process is the main topic of this paper. The goal is to lay the foundations for introducing universal verification into existing and future electoral processes. For this, we look at the commonalities of existing e-voting protocols, propose a high-level summary of the relevant data flow, and finally derive general models for both the election and the verification processes. The paper is written mainly from a technical perspective. Related political, legal, or sociological questions are deliberately left aside.

We will start in Sect. 2 with a general model of the election process, which defines the principal data flow. This model is general enough to be applicable to both electronic and non-electronic election processes. Based on this model, we propose a definition of the verification process. Particular attention is given to the verification result, which we decompose into five main categories. We also discuss the development process of corresponding verification software. In Sect. 3, we use the generality of the election process model to define corresponding processes for hybrid voting systems, which provides multiple (electronic and non-electronic) voting channels simultaneously. In this particular setting, additional considerations are necessary to guarantee the completeness of the verification chain. Section 4 summarizes the findings and concludes the paper.

2   Universally Verifiable Elections

An election system's principal function is to establish the correct election result based on the votes submitted by the voters. This should be done in a way that even the losers of the election will accept the result as correct. In a paper-based election system, this functionality is achieved by involving trustworthy people from all parties in the tallying process. In case of observed or suspected irregularities, election authorities can order a re-tally of the votes by independent third parties to remove any existing doubts. In an electronic election system, this is exactly the purpose of conducting a universal verification, but the evidence necessary for inferring the correctness of the result is derived from cryptographic methods rather than human supervision. Irregularities caused by attacks or software bugs can then be detected in a reliable way. The purposes of re-tallying paper votes and universally verifying electronic votes are therefore largely equivalent.

2.1   Election Process

In order to define universal verification more precisely, we must first introduce an abstract model of an election process. To provide compatibility with most existing election protocols, we suppress technical details as far as possible. A common denominator is the *election period*, during which voters can submit their votes. Independently of the exact length of this period, it defines a natural decomposition of the whole election process into three consecutive phases:

pre-election phase ⇒ election phase ⇒ post-election phase.

Each phase generates its own part of the *election process data*, which contains the auxiliary cryptographic evidence required to perform the verification of the election result. For the general understanding of the election and verification processes, it is not necessary to further specify the exact content of this data, but it is important to keep in mind that this data is public. Usually, it is written to a public bulletin board, from which it can be retrieved by anyone who wants to perform the verification. The election process data is depicted in Fig. 1 as one of the main outputs of the election process.

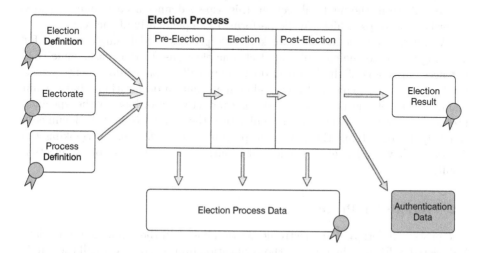

Fig. 1. Abstract model and data flow of an election process.

One of the main inputs of the election process is a document called *election definition*, which defines the details of the election, for example the questions and voting options in a referendum or the list of candidates and election rules in an election. A second input document, which we call *electorate*, contains the list of eligible voters. This document is needed to determine the voter's eligibility and therefore decide about the validity of a submitted vote. Another input document, which we call *process definition*, specifies the details of the election process, for example the start and the end of the election period, but also the identities of the parties and authorities involved in the process or the cryptographic parameters to be used. The party responsible for providing the three input documents is called *election administrator*. Our distinction between election definition and process definition is important in the hybrid setting discussed in Sect. 3, where a single election definition is combined with two or more process definitions.

The most important output of the election process is the *election result*. We do not further specify the contents of this document, except that we assume that it summarizes the outcome of the election tally, for example by summing up the number of yes/no-votes in a referendum or by simply enumerating all decrypted votes in cleartext. This document represents therefore the official result, which is publicly announced in the aftermath of the election. For this, it is important for this document to contain a signature from the election administrator, which guarantees the correctness of its contents.

The same remark about containing a signature holds for the three input documents and for most parts of the elections process data. We summarize this aspect of the model by assuming an additional output called *authentication data* (yellow-highlighted in Fig. 1). In a purely electronic setting, this output will consists of a list of digital signatures with corresponding certificates, from which the authenticity and integrity of all input and output documents can be inferred. As we will see in the next subsection, this aspect defines a particular category of verification steps, which can be performed independently of the rest.

We already mentioned that we kept this process model simple enough for applying it also to the case of non-electronic elections. In that case, some (but not necessarily all) of the involved documents will be paper documents signed by the people that generated them. They may contain declarations that certain manual tasks of the process have been conducted according to the specified procedures. In case of detected irregularities, the existence of such documents can help in identifying the person responsible for causing or overlooking the problem. They are therefore needed for ensuring the plausibility of the election result.

2.2   Verification Process

The process of verifying an electronic election based on the available public data is depicted in Fig. 2. The input of the verification process consists of all the public inputs and outputs of the election process model from the previous section. We refer to it as the *election data* and assume that it is available to any person who wants to perform a verification. Note that we consider the election result as part of the election data, which must be checked for correctness. The purpose of the verification process is to perform a series of tests on the election data, which collectively give enough evidence to assess the correctness of the election result. A compilation of the results obtained from performing the necessary tests is what we call the *verification report*. This document is the principal output of the verification process. The software that generates the verification report based on the election data is called *verifier*.

By defining the verification as a series of individual tests performed by the verifier, it is possible to introduce at least five different top-level categories, according to which the tests can be grouped in a meaningful way (further meaningful categories and sub-categories may exist in more concrete cases). In Table 1, we summarize the meaning of these categories and their differences. One of the purposes of introducing such test categories is to facilitate and systematize the definition of a suitable *test catalog*, which ultimately leads to a fully connected verification chain. This test catalog is the main content of the verifier specification (see Sect. 2.4). Another purpose of introducing categories is to simplify the organization and presentation of the test results in the verification report.

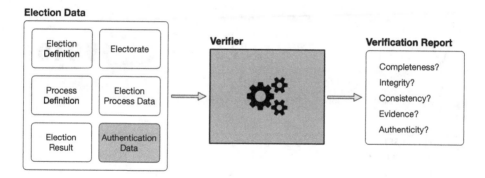

Fig. 2. Abstract model of the verification process.

Table 1. Test categories of the verification process.

Category	Description
Completeness	Do the available data elements cover the whole election process according to the specification? Do they allow a complete verification chain?
Integrity	Do all data elements correspond to the protocol specification? Are they all within the specified ranges?
Consistency	Are related data elements consistent to each other?
Evidence	Are the cryptographic proofs contained in the election data all valid? Do they provide the necessary evidence to infer the correctness of corresponding protocol steps?
Authenticity	Can the data elements be linked unambiguously to the party authorized to create them?

An example of a verifier's user interface is depicted Fig. 3. It shows the upper part of the verification report for an election at the University of Zürich in 2013 using the UniVote system [4,10]. The status bar in the upper right corner indicates that the verification is still in progress. The report also shows the results of the first eleven (out of 61) tests. Nine tests succeeded, one test has been dropped due to a missing certificate, and one test failed due to an invalid signature. Assuming that the verifier itself works properly, this indicates that parts of the implemented voting system have not been working properly, or even worse that the election has been exposed to an attack. In any case, it is clear that both the cause and the impact of the exposed problems have to be investigated. Triggering such an investigation in case of irregularities is the main purpose of performing the verification.

2.3 Impact and Consequences of Failed Tests

As illustrated by the above example, using a verifier to conduct the verification of an election can always lead to a situation, in which some tests from the test

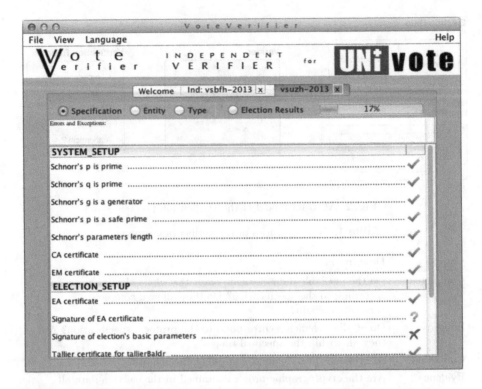

Fig. 3. User interface of the verifier for the UniVote system.

catalog have failed. There are numerous possible causes for a test to fail, but there is presumably no better way for finding the cause than analyzing the particular problem at hand. Giving general recommendations about handling failure cases is therefore quite difficult. Nevertheless, we can at least propose three different evaluation criteria, which may help to classify the impact of the problem and to decide about the next steps.

The first criteria is the maximal number of affected votes. Suppose that N electronic votes have been submitted and that maximally $0 \leq k \leq N$ votes are affected by the problem.[1] Note that this constraint includes the two natural limiting cases of $k = 0$ (no vote affected) and $k = N$ (all votes affected). Another important quantity is the number ΔR of votes, which are necessary to change the winner or the outcome of an election. In a referendum, the general constraint for this number is $1 \leq \Delta R \leq \frac{N}{2}$. For example, for 60 *yes*-votes, 30 *no*-votes, 10 blank votes, and therefore $N = 100$, the outcome could be changed by turning 15 *yes*-votes into *no*-votes. For judging the impact of the problem, it is therefore important to determine if k is smaller or bigger than $\Delta R = 15$. For $1 \leq k < \Delta R$, the impact of the problem may not justify the invalidation of the whole

---

[1] In a hybrid election process, both the number of electronic votes and the total number of votes must be taken into consideration.

election (similar arguments are used to handle minor irregularities in paper-based elections), but in the more severe case of $k \geq \Delta R$, repeating the whole election can probably not be avoided.

The second criteria refers to the security goal violated by the detected problem. Relative to a single submitted vote, three cases must be distinguished: a violation of the vote's secrecy, a violation of the vote's integrity, or a violation of both the vote's secrecy and integrity.[2] Generally, we consider violations of the vote's integrity to be more critical than violations of the vote's secrecy, because they affect the election results in a direct way. The possible consequences are therefore more drastic in such cases. In Fig. 4 we give an overview of the consequences in the scenarios obtained from combining the first two evaluation criteria. It shows for example that vote secrecy violations do not directly invalidate the election result, but that an investigation of the problem's cause is always necessary.

	Vote Secrecy	Vote Integrity	Vote Secrecy & Integrity
k=0	Result confirmed	Result confirmed	Result confirmed
k< ΔR	Result confirmed Initiate investigation Stop using the system	Result questionable Initiate investigation Stop using the system	Result questionable Initiate investigation Stop using the system
k≥ ΔR	Result confirmed Initiate investigation Stop using the system	Result not confirmed Initiate investigation Stop using the system	Result not confirmed Initiate investigation Stop using the system

Fig. 4. Problem scenarios with consequences.

Another important point to consider in case of an unsuccessful verification is the question of whether the problem could possibly be solved by repeating some steps of the election process. For example, the case of a missing or invalid signature could possibly be solved by simply repeating the signature generation. Generally, such recovery procedures mostly exist for data that is not temporarily linked to other parts of the election data. In those cases, only the availability of the data is necessary to conduct the verification, not their moment of creation. Problems encountered with such data can therefore be solved by repeating their creation during a recovery procedure.

---

[2] The main purpose of the universal verification is detecting integrity violations. However, the failing of certain tests can also lead to situations, in which vote secrecy is no longer guaranteed, for example if the signatures of the mixing proofs are all invalid. This could mean that all mixing proofs have been generated by the same party, which can then establish links from cleartext votes to voters.

Assuming that recovery procedures exist, pursuing them will always be the first choice in case of encountering a problem in the verification report. A general business process model for handling failure cases is depicted in Fig. 5. It shows that executing a recovery procedure invokes an additional verification round. If the problem persists—or if no recovery procedure has existed from the beginning—then an investigation of the problem must be invoked and the result of the investigation must be documented in a report.

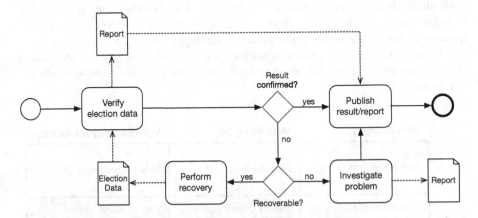

Fig. 5. Process model for handling failure cases and recovering from them.

2.4   Developing the Verifier

The principal technical aid for conducting the verification of an election is the verifier. Clearly, the proper functioning of the verifier is a mandatory precondition for obtaining conclusive verification reports. It is therefore essential that the verifier works exactly in accordance with the specified cryptographic protocol. Any deviation could lead to unpleasant situations in which the verifier reports a failure when everything is correct (false negative) or misses a failure when something went wrong (false positive). In a nutshell, the software development goal for the verifier consists in avoiding these situations altogether.

Given the mathematical and technical complexities of cryptographic voting protocols, developing a verifier directly from the protocol specification is a very big challenge. It requires advanced skills in both applied cryptography and software development. If unqualified personnel is in charge of this task, it is likely that the implemented test catalog will not form a complete verification chain, or that some tests are implemented incorrectly. In both cases, the conclusiveness of the verification report is weakened considerably.

To ensure the required functionality and software quality, we propose a two-step procedure for developing the verifier. The first step consists in deriving a specification document from the specification of the voting system. This task should be performed by cryptography experts that are familiar with voting protocols in general and with the specific technical details of the voting protocol at hand (possibly by the designers of the voting protocol). The main part of this document is the aforementioned test catalog, which together must form a complete verification chain. To assure the completeness of this chain, assembling the test catalog must be carried out with meticulous precision. To detect remaining gaps as early as possible, we also recommend applying a thorough reviewing process to this document. For maximal transparency, we also recommend the publication of this document.

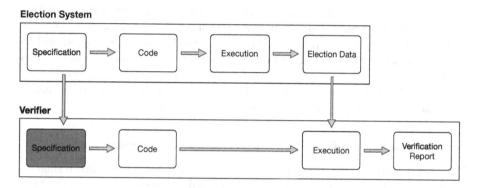

Fig. 6. Developing and executing the verifier based on a separate specification document.

Developing the actual software based on the verifier's specification is the second step of the proposed procedure (see Fig. 6). This task can be delegated to a software engineer with only moderate background knowledge in cryptography and cryptographic protocols. To achieve general software quality properties, standard software design and coding principles should be applied to the development process. Code reviewing is another important method to establish the desired code quality. For maximal transparency, we also recommend to publish the source code and to invite the public to participate in reviewing the code.

Additional preconditions for developing the verifier are a precise interface description for obtaining the election data from the voting system and the availability of some meaningful test data. Both preconditions must be met by the developers of the voting system. Ideally, the test data also contains inconsistencies or flaws, such that the developed software can be tested for false positives and false negatives. Finally, it is also very important to implement a strict versioning policy, because even the slightest change in the voting system or in the election data may be enough to affect the proper functioning of the verifier.

3   Hybrid Election Processes

The election and verification processes as discussed so far are only directly applicable to the simple case of a purely electronic election with a single voting channel. The situation usually gets more complicated if multiple voting channels are offered simultaneously. The simplest way of handling multiple channels is to let the voters choose their preferred channel prior to an election. This leads to a decomposition of the electorate, which finally results in conducting multiple elections independently of each other. In this case, no channel coordination other than summing up the individual election results is necessary. If one of the channels is an electronic one, the verification can therefore be conducted in isolation using the process described in the previous section.

A more complicated situation arises if voters can choose the voting channel spontaneously during the election period. The composition of corresponding election processes is called a *hybrid election process*, and we will see in this section that extra precautions are necessary to handle this case properly. We are particularly interested in hybrid election processes because they correspond to the current plans in Switzerland of offering the electronic channel in addition to the two existing voting channels (postal mail, in person). The question that we want to address here is how to conduct the verification of the electronic votes, if postal voting or voting in person takes place simultaneously.

3.1 Extending the Election and Verification Processes

The major problem that arises in a hybrid election process is to ensure that no voter submits more than one vote over the available channels. This implies that using one channel for submitting a vote must disqualify the voter in every other channel. It is clear that implementing this seemingly simple principle requires accurate coordination between the channels. In practice, it turns out that the submission of multiple votes over multiple channels can not be avoided completely, even if doing so is illegal. If this happens, it should at least not be possible that two votes from the same voter are counted. Double votes from the same voter must therefore be eliminated—together with other invalid ballots—before starting the tallying process. This process, which is called *cleansing*, is a mandatory initial step of the post-election phase.

From the perspective of the election process model of Sect. 2.1, an additional input containing the list of disqualified voters is required to perform the cleansing of the submitted ballots before initiating the tally. This leads to the extended election process model of Fig. 7. The actual electorate that is relevant for the tally is obtained from eliminating the disqualified voters from the electorate. The model depicted in Fig. 7 also shows that the list of actual election participants is an additional output of the process. This list defines the disqualified voters in every other voting channel of the hybrid system. In the next subsection, we will see how to combine two or multiple such election processes into a hybrid election process.

The additional input and output documents in the extended election process model must be taken into account when performing the verification. Note that every single entry in each of these documents is highly critical, because they define somebody's right to submit a vote over some channel. Figure 8, which shows the extended verification process model, illustrates the inclusion of these

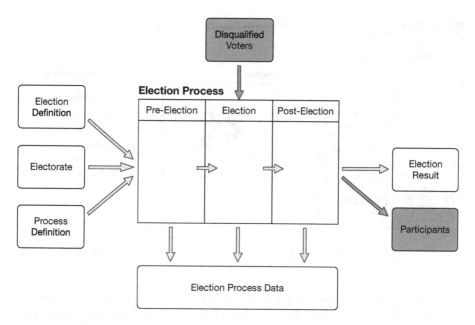

Fig. 7. Extended election process model for hybrid elections.

documents. The purpose of the verification report is still the same, but since two additional inputs are now taken into account, a successful report also validates their contents.

3.2   Composed Election Processes

Let's now have a closer look at actual compositions of multiple election processes. We will restrict ourselves to the simplest case of composing two alternative election processes. As we will see, the result of such a composition is again an election process, which can be further combined with other election processes. In this way, it is possible to construct recursive process models for more complicated combinations of three or more voting channels on the basis of the basic compositions described here.

For analyzing the composition of two election processes, we can distinguish two opposed cases. In the case of a *serial composition*, the temporal availability of the two channels is exclusive, i.e., the election period of the first election process strictly precedes the election period of the second process. Figure 9 depicts the hybrid process model obtained from a serial composition. It shows that the list of participants from the first channel defines the list of disqualified voters in the second channel. Note that the inverse data flow from the second channel back into the first channel is not required to guarantee the detection of double votes. Serial compositions are therefore relatively easy to handle properly.

More complicated situations arise in the case of a *parallel composition*, in which the election periods of the two processes overlap. In this case, the data

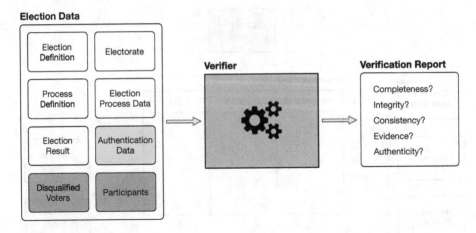

Fig. 8. Extended verification process model for hybrid elections.

exchange between the two channels is mutual. The resulting process model is depicted in Fig. 10. It shows how the list of participants from each of the two channels is given as an additional input into the other channel. The problem here is that the same voter may appear in both lists, which must be taken into account in each of the two cleansing processes. To handle such cases properly, there must be a clear policy of prioritizing one of the two submitted votes.

We see three different general strategies for defining such a policy. We will shortly discuss them in the remaining of this section. For this, we consider the use case from Switzerland, where an electronic voting channel is combined with a

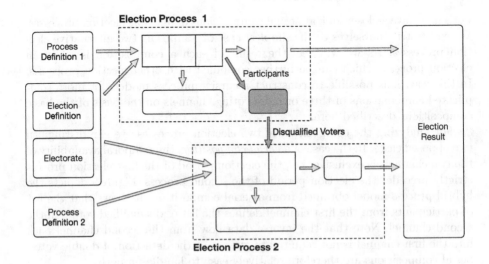

Fig. 9. Serial composition of two election processes.

physical voting channel (postal mail). We assume that an electronic vote counts as "submitted" when the voter terminates the voting process, for example by clicking a button from the voting application's user interface. In case of submitting a paper ballot using postal mail, we assume that the vote counts as "submitted" when the ballot is registered at the polling station. Note that in Switzerland, submitting more than one vote is prohibited by law, regardless of the available voting channels. However, since voters are instructed to submit a paper vote in case of a problem encountered when submitting an electronic vote, enforcing this law will be difficult in practice. In other countries, for example in Norway, submitting multiple votes is explicitly allowed. In such a case, the last submitted vote overrides all previously submitted votes.

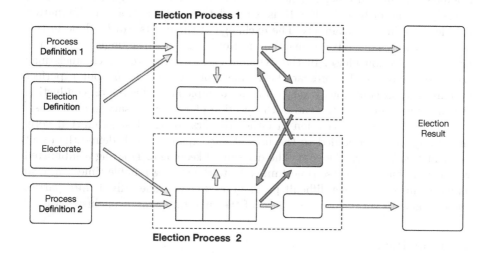

Fig. 10. Parallel composition of two election processes.

Prioritizing the Physical Channel. The rule here is as follows: if the same voter uses both channels to submit a vote, only the vote submitted over the physical channel will be counted. With this policy, paper votes can be counted regardless of the list of participants from the electronic channel. Therefore, the problem of eliminating double votes is only relevant for the electronic channel. Note that this situation is similar to a serial composition, in which the physical channel precedes the electronic channel. This policy is therefore relatively simple to implement. It is also compatible with a current practice in Switzerland, where administrative staff at the electoral office separates paper votes from the signed polling cards right upon receiving the paper ballot.

Prioritizing the Electronic Channel. Here, the rule from above is applied in the opposite way, i.e., only the electronic vote of a voter using both channels is counted. The counting of the electronic votes can therefore be conducted regardless of the list of participants from the physical channel. This also simplifies the verification process, which can be conducted independently of the physical channel, but it makes the counting of the paper ballots at the polling station more complicated. For example, separating the paper votes from the signed polling cards must be postponed until the complete list of participants from the electronic channel is available.

Prioritizing the First or Last Submitted Vote. In this case, if someone submits two votes over both channels, only the first or the last submitted vote will be counted. This is the most complicated policy to implement, because the channels are mutually dependent on each other, i.e., exchanging both lists of participants according the Fig. 10 is a mandatory precondition for eliminating double votes in both channels. The exchange of these lists can be done in two ways, either dynamically during the election phase or in a single step at the end of the election phase. In the dynamic case, the two voting channels may try to sort out double votes at the moment of receiving them, but a perfect synchronization is obviously very difficult to implement. Therefore, conducting the cleansing process at the end of the election phase is necessary in either case.

To enable the prioritization of either the first or the last submitted vote, timestamps must be added to the lists of participants, which define the exact moment of submitting the vote. The decision of keeping or ignoring a submitted vote is then based on these timestamps. Note the issuing reliable timestamps in an electronic context is a difficult problem on its own, especially if third parties must be able to verify the correctness of the timestamps in a conclusive way.

4 Conclusion

This paper is an attempt to define the universal verification process for electronic elections. The motivation for this paper comes from the observation that there is almost no practical experience with conducting actual verifications. On the other hand, since universal verifiability is commonly recognized as one of the most important counter-measures against all sorts of failures or attacks, almost everyone agrees that it must be implemented into future e-voting systems that are used for real political elections. Our analysis of the verification process in this paper shows that conducting an actual verification is more complex than it may appear at first sight. By discussing some of the most apparent questions and problems, we hope to provide some general technical guidelines for people in charge of implementing or organizing a verification process.

In most parts of the paper, for making our analysis and findings as widely applicable as possible, we have adopted a very general perspective. However, relative to a concrete voting system and application use case, many specific questions only arise if all the details about the cryptographic voting protocol, the technical system specification, and the political and legal contexts are available. Therefore, we can not answer these questions here, but we recommend not to underestimate the problems that may arise. More generally, we recommend to pay attention to the difficulties of the verification process well in advance. Election organizers should look at it as a separate important project, which also requires a careful planning, proper management, and adequate budget.

Acknowledgments. We thank the anonymous reviewers for their comments and suggestions. We are also grateful to Timo Bürk, Xavier Monnat, Jörg Schorr, Olivier Esseiva, and Anina Weber for helpful discussions, proofreading, and feedback. This research has been supported by the Post CH Ltd.

References

1. Verordnung der Bundeskanzlei über die elektronische Stimmabgabe (VEleS). Die Schweizerische Bundeskanzlei (BK) (2013)
2. Adida, B.: Helios: web-based open-audit voting. In: Van Oorschot, P. (ed.) SS 2008, 17th USENIX Security Symposium, San Jose, USA, pp. 335–348 (2008)
3. Chaum, D., et al.: Scantegrity: end-to-end voter-verifiable optical-scan voting. IEEE Secur. Priv. **6**(3), 40–46 (2008)
4. Dubuis, E., et al.: Verifizierbare Internet-Wahlen an Schweizer Hochschulen mit UniVote. In: Horbach, M. (ed.) INFORMATIK 2013, 43. Jahrestagung der Gesellschaft für Informatik, LNI P-220, Koblenz, Germany, pp. 767–788 (2013)
5. Galindo, D., Guasch, S., Puiggalí, J.: 2015 Neuchâtel's cast-as-intended verification mechanism. In: Haenni, R., Koenig, R.E., Wikström, D. (eds.) VoteID 2015. LNCS, vol. 9269, pp. 3–18. Springer, Cham (2015). https://doi.org/10.1007/978-3-319-22270-7_1
6. Stenerud, I.S.G., Bull, C.: When reality comes knocking - Norwegian experiences with verifiable electronic voting. In: Kripp, M.J., Volkamer, M., Grimm, R. (eds.) EVOTE 2012, 5th International Workshop on Electronic Voting. LNI, Bregenz, Austria, no. P-205, pp. 21–33 (2012)
7. Haenni, R., Koenig, R.E.: Universelle Verifizierung von Wahlen und Abstimmungen über das Internet. SocietyByte, June 2017
8. Haenni, R., Koenig, R.E., Locher, P., Dubuis, E.: CHVote system specification. IACR Cryptology ePrint Archive, 2017/325 (2017)
9. Häni, K., Denzer, Y.: Visualizing Geneva's next generation e-voting system. Bachelor thesis, Bern University of Applied Sciences, Biel, Switzerland (2018)
10. Scalzi, G., Springer, J.: VoteVerifier: independent vote verifier for UniVote elections. Bachelor thesis, Bern University of Applied Sciences, Biel, Switzerland (2013)
11. Volkamer, M., Spycher, O., Dubuis, E.: Measures to establish trust in internet voting. In: ICEGOV 2011, 5th International Conference on Theory and Practice of Electronic Governance, Tallinn, Estonia (2011)

Model Checking the SELENE E-Voting Protocol in Multi-agent Logics

Wojciech Jamroga, Michal Knapik$^{(\boxtimes)}$, and Damian Kurpiewski

Institute of Computer Science, Polish Academy of Sciences, Warsaw, Poland
{w.jamroga,michal.knapik,damian.kurpiewski}@ipipan.waw.pl

Abstract. SELENE is a recently proposed voting protocol that provides reasonable protection against coercion. In this paper, we make the first step towards a formalization of selected features of the protocol by means of formulae and models of *multi-agent logics*. We start with a very abstract view of the protocol as a public composition of a secret bijection from tracking numbers to voters and a secret mapping from voters to their choices. Then, we refine the view using multi-agent models of strategic interaction. The models define the space of strategies for the voters, the election authority, and the potential coercer. We express selected properties of the protocol using the strategic logic $\mathbf{ATL}_{ir}$, and conduct preliminary verification by model checking. While $\mathbf{ATL}_{ir}$ allows for intuitive specification of requirements like coercion-resistance, model checking of $\mathbf{ATL}_{ir}$ is notoriously hard. We show that some of the complexity can be avoided by using a recent approach of *approximate model checking*, based on fixpoint approximations.

1 Introduction

Designing protocols for secure and verifiable voting is a difficult task. In this work, we present an attempt to use the techniques from multi-agent systems (MAS) in modeling and verification of e-voting. Agents in such systems are equipped with a larger degree of freedom than typical entities in a security protocol. They can have clearly defined objectives, capabilities, and knowledge about the world; they can also form coalitions working towards a joint goal. The benefits of MAS become especially noticeable in analysis of scenarios that involve interaction between human and technical agents, such as electronic voting.

Here, we come up with a simple MAS model of the recently proposed SELENE protocol [19], and characterize several variants of coercion resistance with formulae of Alternating-time Temporal Logic (**ATL** [1]). Coercion resistance is essential in modern elections, and relies on the ability of voters to vote as they intend, and avoid the consequences of not obeying the coercer. Such requirements can be conveniently represented by **ATL** formulae following the scheme:

$$\neg \langle\!\langle \mathit{Coercer} \rangle\!\rangle \, \mathrm{F} \, \big(\text{election ends} \wedge (\text{voters have not obeyed}) \to (\mathit{Coercer} \text{ knows}) \big),$$

interpreted as *"The Coercer has no strategy to make sure that, when the election is over, he will detect disobedience of the coerced voters."* We use the semantics

© Springer Nature Switzerland AG 2018
R. Krimmer et al. (Eds.): E-Vote-ID 2018, LNCS 11143, pp. 100–116, 2018.
https://doi.org/10.1007/978-3-030-00419-4_7

of **ATL**, based on memoryless imperfect information strategies, where agents' strategies assign choices of action to the agents' states of knowledge, rather than global states of the system. This variant of the logic is often referred to as $\mathbf{ATL_{ir}}$ [20]. It is well known that model checking of $\mathbf{ATL_{ir}}$ is $\boldsymbol{\Delta_2^P}$-complete [9,20] and does not have a natural fixpoint characterization [5]. To overcome the prohibitive complexity, we utilize a recently proposed idea of approximate verification based on fixpoint approximations of $\mathbf{ATL_{ir}}$ formulae [10].

The article is organized as follows. We describe SELENE, and discuss some of its formal aspects in Sect. 2. Then, we propose a multi-agent model of the protocol in Sect. 3. In Sect. 4, we present a brief introduction to $\mathbf{ATL_{ir}}$, and propose some $\mathbf{ATL_{ir}}$ formalizations of coercion-resistance. Section 5 reports our attempt at model checking the formulae from Sect. 4 in the models from Sect. 3. We conclude in Sect. 6, and discuss plans for future work.

1.1 Related Work

Over the years, the properties of *receipt-freeness* and *coercion resistance* were recognized as important for an election to work properly. They were studied and formalized in [3,7,8,13,18], see also [17,21] for an overview.

A number of papers used variants of epistemic logic to characterize coercion resistance [11,12]. Moreover, the agent logic **CTLK** together with the modeling methodology of interpreted systems was used to specify and verify properties of cryptographic protocols, including authentication protocols [4,16], and key-establishment protocols [4]. In particular, [4] used variants of the MCMAS model checker to obtain and verify models, automatically synthesized from high-level protocol description languages such as CAPSL, thus creating a bridge between multi-agent and process-based methods.

Our approach is closest to [21] where **ATL**-style formulae were used to encode different flavors of coercion resistance. However, the encodings in [21] were rather informal and imprecise, since neither formal semantics nor concrete model was given to interpret the formulae. In contrast, we use a precise semantics and provide a scalable class of models. Moreover, we use the formulae, the models, and the semantics to conduct verification of the protocol by model checking. Finally, [2] proposed a very simple attempt at model checking of Rivest's ThreeBallot protocol using $\mathbf{ATL_{ir}}$, but the focus was on devising a model equivalence, and ThreeBallot served only to illustrate the idea.

2   Modeling SELENE

We begin with a description of SELENE, followed by a very abstract view of the conceptual backbone of the protocol. After that, we will move on to a more concrete model in Sect. 3.

2.1   Outline of SELENE

SELENE [19] has been proposed recently as a protocol for electronic voting targeted at low-coercion environments. The implemented cryptographic mechanisms should allow the voter to convince the coercer that the voter voted according to the coercer's request. One of the main advantages of the protocol is that, from the voter's perspective, the cryptography is put under the bonnet.

Roughly speaking, SELENE works as follows. The Election Authority executes the initial setup of the system, which includes generation of the election keys and preparation of the cryptographic vote trackers, one for each voter. The trackers are then encrypted and mixed, and published on the Web Bulletin Board (WBB). The aim is to break any link between the voter and her encrypted tracker. Hence, the pool of trackers is public, while the assignment of the trackers is secret.

In the voting phase, each voter fills in, encrypts, and signs her vote. The signed and encrypted ballot is then collected by the system. After several intermediate steps, a pair $(Vote_v, tr_v)$ is published in WBB for each $v \in Voters$, where $Vote_v$ and tr_v are, respectively, the decrypted ballot and the tracker of v. At this stage, no voters know their tracker numbers. All the cast votes are presented in plaintext in WBB.

The final stage consists of the notification of tracker numbers. If the voter is not coerced, then she requests the special α_v term, which allows for obtaining the correct tracker tr_v. If some pressure was exerted on the voter to fill her ballot in a certain way, she sends a description of the requested vote to the election server. A fake α'_v term is sent, which can be presented to the coercer. The α'_v token, together with the public commitment of the voter, reveals a tracker pointing out to a vote compatible with the coercer's demand, assuming that there is one.

2.2   An Abstract View of the Protocol

We now propose a convenient way of describing the scheme behind SELENE at the abstract level. Social choice can be seen as a function that, given a set of voters, produces a collective decision for the society. This can be decomposed into a mapping between voters and their individual choices, and a mapping from the choices to the collective decision. End-to-end voter-verifiable protocols strive to make the former individually verifiable (so that each voter can verify her part of the function), and the latter universally verifiable (so that the whole function can be verified by everybody). On the other hand, coercion resistant protocols strive to make the first part secret to anybody except for the voter in question. SELENE's idea of how to combine the two objectives is to further decompose the connection between voters and their cast ballots by means of the trackers.

Formally, let *Voters*, *Trackers*, and *Choice* be three finite sets such that $|Voters| = |Trackers|$. The first part of the protocol corresponds to a random choice of a secret *tracker bijection* $\mathcal{F}_T \colon Voters \to Trackers$ that assigns a unique tracker to each voter. We denote the set of all such bijections by $\mathcal{T}$. Moreover, the final part of SELENE can be presented as a *public bulletin function* $\mathcal{F}_P \colon Trackers \to Choice$ that assigns to each $tr \in Trackers$ the vote $\mathcal{F}_P(tr)$ cast by the owner of the tracker. The secret *choice function* $\mathcal{F}_I = \mathcal{F}_P \circ \mathcal{F}_T \colon Voters \to Choice$ connects voters with their ballots. The Election Authority is the only entity in the process that can observe the choice function. Note that this view can be applied to any voting system based on publicly visible trackers.

2.3 Combinatorial Aspects

Let $\mathcal{F}_P, \mathcal{F}_I$, and $\mathcal{F}_T$ be the public bulletin function, the choice function, and the tracker bijection. We will now estimate the range of uncertainty of the coercer, with the intuition that the less he knows about the real tracker assignment $\mathcal{F}_T$, the more room is available for coercion resistance. For each $tr, tr' \in Trackers$, let $tr \approx_{\mathcal{F}_P} tr'$ iff $\mathcal{F}_P(tr) = \mathcal{F}_P(tr')$, i.e., two trackers are "vote-equivalent" if they point to identical votes. Moreover, let $Trackers/\approx_{\mathcal{F}_P}$ denote the set of equivalence classes of $\approx_{\mathcal{F}_P}$. The uncertainty of the coercer can be measured by the number of permutations in the set of trackers, that he cannot distinguish from the actual tracker assignment.

Formally, let $\Pi(Trackers)$ denote the set of all permutations of trackers, i.e., bijections $\pi \colon Trackers \to Trackers$. Now, $\mathcal{T}_{\mathcal{F}_P} = \{\pi \in \Pi(Trackers) \mid \mathcal{F}_P = \mathcal{F}_P \circ \pi\}$ is the set of all permutations of trackers that are consistent with the public outcome of the election. To see this, observe that for each $\pi \in \mathcal{T}_{\mathcal{F}_P}$ we have $\mathcal{F}_I = \mathcal{F}_P \circ \mathcal{F}_T = \mathcal{F}_P \circ \pi \circ \mathcal{F}_T$. The size of $\mathcal{T}_{\mathcal{F}_P}$ reflects the space of defensive capabilities against coercion, should a part of the secret tracker bijection become public, under the assumption that voting is one-shot rather than repeated.

Definition 1 (Anti-coercion space). *The* anti-coercion space *of an election, given the public bulletin function $\mathcal{F}_P$, is defined as $acspace(\mathcal{F}_P) = \{\mathcal{F}_P \circ \pi \mid \pi \in \Pi(Trackers)\}$. Intuitively, $acspace(\mathcal{F}_P)$ corresponds to all the possible choice functions $\mathcal{F}_I$ consistent with $\mathcal{F}_P$.*

Theorem 1. *If the result of the election consists of n votes for candidates $c_1, \ldots, c_k$, s.t. each candidate c_i got m_i votes, then $|acspace(\mathcal{F}_P)| = \frac{n!}{(m_1!) \cdot \ldots \cdot (m_k!)}$.*

Proof. Notice that $|\mathcal{T}_{\mathcal{F}_P}| = \prod_{\rho \in Trackers/\approx_{\mathcal{F}_P}} (|\rho|!)$. By the orbit-stabilizer theorem [14] we have $|acspace(\mathcal{F}_P)| = \frac{|T|}{|\mathcal{T}_{\mathcal{F}_P}|}$, which concludes the proof.

Note that the space is typically vast, unless for very small elections or when almost all the voters voted for the same candidate. This is good news, as it makes it potentially hard for the coercer to obtain useful information about the real choices of the voters. On the other hand, a faithful representation of the coercer's state of knowledge leads to state-space explosion, which makes verification more complex. We will see it clearly in the next section.

3   Multi-agent Model of SELENE

In this section we present in detail a multi-agent model of SELENE. We start with defining the formal structures used for modeling the entities participating in the protocol and their interactions, and move on to presenting the model of SELENE, together with selected details of its implementation.

3.1   Models of Multi-agent Interaction

Multi-agent systems are often modeled by a variant of transition systems where transitions are labeled with combinations of actions, one per agent. Moreover, epistemic relations are used to indicate states that look the same to a given agent. Formally, an *imperfect information concurrent game structure* or *iCGS* [1] is given by $M = \langle Agt, St, PV, V, Act, d, o, \{\sim_a | a \in Agt\} \rangle$ which includes a nonempty finite set of all agents $Agt = \{1, \ldots, k\}$, a nonempty set of states St, a set of atomic propositions PV and their valuation $V : PV \to 2^{St}$, and a nonempty finite set of (atomic) actions Act. The protocol function $d : Agt \times St \to 2^{Act}$ defines nonempty sets of actions available to agents at each state; we will write $d_a(q)$ instead of $d(a, q)$, and define $d_A(q) = \prod_{a \in A} d_a(q)$ for each $A \subseteq Agt, q \in St$. Furthermore, o is a (deterministic) transition function that assigns the outcome state $q' = o(q, \alpha_1, \ldots, \alpha_k)$ to each state q and tuple of actions $\langle \alpha_1, \ldots, \alpha_k \rangle$ such that $\alpha_i \in d(i, q)$ for $i = 1, \ldots, k$.

Every $\sim_a \subseteq St \times St$ is an epistemic equivalence relation with the intended meaning that, whenever $q \sim_a q'$, the states q and q' are indistinguishable to agent a. The *iCGS* is assumed to be *uniform*, i.e., $q \sim_a q'$ implies $d_a(q) = d_a(q')$.

It should be mentioned that *iCGS* generalize transition networks as well as normal form games, repeated games, and extensive form games. Moreover, it is possible to define the notions of *strategic play* and *strategic ability* in *iCGS*.

3.2   A Multi-agent Model of Selene

In what follows, we describe our multi-agent model of SELENE. The system consists of the set *Voters* of voter agents, the single *Coercer*, the Election Defense System *ElectionDS*, and the *Environment* agent. We denote the set of all these agents by *Agents*. The local states of each agent are defined by its local variables. A global state of the system is a valuation of local variables of all the agents. Each agent can observe its local variables and selected local variables of the *Environment*. For simplicity, we assume a single coercer. This precludes the case when, e.g., two coercers request two different votes from the same voter and then compare the results. We plan to study this type of interactions in the future.

The model is parameterized by the following natural numbers: n voters; k possible choices (i.e., the ways that a ballot can be filled); *maxCoerced* voters that can be influenced by the coercer; *votingWaitTime* and *helpRequestTime* that reflect the maximal number of steps the system waits for votes and notifications about being coerced, respectively. We denote such model by $\mathcal{M}(n, k, maxCoerced, votingWaitTime, helpRequestTime)$.

In what follows, we omit auxiliary variables and actions that are not relevant to understanding the interplay between agents.

Agent *Environment*. The purpose of the *Environment* agent is twofold. Firstly, it serves as a container for variables shared by selected agents. The agents can have read-only or write-only access to the variables (denoted by *Can observe* and *Can set*, respectively, in agent interfaces in Figs. 1, 2, and 3). Secondly, it traces

Variables

- *vote*: 0...k
- *demandedVote*: 0...k

Actions

- $Vote_i$, for $i \in \{1, \ldots, k\}$
- $INeedVote_i$, for $i \in \{1, \ldots, k\}$
- *FetchGoodTracker*
- *CopyRealTracker*
- *Wait*
- *Finish*

Can observe

- WBB: *public election function*
- *elections' stage (init/voting/defense)*
- *his real tracker (when permitted)*
- *his exposed tracker*

Can set

- *his exposed tracker (via CopyRealTracker)*

Fig. 1. A voter agent

the passage of time and changes the stage of elections. Namely, the elections start in the **initial stage,** when the secret bijection is non-deterministically prepared. Then, the **voting phase** is open and the clock is started. This phase ends when either all the voters send their choices or time exceeds *votingWaitTime*. Then, the system enters the **defense stage** and the clock restarts. The defense stage ends either when the clock exceeds *helpRequestTime* or all the voters execute the *Finish* action. Note that every agent can observe WBB, i.e., public election function, the stage, and the clock value. The clock limits are also public knowledge.

Voter Agents. Each *Voter* shares the same structure, presented in Fig. 1. It is able to record via the *vote* variable the vote cast for choice $i \in \{1, \ldots, k\}$ by executing the action $Vote_i$. This action can be used only once, in the voting phase. It also records the coercer's request to vote for *demandedVote*. In both the cases 0 denotes that the variable is not set, i.e. the agent did not vote yet and has not been contacted by the coercer, respectively. In addition to the public variables of *Environment,* each *Voter* can observe his real tracker, obtained in the defense phase by executing action *FetchGoodTracker*. The agent can also observe his exposed tracker, i.e., the number assigned by *ElectionDS,* as presented to the *Coercer* agent. This becomes possible after requesting in the defense phase a tracker that points to a specific choice $i \in \{1, \ldots, k\}$, by firing action $INeedVote_i$. After obtaining his real tracker a *Voter* can decide to make it visible to the coercer

---

Variables

- $falseTrackerSentToVoter_i$: Boolean, for $i \in \{1, \ldots, n\}$

Actions

- $SetFalseTrackerOfVoter_i To_j$, for $1 \leq i \leq n$, $1 \leq j \leq k$
- $Wait$

Can observe

- WBB: *public election function*
- *the secret bijection*
- *elections' stage (init/voting/defense)*

Can set

- *the exposed tracker of every Voter*

Fig. 2. The *ElectionDS* agent

by executing action *CopyRealTracker*. Finally, the agent can always *Wait*, unless the clock reaches the limit set for a phase. In the latter case, if it is the voting phase, then the *Voter* needs to decide on the vote immediately, and if it is the defense phase, then it automatically ends his participation by firing action *Finish*. It should be noted that these actions are autonomous, e.g., a *Voter* can signal *ElectionDS* that he is coerced to vote in a selected way, even if coercion does not take place.

Agent *ElectionDS*. The structure of *ElectionDS* agent is presented in Fig. 2. The agent can, in addition to the public variables of *Environment*, observe the secret bijection function. This gives *ElectionDS* the full knowledge of the secret election function. The boolean variables $falseTrackerSentToVoter_i$ record that a voter $i \in \{1, \ldots, n\}$ requested and has been provided with a false tracker. This request is fulfilled by executing an action $SetFalseTrackerOfVoter_i To_j$ that sets the exposed tracker of voter $1 \leq i \leq n$ to choice $1 \leq j \leq k$. Note that while *ElectionDS* can set the value of the exposed tracker of any *Voter*, it cannot read the current value of the variable. Therefore, each *Voter* can first request a false tracker pointing to any choice and expose his real tracker afterwards, unknowingly to *ElectionDS*. Finally, *ElectionDS* can always *Wait*.

Agent *Coercer*. The structure of *Coercer* is presented in Fig. 3. Starting from the initial phase until the votes are published, the agent can demand from any voter $1 \leq j \leq n$ to vote for $1 \leq i \leq k$, by executing $ReqVote_i FromVoter_j$ action. Such a request can be made at most once per voter and the total number of requests cannot exceed $maxCoerced$. These choices are recorded using variables $voteDemandedFromVoter_i$, where $1 \leq i \leq n$. As previously, the value of 0 signifies that no request has been made. The agent can observe all public variables of *Environment* and all the exposed trackers of all voters. At any step, the *Coercer* agent can *Wait*.

Variables

- $voteDemandedFromVoter_i: 0, \ldots, k$, for $i \in \{1, \ldots, n\}$

Actions

- $ReqVote_iFromVoter_j$, for $1 \leq i \leq k$, $1 \leq j \leq n$
- *Wait*

Can observe

- WBB: *public election function*
- *elections' stage (init/voting/defense)*
- *the exposed tracker of every Voter*

Fig. 3. The *Coercer* agent

Atomic Propositions. In order to construct formulae that can be interpreted in the model, we need some atomic propositions. We set $PV = \{\text{finished}\} \cup \{\text{vote}_{v,i} \mid 1 \leq v \leq n, 1 \leq i \leq k\}$. Proposition finished denotes that the execution of the protocol has come to an end, and it holds iff all the voters have executed *Finish* or the clock has exceeded *helpRequestTime*. Formula $\text{vote}_{v,i}$ says that voter v has voted for candidate i; it holds iff v's variable *vote* contains i.

3.3 Implementation of the Model

We have used two different model checkers to verify properties of the model presented in Sect. 3.2. For exact model checking, we used MCMAS [15], which is the only publicly available tool for **ATL**$_{ir}$. MCMAS is based on the Interpreted Systems Programming Language (ISPL), which allows for higher-level descriptions of agents and their interaction. In Fig. 4, we present the ISPL code implementing the *Coercer* agent. The local variables of the agent are denoted by *Vars*, *Lobsvars* denotes the set of the environment variables that the agent can observe, and *Actions* are action labels. The *protocol* section specifies which actions are available at what states; the *evolution* section defines the consequences of their execution. We refer to [15] for more details about MCMAS and ISPL. Unfortunately, exact model checking of abilities under imperfect information works only for very small models. To overcome this, we used the approximate model checking technique from [10]. We have developed a prototype tool implementing the technique, in which the explicit state variant of the model from Sect. 3.2 is hard-coded. The explicit state representation is completely isomorphic with the ISPL code. Both the ISPL code generator and the prototype tool are available online at https://github.com/SeleneMC16/SeleneModelChecker.

```
Agent  Coercer

Lobsvars = {exposedTrackerOfVoter1 , exposedTrackerOfVoter2 };

Vars :
     coercedVoters :  0..2;
     voteDemandedFromVoter1 :  0..2;
     voteDemandedFromVoter2 :  0..2;
end  Vars

Actions = {ReqVote1FromVoter1 , ReqVote2FromVoter1 ,
             ReqVote1FromVoter2 , ReqVote2FromVoter2 , Wait };

Protocol :
     coercedVoters < maxCoerced and voteDemandedFromVoter1 = 0
     and Environment . votesPublished = false :
     {ReqVote1FromVoter1 , ReqVote2FromVoter1 , Wait };

     coercedVoters < maxCoerced and voteDemandedFromVoter2 = 0
     and Environment . votesPublished = false :
     {ReqVote1FromVoter2 , ReqVote2FromVoter2 , Wait };

     Other : {Wait };
end  Protocol

Evolution :
     coercedVoters = coercedVoters + 1 if
     ( Action = ReqVote1FromVoter1
     or  Action = ReqVote2FromVoter1
     or  Action = ReqVote1FromVoter2
     or  Action = ReqVote2FromVoter2 );

     voteDemandedFromVoter1 = 1 if Action = ReqVote1FromVoter1 ;
     voteDemandedFromVoter1 = 2 if Action = ReqVote2FromVoter1 ;
     voteDemandedFromVoter2 = 1 if Action = ReqVote1FromVoter2 ;
     voteDemandedFromVoter2 = 2 if Action = ReqVote2FromVoter2 ;
end  Evolution

end  Agent
```

Fig. 4. ISPL code of the *Coercer* agent

4   Specification of Properties

In this section, we provide a list of example coercion-related specifications, formulated in the strategic logic **ATL**$_{ir}$. We reduce vulnerability to coercion to the ability of the coercer to learn about the value of the voter's vote. We also assume that the voter prefers to evade coercion, rather than cooperate with the coercer. Intuitively, this reflects the typical voters' attitude towards intimidation, rather than vote buying and bribery. We begin by a brief introduction to the logic.

4.1   Alternating-Time Temporal Logic

Alternating-time temporal logic with imperfect information and imperfect recall (**ATL**$_{ir}$ [1,20]) generalizes the branching-time temporal logic **CTL** by replacing the path quantifiers E, A with *strategic modalities* $\langle\!\langle A \rangle\!\rangle$. Informally, $\langle\!\langle A \rangle\!\rangle \gamma$ expresses that the coalition A has a collective strategy to enforce the temporal property γ. The formulae make use of temporal operators: "X" ("next"),

"G" ("always from now on"), "F" ("now or sometime in the future"), and U ("until").

Syntax. The language of $\mathbf{ATL}_{ir}$ formulae is defined by the following grammar:

$$\varphi ::= p \mid \neg\varphi \mid \varphi \wedge \varphi \mid \langle\langle A \rangle\rangle X\varphi \mid \langle\langle A \rangle\rangle G\varphi \mid \langle\langle A \rangle\rangle F\varphi \mid \langle\langle A \rangle\rangle \varphi\, U\, \varphi,$$

where p stands for atomic propositions, and $A \subseteq \text{Agt}$ for any coalition of agents.

Strategies. A *strategy* of agent $a \in \text{Agt}$ is a conditional plan that specifies what a is going to do in every possible situation. Formally, it can be represented by a function $s_a : St \rightarrow Act$ satisfying $s_a(q) \in d_a(q)$ for each $q \in St$. Moreover, we require that $s_a(q) = s_a(q')$ whenever $q \sim_a q'$, i.e., strategies specify same choices in indistinguishable states. A *collective strategy* s_A for coalition $A \subseteq \text{Agt}$ is a tuple of individual strategies, one per agent from A. By $s_A[a]$ we denote the strategy of agent $a \in A$ selected from s_A.

Outcome Paths. A *path* $\lambda = q_0 q_1 q_2 \ldots$ is an infinite sequence of states such that there is a transition between each q_i, q_{i+1}. We use $\lambda[i]$ to denote the ith position on path λ (starting from $i = 0$). Function $out(q, s_A)$ returns the set of all paths that can result from the execution of strategy s_A from state q. Formally:

$$out(q, s_A) = \{\lambda = q_0, q_1, q_2 \ldots \mid q_0 = q \text{ and for each } i = 0, 1, \ldots \text{ there exists}$$
$$\langle \alpha_{a_1}^i, \ldots, \alpha_{a_k}^i \rangle \text{ such that } \alpha_a^i \in d_a(q_i) \text{ for every } a \in \text{Agt}, \text{ and } \alpha_a^i = s_A[a](q_i)$$
$$\text{for every } a \in A, \text{ and } q_{i+1} = o(q_i, \alpha_{a_1}^i, \ldots, \alpha_{a_k}^i)\}.$$

Function $out^{ir}(q, s_A) = \bigcup_{a \in A} \bigcup_{q \sim_a q'} out(q', s_A)$ collects all the outcome paths that start from states indistinguishable from q to at least one agent in A.

Semantics. Let M be an *iCGS* and q its state. The semantics of **ATL** can be defined by the clauses below. We omit all the clauses for temporal operators except for "sometime", as they are not relevant for this paper.

- $M, q \models p$ iff $q \in V(p)$, and $M, q \models \neg\varphi$ iff $M, q \not\models \varphi$,
- $M, q \models \varphi \wedge \psi$ iff $M, q \models \varphi$ and $M, q \models \psi$, and $i \in \mathbb{N}$ we have $M, \lambda[i] \models \varphi$,
- $M, q \models \langle\langle A \rangle\rangle F\varphi$ iff there exists a collective strategy s_A such that for all $\lambda \in out^{ir}(q, s_A)$ there exists $i \in \mathbb{N}$ such that $M, \lambda[i] \models \varphi$.

In order to reason about the knowledge of agents, we add *modalities* K_a:

- $M, q \models K_a\varphi$ iff $M, q' \models \varphi$ for all q such that $q \sim_a q'$.

That is, $K_a\varphi$ says that φ holds in all the states that agent a considers possible at the current state of the world q.

4.2   Formulae for Coercion

Let us consider a coercer attempting to force a group of voters $A \subseteq \text{Agt}$ to vote for his preferred candidate. We can assume w.l.o.g. that the number of the candidate is 1. The formulae in Fig. 5 express different "flavors" of the coercer's coercive ability, with the following reading:

- Φ_1 expresses that the coercer can enforce a state where the elections are over and, if no one in A followed his orders, then the coercer knows that at least one of them disobeyed (but does not necessarily know who);
- Φ_2 says that if some of the voters did not vote as ordered, then the coercer will identify at least one of them.

Conceptually, the formulae capture the extent to which the coercer can identify the disobedience of the coerced voters, and hence knows when to execute his threats. Note that, when $A = \{v\}$, then both formulae are equivalent.

$$\Phi_1 \equiv \langle\!\langle Coercer \rangle\!\rangle\, \mathrm{F}\left(\text{finished} \wedge \left(\bigwedge_{v \in A} \neg\mathsf{vote}_{v,1} \to \mathsf{K}_{Coercer}\left(\bigvee_{v \in A} \neg\mathsf{vote}_{v,1} \right)\right)\right.$$

$$\Phi_2 \equiv \langle\!\langle Coercer \rangle\!\rangle\, \mathrm{F}\left(\text{finished} \wedge \left(\bigvee_{v \in A} \neg\mathsf{vote}_{v,1} \to \bigvee_{v \in A} \mathsf{K}_{Coercer}(\neg\mathsf{vote}_{v,1}) \right)\right.$$

Fig. 5. Formulae for model checking

5 Verification

SELENE is supposed to provide protection against coercion, so the formulae in Sect. 4 should in principle be all false. However, every protection mechanism has its limits. As noted in [19], even a single coercer can defeat the election defense system if the number of ballots is small or the coerced voter is particularly unlucky and the vote demanded by the coercer is not present in WBB. Also, the coercer's power intuitively increases with the number of voters he can simultaneously coerce. Finally, the exact limits of the coercer's ability to coerce become unclear when we consider more complex models, due to their combinatorial complexity. This is exactly when model checking can help to detect threats or verify correctness. In this section, we provide a preliminary attempt at model checking of the properties specified in Sect. 4.2 with respect to the models proposed in Sect. 3.2.

5.1 Exact and Approximate Model Checking of ATL$_{\mathrm{ir}}$

Synthesis and verification of strategies under partial observability is hard. More precisely, model checking of **ATL** variants with imperfect information has been proved Δ_2^P- to **PSPACE**-complete for agents that play memoryless strategies [9,20]. In our case, the following result applies.

Proposition 1 ([9,20]). *Model checking* **ATL**$_{\mathrm{ir}}$ *is* Δ_2^P-*complete with respect to the number of the transitions in the model and length of the formula.*

The only publicly available tool for verification of imperfect information strategies is MCMAS [15], which essentially searches through the space of all the possible strategies. Nevertheless, no better algorithm is currently known, despite some recent attempts [6]. We employ MCMAS for *exact* model checking of our coercion specifications for SELENE. An interesting alternative has been proposed recently in the form of *approximate model checking* based on fixpoint approximations of formulae [10]. The idea is to model check, instead of formula $\varphi \equiv \langle\!\langle A \rangle\!\rangle F\mathsf{p}$, its upper and lower approximations $tr_U(\varphi)$ and $tr_L(\varphi)$:

- $tr_U(\varphi)$ verifies the existence of a *perfect information strategy* that achieves $F\mathsf{p}$. Clearly, when there is no perfect information strategy to achieve it, then $\langle\!\langle A \rangle\!\rangle F\mathsf{p}$ must also be false;
- $tr_L(\varphi)$ is a more sophisticated property, expressed in Alternating Epistemic μ-Calculus with Steadfast Next Step, with the property that the truth of $tr_L(\varphi)$ always implies φ. We refer the interested readers to [10] for details.

We have implemented the approximate algorithm from [10], together with a model generator for SELENE, and ran a number of experiments with both exact and approximate model checking. The setup of the experiments, as well as the results, are presented in the rest of the section.

configuration	#states	tgen	Lower approx.		Upper approx.		Approx.	Exact	
			tverif	result	tverif	result	result	(tg+tv)	result
$(2,1,1,1,1)$	427	<1	<1	False	<1	True	?	<1	True
$(2,1,1,4,4)$	16777	1	<1	False	<1	True	?	249	True
$(2,1,2,4,4)$	22365	1	<1	True	<1	True	True	timeout	
$(2,2,1,4,4)$	331441	19	1	False	16	True	?	timeout	
$(2,2,2,4,4)$	596577	36	2	True	31	True	True	timeout	
$(3,2,1,1,1)$	281968	40	<1	False	4	True	?	timeout	
$(4,1,1,1,1)$	146001	2	<1	False	2	True	?	timeout	
$(4,2,1,1,1)$				memout				timeout	

Fig. 6. Experimental results for formula Φ_1

5.2   Experiments and Results

We collect the results of the evaluation for each of the specified formulae in tables presented in Figs. 6 and 7. We show performance results for the approximation algorithms, both for the lower and the upper bound, and compare them to the exact verification done with MCMAS. Each row in a table corresponds to a single run of an experiment over the selected model. The columns contain the following information:

- the parameters of the model (*configuration*), consisting of the numbers of voters and available candidates, the maximal numbers of voters that the coercer can try to coerce and the clock steps that the system waits for incoming votes and for notifications from the voters about coercion attempts. E.g., configuration $(2, 2, 2, 4, 4)$ describes the model with 2 voters, 2 candidates, the coercer coercing up to 2 voters, and the maximal time units for the system to wait for votes and coercion notifications being both set to 4;

configuration	#states	tgen	Lower approx.		Upper approx.		Approx.	Exact	
			tverif	result	tverif	result	result	(tg+tv)	result
$(2, 1, 1, 1, 1)$	427	<1	<1	False	<1	True	?	<1	True
$(2, 1, 1, 4, 4)$	16777	1	<1	False	1	True	?	257	True
$(2, 1, 2, 4, 4)$	22365	1	<1	True	<1	True	True	timeout	
$(2, 2, 1, 4, 4)$	331441	19	1	False	4	False	False	timeout	
$(2, 2, 2, 4, 4)$	596577	36	1	False	7	False	False	timeout	
$(3, 2, 1, 1, 1)$	281968	40	<1	False	1	False	False	timeout	
$(4, 1, 1, 1, 1)$	146001	2	<1	False	3	True	?	timeout	
$(4, 2, 1, 1, 1)$	memout							timeout	

Fig. 7. Experimental results for formula Φ_2

- The size of the state space (*#states*) and the time that the algorithm spent on generating the data structures for the model (*tgen*);
- The running time and output of the verification algorithm (*tver, result*) for model checking the lower approximation $tr_L(\phi)$, and similarly for the upper approximation $tr_U(\phi)$;
- The result of the approximation (*Approx. result*), with "?" in case of inconclusive output;
- The total running time (*tg+tv*) and the result (*result*) of the exact ATL_{ir} model checking with MCMAS.

The running times are given in seconds. *Timeout* indicates that the process did not terminate in 2 h. *Memout* indicates that the process is terminated by the system due to allocating too much memory.

The exact ATL_{ir} model checking is performed with MCMAS 1.3.0. To perform the approximate verification, we used the explicit representations of models from Sect. 3.2, and an implementation of the fixpoint algorithms from [10] in a stand-alone tool written in C++. The models used in both approaches were isomorphic. The tests were conducted on a Intel Core i7-6700 CPU with dynamic clock speed of 2.60–3.50 GHz, 32 GB RAM, running 64bit Ubuntu 16.04 Linux.

5.3   Discussion of the Results

As confirmed by the experiments, the question posed by formula Φ_2 is the most restrictive. Namely, in Φ_2 we ask whether the coercer has a general strategy to find out exactly which voter voted against his demands, assuming that there was a disobedient one. The answer to this question is true only in special cases of a single candidate. On the other hand, the results of verification of Φ_1 reveal that the system is sometimes not able to fully defend a coerced group and the coercer can detect that at least one of the members did not follow the demands. To illustrate this on a simple example, in a model of two voters and two ballots the coercer has a trivial strategy: request a vote for candidate 1 from both the voters. Moreover, in this case the coercer has even more knowledge, as he knows which one of the voters deceived (they both did).

$$\Phi_2^{dist_{A'}} \equiv \langle\!\langle Coercer \rangle\!\rangle \, F \left(finished \wedge \left(\left(\bigvee_{v \in A} \neg vote_{v,1} \wedge \bigwedge_{v' \in Agents \setminus A} dist_{A'}(v') \right) \rightarrow \bigvee_{v \in A} K_{Coercer}(\neg vote_{v,1}) \right) \right.$$

Fig. 8. A formula for quantitative analysis

Exact model checking with MCMAS seems infeasible in most of the cases, except for the small models up to hundreds of states. The approximations offer a dramatic speedup, enabling verification of models up to hundreds of thousands of states. Although the approximate method is faster, the results can be inconclusive; namely, we observe cases where the truth value of $tr_L(\varphi)$ differs from the value of $tr_U(\varphi)$. It should be noted that in the approximate approach the graphs are represented explicitly in memory, unlike in the case of BDD-based symbolic methods. Still, memory is cheaper and easier to buy than time.

5.4   Counting Coercion-Friendly Configurations

The validity of a property is a strong result: if a formula is true in the model, then the coercer has a strategy to achieve his goal under all possible circumstances. The system is therefore completely insecure against the considered type of attack. If, however, the formula turns out false, it does not mean that the system is always able to defend itself. In such case we only know that there is no uniform strategy that allows the coercer to break the system's defenses, given no information about the initial state of affairs (e.g., a partially uncovered choice function). We thus attempt to quantitatively estimate the extent to which our model is safe from the attacks expressed by Φ_2. To this end we inspect in detail all the possible distributions $D_{A'}$ of votes of voters outside of the coerced group A and check under which of these the coercer can precisely point to a disobedient voter. Formally, $dist_{A'} \in D_{A'}$ iff $dist_{A'}$ is a function from $Agents \setminus A$ to PV such that for each $v \in Agents \setminus A$ there exists $1 \leq i \leq k$ such that $dist_{A'}(v) = vote_{v,i}$.

To perform quantitative analysis we utilise the formula $\Phi_2^{dist_{A'}}$ presented in Fig. 8. Note that the formula depends on $dist_{A'} \in D_{A'}$ and $A \subseteq Agents$. Intuitively, it expresses the ability of the coercer to enforce that if some of the agents in A did not vote for candidate 1 and the remaining voters voted according to $dist_{A'}$, then the coercer can identify a voter in A that did not vote for 1.

The process of quantitative analysis is performed as follows. For a given model configuration, we fix an arbitrary coalition A. Then, for each distribution $dist_{A'} \in D_{A'}$ the formula $\Phi_2^{dist_{A'}}$ is verified. Our approach is based on state-labelling, hence we can inspect all the states reached just after publishing votes.

configuration	#states	tgen	result	#vote	#rvote	pvote $= \frac{\#rvote}{\#vote} \times 100\%$
$(2,2,1,4,4)$	331441	14	False	200	50	25%
$(2,2,2,1,1)$	9651	<1	False	144	36	25%
$(2,2,2,4,4)$	596577	24	False	360	90	25%
$(2,3,1,2,2)$	289423	10	False	378	168	44%
$(2,3,2,1,1)$	64829	1	False	576	256	44%
$(2,3,2,2,2)$	661501	22	False	864	384	44%
$(2,3,2,2,2)$	281968	15	False	672	84	12%
$(2,3,2,2,2)$	765232	41	False	1824	228	12%
$(4,1,1,1,1)$	146001	2	False	240	0	0%

Fig. 9. Experimental results for formula $\Phi_2^{dist_{A'}}$ with percentage coverage

In Fig. 9 by #vote we denote the aggregate number of such states that are consistent with any $dist_{A'} \in D_{A'}$ and #rvote collects the count of how many of these states satisfy $\Phi_2^{dist_{A'}}$. As we can observe, there are cases where the coercer can gain advantage in nearly half of considered distributions.

It should be emphasized that approximate algorithms are used for model checking $\Phi_2^{dist_{A'}}$. Thus, the *pvote* shows only the percentage of *confirmed cases* where a successful coercion strategy exists. The actual counts may be larger, since the approximations provide only guaranteed lower bound estimation.

6   Conclusions

In this paper, we present our first step towards model checking of e-voting protocols with respect to strategic abilities of their participants. We propose a simple multi-agent model of SELENE, together with several formulae of **ATL**$_{ir}$ expressing coercion, and conduct preliminary experiments with model checking.

Our construction of the model is based on a natural pattern of dividing the outcome of an election into the public bulletin and the secret choice function, together with a secret bijection. We argue that the MAS approach provides a flexible framework for modelling security properties of voting protocols. In particular, it offers a natural separation of social and technical components and their interactions. Moreover, **ATL**$_{ir}$ offers a sensible trade-off between expressivity and veracity as the property specification language.

Model checking is done in two variants: exact, using MCMAS [15], and approximate, using the recently proposed methodology of fixpoint approximations [10]. As the experiments show, despite the prohibitive complexity of model checking with **ATL**$_{ir}$, the approximate method enables the analysis of many instances of our models, even in the presence of combinatorial explosion.

In the future, we plan to apply some recent developments in model reduction methods for strategic logics and allow for verification of more complex models. These include techniques such as abstraction, bisimulation-based reduction, and partial-order reduction. Moreover, we would like to extend the model of SELENE with additional actors, such as coercers with conflicting goals.

Acknowledgements. The authors acknowledge the support of the National Centre for Research and Development (NCBR), Poland, under the PolLux project VoteVerif (POLLUX-IV/1/2016).

References

1. Alur, R., Henzinger, T.A., Kupferman, O.: Alternating-time temporal logic. J. ACM **49**, 672–713 (2002)
2. Belardinelli, F., Condurache, R., Dima, C., Jamroga, W., Jones, A.V.: Bisimulations for verification of strategic abilities with application to ThreeBallot voting protocol. In: Proceedings of AAMAS, pp. 1286–1295. IFAAMAS (2017)
3. Benaloh, J., Tuinstra, D.: Receipt-free secret-ballot elections. In: Proceedings of the 26th Annual ACM Symposium on Theory of Computing, pp. 544–553. ACM (1994)
4. Boureanu, I., Kouvaros, P., Lomuscio, A.: Verifying security properties in unbounded multiagent systems. In: Proceedings of AAMAS, pp. 1209–1217 (2016)
5. Bulling, N., Jamroga, W.: Alternating epistemic mu-calculus. In: Proceedings of IJCAI 2011, pp. 109–114 (2011)
6. Busard, S., Pecheur, C., Qu, H., Raimondi, F.: Reasoning about memoryless strategies under partial observability and unconditional fairness constraints. Inf. Comput. **242**, 128–156 (2015)
7. Delaune, S., Kremer, S., Ryan, M.: Coercion-resistance and receipt-freeness in electronic voting. In: 19th IEEE Computer Security Foundations Workshop, p. 12-pp. IEEE (2006)
8. Dreier, J., Lafourcade, P., Lakhnech, Y.: A formal taxonomy of privacy in voting protocols. In: 2012 IEEE International Conference on Communications (ICC), pp. 6710–6715. IEEE (2012)
9. Jamroga, W., Dix, J.: Model checking ATL_{ir} is indeed Δ_2^P-complete. In: Proceedings of EUMAS 2006. CEUR Workshop Proceedings, vol. 223. CEUR-WS.org (2006)
10. Jamroga, W., Knapik, M., Kurpiewski, D.: Fixpoint approximation of strategic abilities under imperfect information. In: Proceedings of AAMAS, pp. 1241–1249 (2017)
11. Jonker, H.L., Pieters, W.: Receipt-freeness as a special case of anonymity in epistemic logic. In: Proceedings of the 19th Computer Security Foundations Workshop, pp. 28–42 (2006)
12. Kusters, R., Truderung, T.: An epistemic approach to coercion-resistance for electronic voting protocols. In: Security and Privacy, pp. 251–266 (2009)
13. Küsters, R., Truderung, T., Vogt, A.: A game-based definition of coercion-resistance and its applications. In: 2010 23rd IEEE Computer Security Foundations Symposium, pp. 122–136. IEEE (2010)
14. Lang, S.: Algebra. Addison-Wesley, Boston (1993)
15. Lomuscio, A., Qu, H., Raimondi, F.: MCMAS: an open-source model checker for the verification of multi-agent systems. Int. J. Softw. Tools Technol. Transf. **19**(1), 9–30 (2017)
16. Lomuscio, A., Penczek, W.: LDYIS: a framework for model checking security protocols. Fundamenta Informaticae **85**(1–4), 359–375 (2008)
17. Meng, B.: A critical review of receipt-freeness and coercion-resistance. Inf. Technol. J. **8**(7), 934–964 (2009)

18. Okamoto, T.: Receipt-free electronic voting schemes for large scale elections. In: Christianson, B., Crispo, B., Lomas, M., Roe, M. (eds.) Security Protocols 1997. LNCS, vol. 1361, pp. 25–35. Springer, Heidelberg (1998). https://doi.org/10.1007/BFb0028157
19. Ryan, P.Y.A., Rønne, P.B., Iovino, V.: Selene: voting with transparent verifiability and coercion-mitigation. In: Clark, J., Meiklejohn, S., Ryan, P.Y.A., Wallach, D., Brenner, M., Rohloff, K. (eds.) FC 2016. LNCS, vol. 9604, pp. 176–192. Springer, Heidelberg (2016). https://doi.org/10.1007/978-3-662-53357-4_12
20. Schobbens, P.Y.: Alternating-time logic with imperfect recall. Electron. Notes Theor. Comput. Sci. 85(2), 82–93 (2004)
21. Tabatabaei, M., Jamroga, W., Ryan, P.Y.A.: Expressing receipt-freeness and coercion-resistance in logics of strategic ability: preliminary attempt. In: Proceedings of the PrAISe@ECAI Workshop, pp. 1:1–1:8. ACM (2016)

How Much Does an e-Vote Cost? Cost Comparison per Vote in Multichannel Elections in Estonia

Robert Krimmer[1] , David Duenas-Cid[1(✉)] ,
Iuliia Krivonosova[1] , Priit Vinkel[2] , and Arne Koitmae[2]

[1] Tallinn University of Technology, Akadeemia tee 3, 12618 Tallinn, Estonia
{robert.krimmer,david.duenas,iuliia.krivonosova}@ttu.ee
[2] State Electoral Office of Estonia, Tallinn, Estonia
{priit.vinkel,arne.koitmae}@valimised.ee

Abstract. We are presenting the results of the CoDE project in this paper, where we investigate the costs per vote of different voting channels in Estonian Local Elections (2017). The elections analyzed involve different processes for casting a vote: Early Voting at County Centers, Advance Voting at County Centers, Advance Voting at Ordinary Voting District Committees, Electronic Voting, Election Day Voting, and Home Voting. Our analysis shows how the administrative costs per e-vote (an electronic vote) are half the price of the second cheapest option (Election Day Voting), representing the most cost-efficient way of organizing elections, given the conditions of this Case Study. Otherwise, different forms of convenience voting have much higher costs, giving us subjects for further discussion on how to organize multichannel elections.

Keywords: Multi-channel elections · Calculation of costs · TDABC
BPR

1 On e-Government, e-Voting and Calculation of Costs

Since McLuhan coined the notion of a global village [42] for the current Information Society [56] we adopted, naturalized and routinized the use of technology for several constituents of our daily life. The leap to an online world of Public Administration [36] had often been regarded as a potential cornerstone for managerial reform and creating future systems of governance [45]. In relation to this, e-government, following Yildiz [61] can facilitate better structures for interconnectivity, service delivery [5], efficiency and effectiveness [24, 50], decentralization, transparency and accountability. Citizens, already used to relating with others (friends, family and businesses) use online tools and consider the use of e-government measures as a normal step in the development of technology-based relationships [8].

Estonia is one of the pioneering and leading countries in adopting e-government tools [1, 27, 32, 51], thanks to the three layers forming the backbone of their government services: the X-road system, the electronic ID and the service provision eesti.

© Springer Nature Switzerland AG 2018
R. Krimmer et al. (Eds.): E-Vote-ID 2018, LNCS 11143, pp. 117–131, 2018.
https://doi.org/10.1007/978-3-030-00419-4_8

ee [41]. Amongst the causes for this success Kalvet [27] lists: (1) utilizing an e-commerce role model for the use of ICT in the public sector [55]; (2) the presence of enthusiastic and visionary civil servants who developed information systems in the public sector [63] and politicians focused on developing a program of e-government [17]; (3) a favorable legislative environment towards ICT; (4) stable funding for ICT expenditures; (5) the adoption of the Estonian ID-Card by public administration; and (6) cooperation between the public and private sectors, especially the banking sector *as a generator of expectations regarding e-government services and as a general catalyst for e-government* (p. 146). As a result, Estonia represents an ideal venue for observing different dimensions of e-related expressions such as e-government, e-voting, e-banking or e-commerce [30].

1.1 Convenience Voting and Electoral Complexity

The adoption of e-voting strategies can be inserted into the context of the battle against the consolidated tendency for a declining turnout [4, 39], which is challenging global understanding and the functioning of the democratic process. Some of the causes described for understanding this decline have been summarized as (1) the transition to a less competitive electoral scenario, (2) a generational decline in the will to participate in the political process and (3) a transformation of values that lead to political engagement [6]. The disengagement of citizens at elections threatens the correct functioning of democracy by unbalancing the distribution of power and representation between those who participate and those who do not [37], having spillover effects on the global legitimacy of the system of governance and its decision-making [9, 48]. Many governments and Electoral Management Bodies react by actively seeking out, testing and/or implementing improvements to traditional voting systems, presuming that a more convenient voting system will have positive impacts on the turnout at elections [57].

As a result, new systems for early or convenience voting had been proposed in a number of countries [31, 34], and administrative rules and procedures have been adapted to allow citizens to cast their vote at different moments in the election cycle [20], trying to increase the comfort of voters and ease voters' comfort [2, 7]. Administration of elections represents a necessary factor influencing voter turnout: an adequate voting system might not increase the number of voters, but an inadequate one will definitely decrease it. Although election administration differs from context to context, it is still commonplace that new voting channels cannot replace but can only complement existing methods of participation in elections due to the responsibility to provide a service to the entire electorate [19, 62]. However, the opportunity to rethink and optimize electoral administrative procedures when introducing these additional voting channels is often missed.

The Estonian e-vote remote online voting system, in use since 2005, turns Estonia into the only country in Europe (if not in fact the world) to use this without restriction in all types of elections [54]. The Estonian I-voting project was established in order to sustain and increase voter turnout by creating an additional and convenient voting channel that would be in coherence with efficient use of the infrastructure already in existence [28]. Estonian e-voting systems can be considered a successful and widely used voting mode (over 30% in the last three elections) but with an unequal impact in different subpopulations [52].

The adoption of multi-channel electoral systems poses a set of new challenges to be considered by public administrations, including additional workloads for electoral administrations, increased vulnerability from double voting, increased length of voting periods or difficulties derived from overlapping voting periods [59]. Previous research studies to evaluate multichannel elections [34, 60] indicated the three main areas of concern: (1) multiple-channel elections increase the complexity for election administrations; (2) the increase in complexity requires business process reengineering of electoral processes; and (3) it involves analyzing the cost of introducing new voting channels. This situation addresses a different dimension in the debate on elections, how to achieve the desired social goals with a reduced economic impact.

1.2   Cost Accounting

The analysis of the costs arising from running elections has attracted researchers' and practitioners' interest, but a large share of the research already conducted on this issue had been focused on the costs for candidates and campaigns [22, 26, 47], the costs for voters [14, 16, 23, 46] or the costs of public information systems [12, 40]. Other projects that addressed the topic revealed (1) the increase in the cost of elections all over the world [44], (2) the need to define different kinds of electoral costs and the analytical scope of the methodology [38], (3) the need to include costs incurred by adding new voting channels, either high one-off costs (e-votes) or transaction costs (postal voting) [35] and (4) the need to overcome the reduced level of transparency and limited opportunities for scrutinizing certain voting modalities [13]. A clear and successfully proven methodology for facing this challenge is still lacking [58], permitting the calculation of costs of multichannel elections overcoming the previous difficulties, amongst others, (1) the lack of depth in approaches for calculating costs based on the assessment of administrative costs through electoral budgets and their division by the number of voters participating [18], the difficulties of uncovering hidden costs and dealing with different accounting systems and governance structures [10, 38] or difficulties relating to the choice of methodology of directly questioning the source (levels of response, overall quality of responses) [25]. Three main problems can summarize the access to the costs of elections: (1) the difficulties in accessing election costs [11], as many democratic governments are not obliged to divulge this information; (2) the difficulties in recovering hidden costs from budgets; and (3) the difficulties of allocating the costs of public infrastructures to the organization of the election.

2   Methodology

For developing the research methodology, we referred to a broader research field of governmental cost accounting and business-oriented methodologies adapted for calculating administrative management costs. Our goal not only relates to detecting potential inefficiencies in the electoral process or to raising awareness of the costs [43], but also, in particular to deliver comparative results of the costs of different voting channels, in order to enrich the existing literature on e-voting and electoral analysis. To achieve this, our proposed methodology relies on the use of (1) Business Process Reengineering (BPR) [3, 21] for facilitating workflow analysis of complex systems (elections); and (2) Activity-Based Costing (ABC) [15, 33] for calculating costs per service/unit produced by the electoral system (votes), in particular, the use of Time-Driven ABC (TDABC) [29], which reduces the volume of data required for conducting the ABC analysis of (1) the practical capacity of resources committed and the costs involved and (2) unit times for performing transactional activities.

Based on this, a model was developed with the following steps:

1. Conducting electoral process modeling based on the analysis of electoral legislation and publicly available internal instructions, complemented with interviews with stakeholders and on-site observations.
2. Creating a list of activities based on findings from Step 1. Select only those activities which are organized differently depending on the voting channel.
3. Identifying resource pools and determining costs assigned to each resource pool.
4. Attributing costs to activities (attribute directly if possible; attribute by proportional time in other cases) in order to receive total cost per activity.
5. Calculating the practical capacity of resources (we set it at 80% of the theoretical full capacity in line with the standard established in accounting research).
6. Dividing total cost per activity by the practical capacity, to receive cost per minute per activity.
7. Dividing time spent on every activity by output to receive cost per output (in our case, per vote or ballot paper) per activity[1]. Multiply this number by the unit cost of a resource pool in order to receive the cost per vote or ballot paper per activity. Total the cost per vote cast for all activities considered, in order to receive the cost per vote used per voting channel.
8. Comparing costs per vote cast for different voting channels.

3 Case-Study

3.1 Case Selection

As was mentioned above, Estonia has a leading position in the development of e-government and I-voting tools, having aroused the interest of many scholars trying to understand the adoption of these tools by citizens [1], its impact on electoral turnout [53] or internal processes in the I-voting system [40], leading many to consider Estonia as a critical case in any relevant research on e-democracy.

Administration of Estonian elections is rather complex, permitting the multichannel analysis proposed. Voters are simultaneously offered multiple voting channels (Fig. 1). However, not all the voting channels are active during every election (voters residing

---

[1] In traditional TD ABC the time per item of output is estimated. However, as is the case with elections, we know precisely how much time is spent on every activity, we receive time per item of output in the manner described above.

outside Estonia cannot participate in Local Elections) and some of the voting channels, when occurring, overlap both in their periods, like advance voting at county centers, advance voting in ordinary Voting District Committees and Internet voting.

Two more elements endorse developing a case study in Estonia. Firstly, the fact that Estonian elections by and large use the existing infrastructure, providing an excellent opportunity to test analytical methodologies directed towards delving into hidden costs. Secondly, the involvement of the Estonian Electoral Management Bodies (State Electoral Office) in developing the case study and also the interests of Estonian administration in implementing a similar cost calculation methodology to the one proposed in this research by 2020.

With this background, Estonia has been selected as the first case for us to test our methodology and model. For this analysis, we focus on the most recent elections in Estonia which happened to be the Local Elections taking place in October, 2017.

3.2 Case Description

Estonian local elections took place from October 5–15, 2017, and offered voters seven different voting channels. Overall, it provided a turnout of 586,519 voters (53.3% of the electorate), including 120,888 early and advance voters (20.6% of turnout) and 186,034 e-voters (31.7% of turnout). 279,597 voters cast their votes on Election Day (47.7% of turnout). The results do not represent a big change from previous local elections in terms of overall turnout, following the series of declining turnouts starting in 2009, but indicate a consolidation of the use of e-voting (31.7% of votes cast) and the popularity of voting in county centers (40% of all early and advance votes were cast in 28 county centers, compared to only 60% of advance votes cast in 549 ordinary polling stations).

In order to conduct the cost analysis, we divided voting channels occurring in relation to time of voting:

- *I-voting* (10th to 4th day before Election Day).
- *Early Voting* (10th to 7th day before Election Day).
- *Advance Voting* (6th to 4th day before Election Day).
- *Election Day Voting*.

In relation to the voting location, we consider:

- *Supermarket Voting* - Voting organized in county centers (Early, Advance and Election Day Voting).
- *VDC Voting* - Voting organized in ordinary Polling Stations – Voting District Committees (VDC) according to the Estonian legal system (Advance and Election Day Voting).
- *I-voting*.

This division is based on the following criteria: (1) The differentiation between voting organized online and voting at physical locations (Early, Advance and Election Day Voting) is due to the obvious organizational differences and, as a result, activities and costs involved; (2) voting organized in county centers and voting organized in ordinary VDCs are analyzed separately due to a significant difference in the number of locations (28 county centers compared to 549 ordinary VDCs), staff involved (3–6

Voting Channels for voting in Estonia	
1)	Early voting at county centers
2)	Advance voting at county centers
3)	Advance voting at ordinary VDCs
4)	Custodial voting
5)	Electronic voting
6)	Election day voting
7)	Home voting
Voting Channels for voting from abroad	
1)	By Post
2)	At the Diplomatic Missions
3)	Electronic voting

Fig. 1. Voting channels in Estonia.

members of staff per ordinary VDC and, at least 8 officers per county center), and voting channels offered in these locations (Early Voting is only organized in county centers). Home voting is considered as a subtype of Election Day Voting and, as a result, it is included in this category of our analysis. To analyze it separately, further observations would be required to accurately establish travel time and average number of voters per polling station.

Early voting in county centers is a relatively new voting innovation in Estonia, and it implies that for four days from the 10th to 7th day before Election Day, voters could vote at any of the county centers regardless of the voting district of their residence. In 2017 local elections, 28 county centers were open throughout the country. Half of them were situated in shopping malls, expecting a significant increase in turnout by making the voting process more convenient.

Another important feature of Estonian elections is that early, advance and e-voters are not permitted to override their votes on Election Day. The principle of the precedence of ballot paper voting allows e-voters to override their e-vote with a paper vote but only during the period of early and advance voting, not on Election Day.

3.3 Time Frame, Processes and Activities

As our focus is on cost variation between the different electoral channels present in the Estonian electoral system, we considered the processes occurring in one particular period of the election cycle: the election period [34] (Fig. 2). In Estonia the election period starts 90 days before Election Day with "Informing EU citizens of their right to vote" and finishes three days after the Election Day with the "Resolution of complaints on electoral management". The activities and processes occurring before and after the election period would not add differences to the costs analyzed amongst voting channels, as the activities occurring are the same for every channel.

Based on the analysis of electoral legislation and publicly available internal instructions, complemented by interviews with municipal secretaries responsible for organizing elections, members of EMBs, members of the National Electoral

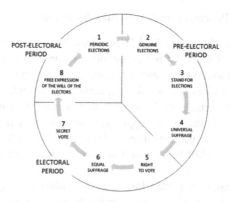

Fig. 2. The electoral cycle [34].

Committee, and the I-voting auditor, as well as multiple on-site observations across the country, we mapped the electoral processes occurring in the time frame under consideration. Overall, we identified 31 processes with 177 activities among which we selected only major processes which are organized differently, depending on a voting channel which constitutes the third step of our analysis. These processes are as follows:

1. Organization of the voting place.
2. Voter identification.
3. Processing votes.
4. Counting votes.

These four major processes consist of different sets of activities depending on voting channel and voting location. There are 22 activities for I-voting, 8 activities for early and advance voting, and 7 activities for election day voting, all of which will be described in more detail in the following section. This represents our list of activities for TD ABC analysis. During the third step of analysis, we identified the following resource pools: labor costs, printing costs, stationery costs, transportation costs, rental costs, costs of equipment and depreciation costs. We assigned costs to those pools based on electoral budgets available, information derived from procurement contracts, interviews, observations and estimates. In order to assign costs we also considered: the ratio of activities consumed by different voting channels to avoid double counting; the number of times an activity is repeated during the electoral period; the time spent in conducting a certain activity; the number of people participating in a certain activity; and the final number of votes cast through every voting channel. For calculating time, we derived data from log files, on-site observations, legislative regulation and interviews. For the fourth step, labor and transportation costs were attributed directly to activities; other costs were attributed based on the proportion of time every activity consumes. Finally, the steps from the fifth to eighth step were calculated according to the model.

3.4 Description of Processes and Activities Analyzed

Organization of the voting place for Election Day Voting consists of many activities from the delivery of ballots, ballot boxes and other equipment to putting the seal on all paper ballots allocated to a polling station. Moreover, the organization of voting places for Advance Voting requires additional equipment and particular skills from the staff. For Electronic Voting, setting up the voting place is no less complicated. For an e-voter, the voting place is the voting application through which a voter casts a vote. However, the supporting infrastructure without which e-votes could not be cast includes: an electronic ballot box (which is a vote storage server), vote forwarding server and the log server [49].

The process of voter identification differs significantly for the different voting channels. During the Election Day, voter identification occurs based only on the printed voters list. During Advance Voting, those polling places allowing voters from outside their place of residence (county centers) conduct voter identification with the help of the electronic voter registers which are updated daily. Therefore, such voting locations must have computers with access to an updated electronic voter register. For voter identification in I-voting, the voter identifies himself/herself with an ID card used via a card-reader in the voter application. Based on the information retrieved from an ID card, the voter application gives a voter an appropriate list of candidates. To cast a vote, a voter puts a digital signature onto the ballot. Alternatively, identification may be completed with the help of digi-ID or mobile-ID.

Processing votes is the least complicated activity for Election Day Voting, as all votes are stored in ballot boxes, and no additional steps are required before the count. Otherwise, processing votes cast during Advance Voting requires transportation of votes from outside the Voting District (VD) to the appropriate VD/County/National Electoral Commission. For this purpose, votes should first be sorted according to their VD. This process also requires delivering votes belonging to this VD. Processing e-votes takes place with the help of an electronic ballot box. All other activities associated with it such as removing the information on a voter from a vote take place during the counting process.

Counting votes depends on the format of votes cast: manual counting of paper votes and automated counting of e-votes. All paper votes in Estonia are counted manually, at least two times. No equipment such as scanners is used in the counting process. However, counting advance votes and election day votes also differ from one another. To count advance votes, first votes should be removed from their envelopes. Then, the second stamp should be stamped on every ballot paper. Finally, advance votes are mixed with election day votes and counted together.

Now, when the differences in how four major processes are organized for every voting channel are explained, we move to the description of different sets of activities constituting those processes for every voting channel.

Regarding **Internet-voting**, we consider such activities as: auditing the I-voting system; organizing seminars and training sessions for observers, the media and all those interested in I-voting (activities aimed at building trust); conducting the penetration test of the I-voting system; monitoring the network; activities concerning harmonization between I-voting and paper-based voting (printing and transportation of e-voters' lists, manual transfer of e-voters into printed voter lists); counting and recounting of votes (these processes are automated, but by law require certain numbers of officers to be present); storage and destruction of e-votes, voter ID cards, and hard drives. Hence, calculating I-voting costs also considers such **cost pools** as transportation and printing costs, alongside labor costs and depreciation costs which take into consideration the expected life span, initial costs of I-voting system acquisition and the cost of updates and replacement.

Regarding **voting organized in ordinary polling stations**, we consider the following activities: delivery of equipment before voting starts (voting booths, ballot boxes, stamps and others); setting up a voting place (installing voting booths, setting up signs giving directions, setting up tables for voting district committee officers); stamping ballot papers before voting (as in Estonia, every ballot must have a stamp from the voting district where it would be issued to a voter); voter identification during voting days; counting ballot papers; transportation of ballot papers for recounting; recounting. Therefore, among the **cost pools** we consider labor costs, transportation costs, printing costs, stationery costs, rental costs for equipment (mainly renting printers and laptops which polling stations need for advance voting and election day voting, but also rental of voting booths as according to our estimation based on interviews and observation, around 25% of VDCs must hire voting booths for elections as they do not possess their own ones).

Regarding **voting organized in county centers**, we consider all the same activities as for voting organized in ordinary polling stations, with one additional activity, which is processing of advance votes from outside the voting district: two members of staff for every county center are obliged to transport votes from outside their voting district to the National Electoral Commission, then, collect home votes, and transport them back to their county. That is how the exchange of votes from outside cast during the advance voting period is currently organized. Another thing to consider is that counting advance votes always requires more resources than counting election day votes, even when it occurs in the same voting settings, because it requires the additional activities which are removing ballots from envelopes and putting a stamp of an appropriate VDC onto a ballot paper for votes cast. In our model, we take this into consideration. Regarding **cost pools**, we consider labor costs, transportation costs, printing costs, stationery costs, and equipment rental costs. Early voting in county centers requires allocating additional voting booths, ballot boxes, envelopes, laptops and printers for those who decide to vote in a different voting place than their own. Such voting places should also have printed lists of candidates available on request for all voting districts. Such voting districts should also have at least part of their staff trained and able to operate laptops with electronic voter registers and printers.

4   Results and Costs

The use of TDABC analysis allowed us:

- to consider the different pools of administrative costs incurred during the management of local elections in Estonia, including (a) wages, (b) depreciation, (c) transportation, (d) rental, (e) printing and (f) stationery costs;
- to track the electoral expenses incurred by the different protagonists involved in managing elections, including (a) Local Municipalities, (b) State Electoral Office, (c) Estonian Information System Authority (RIA) and (d) others;
- and to allocate those costs to the voting channels, (a) Early Voting at County Centers, (b) Advance Voting at County Centers, (c) Advance Voting at Ordinary VDCs, (d) Electronic Voting, (e) Election Day Voting (including Home Voting) at County Centers and (f) Election Day Voting (including Home Voting) at Ordinary VDCs.

Through process modeling (BPR) we could understand the internal steps for every voting channel and estimate the unused capacity for every model (see Fig. 3). As a result, the TDABC analysis of existing voting channels allows us to allocate numbers to some aprioristic ideas regarding how the costs rise or decline. In particular, the combination of a reduction of use for certain voting channels due to a decline in its popularity but deployment of the same structures and resources (workforce, number of polling stations and working hours), leads to an increase in cost per vote. In particular, our data permits stating that certain forms of Advance Voting have large amounts of unused capacities resulting in low cost-efficiency (higher cost per vote cast) compared to other voting channels.

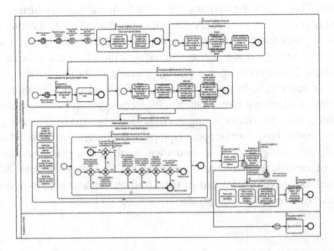

Fig. 3. Model of the activity "Ascertaining voting results in a Voting District Committee".

The analysis conducted shows (Fig. 4) that for the Local Elections in Estonia (2017), the most expensive voting channel was Advance Voting in Ordinary VDCs (3) for which the costs considered constituted 20.40 euros per ballot paper. Next comes Advance Voting in County Centers (2) with 6.24 euros per ballot paper and Early Voting in County Centers (1) with 5.07 euros per ballot paper. Regarding Election Day Voting (6), the costs considered constitute around 4.50 euros per vote cast with almost no difference between county centers and ordinary VDCs. I-voting (5) represents the cheapest option carried out in the 2017 Estonian elections, with 2.30 euros per e-vote cast.

Voting Channel	Cost per ballot (in Euro)
Early Voting in country centres	5,07
Advance Voting in country centres	6,24
Election Day Voting in country centres	4,61
Advance Voting in VDC	20,41
Election Day Voting in VDC	4,37
I-Voting	2,32

Fig. 4. Costs for the different voting channels for Estonian Local Elections (2017).

5   Discussion and Conclusions

This research has a double and complementary goal to take one step forward in the approach to costs involved for elections. First of all, we aim to use an innovative method in order to count the costs of voting systems to be used in multichannel elections, proving the suitability of its use. Secondly, we aim to put our method into practice in a real electoral context, promoting reflection of the costs of different voting channels and their efficiency.

Regarding the methodological dimension, the methodology we proposed could and should be used in different case studies, should be adapted to the context, or in further elections in the Estonian context, in order to allow more general conclusions to be reached. Accordingly, the results we obtained are valid for the case study we analyzed (Local Elections in Estonia, 2017).

The proposed methodology allowed us to assess with greater accuracy the administrative costs of running elections. The definition of direct and indirect costs incurred by the different protagonists that occur in the organization and development of elections gives a more realistic view of electoral costs, improving previous approaches based on assessing costs by adding up shares of total costs collected from electoral budgets. Secondly, the TDABC methodology allows a more accurate allocation of costs of voting channels, revealing the activities with the heaviest drain on resources that trigger the cost expenditure, facilitating further reflection in the drive for efficiency.

Finally, the use of observation as the main strategy for collecting data allows us to surpass some traditional limitations of calculating electoral costs. Amongst other things, previous researches pointed out the limited access to data on electoral costs and the lack of ability to track expenses as the main constraints for a better fit for analyses. Moreover, this observational approach allows replicating research in other contexts where the availability of information on electoral costs is poor but observation of the electoral process is allowed. In order to test the assumptions derived from our observations, the approach was complemented by a significant number of interviews with polling officers and staff, members of local electoral councils, National Electoral Commission, State Electoral Office of Estonia and other agencies involved in elections. The support of Electoral Management Bodies when providing information and experience-based opinions improves the validity and credibility of the results.

Regarding the cost analysis, we can raise some general statements regarding the Estonian Local Elections (2017): (1) E-voting is the cheapest voting channel proposed in the electoral context analyzed due to the tool's acceptation by citizens and reduced costs involved in deployment. The cost per e-vote cast is half the cost of the second cheapest option; (2) Election Day Voting represents the second cheapest option per vote due to the fact it is a frequently used voting channel and even with the increased amount of resources deployed; (3) Early and Advance Voting channels are more expensive due to the length of deployment and the lower number of participants that use these channels by comparison; (4) Advance Voting in Ordinary VCD is by far the most expensive channel, at around 18.00 euros per vote more expensive than the cheapest voting channel.

Costs per vote are correlated with resources invested and the popularity of the voting channel. In the search for convenience for voters, e-voting seems to be a good bet in terms of efficiency and success amongst voters, refocusing the debate on suitability to other dimensions (trust, security). The consolidation and success of e-voting in the Estonian electoral context, and its consequent cost efficiency clearly contrasts with other voting channels that consume more resources without achieving such high levels of success. Even so, we would like to stress that the results presented are valid for the elections analyzed, and that a change of voters' electoral behavior in further elections could impact on the distribution of costs by changing them substantially. To better understand electoral costs, this research should be repeated in the same electoral context allowing a comparison between elections.

Finally, the use of TDABC methods in this research, and in future research studies, may have practical implications in terms of rethinking the way elections are organized and formulated; consequently, less efficient voting channels try to maintain the conditions to allow voters to cast their votes in a convenient way but have less impact on reducing public expenditure. Multi-channel elections including e-voting, such as the one analyzed, represent a different and complex reality that can challenge the viability of some paper-based voting channels, especially those with higher unused capacities that reduce the efficiency of the tool.

Acknowledgment. We extend sincere thanks to Breck Shuyler who was assisting us with modelling of BMPNs and on-site observation during the electoral process. This article is based upon work supported by the Estonian Research Council grant (PUT 1361 "Internet Voting as Additional Channel for Legally Binding Elections: Challenges to Voting Processes Re-engineering", 2017–2020).

References

1. Alvarez, M.R., et al.: Internet voting in comparative perspective: the case of Estonia. PS Polit. Sci. Polit. **42**(3), 497–505 (2009)
2. De Araújo, J.: Improving public service delivery: the crossroads between NPM and traditional bureaucracy. Public Adm. **79**(4), 915–932 (2001)
3. Attaran, M.: Exploring the relationship between information technology and business process reengineering. Inf. Manag. **41**(5), 585–596 (2004)
4. Barrat Esteve, J., et al.: Votacions electròniques: una eina de gestió pública per a la millora de la qualitat democràtica i la participació política. Escola d'Administració Pública de Catalunya, Barcelona (2018)
5. Bekkers, V.J.J.M., Zouridis, S.: Electronic service delivery in public administration: some trends and issues. Int. Rev. Adm. Sci. **65**(2), 183–195 (1999)
6. Blais, A., Rubenson, D.: The source of turnout decline: new values or new contexts? Comp. Polit. Stud. **46**(1), 95–117 (2013)
7. Buckley, J.: E-service quality and the public sector. Manag. Serv. Qual. **13**(6), 453–462 (2003)
8. Carter, L., Bélanger, F.: The utilization of e-government services: citizen trust, innovation and acceptance factors. Inf. Syst. J. **15**(1), 5–25 (2005)
9. Cavanagh, T.: Changes in American voter turnout 1967–1976. Polit. Sci. Q. **96**(1), 53–65 (1981)
10. Chowdhury, A.: Cost of voting: estimating the impact of online voting on public finances. The Institute for Digital Democracy, London (2017)
11. Clark, A.A.: The cost of elections: money well spent? Polit. Insight **5**(3), 16–19 (2014)
12. Codagnone, C.: Measuring e-government: reflections from eGEP measurement framework experience. Eur. Rev. Polit. Technol. **4**, 89–106 (2007)
13. Coleman, S.: Elections in the 21st century: from paper ballot to e-voting. Report by the Independent Commission on Alternative Voting Methods. Electoral Reform Society, London (2002)
14. Colomer, J.M.: Benefits and costs of voting. Elect. Stud. **10**(4), 313–325 (1991)
15. Kaplan, R.S., Cooper, R.: Activity-based systems: measuring the costs of resource usage, pp. 1–13. Accounting Horizons, September 1992
16. Downs, A.: An economic theory of political action in a democracy. J. Polit. Econ. **65**(2), 135–150 (1957)
17. Ernsdorff, M., Berbec, A.: Estonia: the short road to e-government and e-democracy. In: Nixon, P., Koutrakou, V. (eds.) E-Government in Europe: Re-booting the State, pp. 228–241. Routledge, New York (2007)
18. Ernst & Ernst: Election administration Volume III: Costing Elections. Clearinghouse on Election Administration, Washington (1979)
19. Grabenwarter, C.: Report on the compatibility of remote voting and electronic voting with the standards of the Council of Europe. Council of Europe, Strasbourg (2004)
20. Gronke, P., et al.: Convenience voting. Annu. Rev. Polit. Sci. **11**(1), 437–455 (2008)

21. Grover, V., et al.: The implementation of business process reengineering. J. Manag. Inf. Syst. **12**(1), 109–144 (1995)
22. Harada, M., Smith, D.M.: You have to pay to play: candidate and party responses to the high cost of elections in Japan. Elect. Stud. **36**, 51–64 (2014)
23. Haspel, M., Gibbs Knotts, H.: Location, location, location: Precinct placement and the costs of voting. J. Polit. **67**(2), 560–573 (2005)
24. Heeks, R.: Understanding e-Governance for Development. i-Government Working Paper Series, vol. 20, no. 2, pp. 1–27 (2001)
25. James, T.S., Jervier, T.: The cost of elections: the effects of public sector austerity on electoral integrity and voter engagement. Public Money Manag. **37**(7), 461–468 (2017)
26. Johnston, R., Pattie, C.: How much does a vote cost? Incumbency and the impact of campaign spending at English general elections. J. Elections Public Opin. Parties **18**(2), 129–152 (2008)
27. Kalvet, T.: Innovation: a factor explaining e-government success in Estonia. Electron. Gov. Int. J. **9**(2), 142–157 (2012)
28. Kalvet, T.: Management of technology: the case of e-voting in Estonia. In: 2009 International Conference on Computer Technology and Development, ICCTD 2009, pp. 512–515 (2009)
29. Kaplan, R.S., Anderson, S.R.: Time-driven activity-based costing: a simpler and more powerful path to higher profits, vol. 82, p. 266. Harvard Business School Press Books, Boston (2007)
30. Kassen, M.: Open data and e-government – related or competing ecosystems: a paradox of open government and promise of civic engagement in Estonia. Inf. Technol. Dev. 1–27 (2017)
31. Kersting, N., Baldersheim, H.: Electronic Voting and Democracy. Palgrave - MacMillan, New York (2004)
32. Kitsing, M.: Success without strategy: e-government development in Estonia. Policy Internet **3**(1), 1–21 (2011)
33. Kont, K.-R.: What do acquisition activities really cost? A case study in Estonian university libraries. Libr. Manag. **36**(6/7), 511–534 (2015)
34. Krimmer, R., Triessnig, S., Volkamer, M.: The development of remote e-voting around the world: a review of roads and directions. In: Alkassar, A., Volkamer, M. (eds.) Vote-ID 2007. LNCS, vol. 4896, pp. 1–15. Springer, Heidelberg (2007). https://doi.org/10.1007/978-3-540-77493-8_1
35. Krimmer, R., Wendt, F.: Costs of Electronic Voting: An Overview. E-Voting.cc, Vienna (2010)
36. Layne, K., Lee, J.: Developing fully functional E-government: a four stage model. Gov. Inf. Q. **18**(2), 122–136 (2001)
37. Lijphart, A.: Unequal participation: democracy's unresolved dilemma. Am. Polit. Sci. Rev. **91**(1), 1–14 (1997)
38. López-Pintor, R., Fisher, J.: Getting to the Core. A Global Survey on the Cost of Registration and Elections. United Nations Development Programme, New York (2006)
39. López-Pintor, R., Gratschew, M.: Voter Turnout Since 1945: A Global Report. IDEA Institute for Democracy and Electoral Assistance, Stockholm (2002)
40. Maaten, E., Hall, T.: Improving the transparency of remote e-voting: the Estonian experience. In: Krimmer, R., Grimm, R. (eds.) 3rd International Conference on Electronic Voting 2008, pp. 31–45. Gesellschaft für Informatik, Bregenz (2008)
41. Margetts, H., Naumann, A.: Government as a Platform: What can Estonia Show the World? Oxford Internet Institute, Oxford (2017)
42. McLuhan, M.: Understanding Media: The Extensions of Man. MIT Press, Cambridge (1964)

43. Anderson, S., Young, S.: Implementing Management Innovations, Lessons Learned from Activity Based Costing in the US Automobile Industry. Springer, Heidelberg (2002)

44. Montjoy, R.S.: The changing nature ... and costs ... of election administration. Public Adm. Rev. **70**(6), 867–875 (2010)

45. Moon, M.J.: The evolution of e-government among municipalities: rhetoric or reality? Public Adm. Rev. **62**(4), 424–433 (2002)

46. Niemi, R.G.: Costs of voting and nonvoting. Public Choice **27**(1), 115–119 (1976)

47. Petithomme, M.: Second-order elections, but also 'low-cost' campaigns? National parties and campaign spending in European elections: a comparative analysis. Perspect. Eur. Polit. Soc. **13**(2), 149–168 (2012)

48. Salisbury, R.: Research on political participation. Am. J. Pol. Sci. **19**(2), 323–341 (1975)

49. Springall, D., et al.: Security analysis of the Estonian internet voting system. In: Proceedings of the 2014 ACM SIGSAC Conference on Computer and Communications Security - CCS 2014, pp. 703–715. ACM Press, New York (2014)

50. Szopiński, T., Staniewski, M.W.: Manifestations of e-government usage in post-communist European countries. Internet Res. **27**(2), 199–210 (2017)

51. Toots, M., Kalvet, T., Krimmer, R.: Success in eVoting – success in eDemocracy? The Estonian paradox. In: Tambouris, E., et al. (eds.) ePart 2016. LNCS, vol. 9821, pp. 55–66. Springer, Cham (2016). https://doi.org/10.1007/978-3-319-45074-2_5

52. Vassil, K., et al.: The diffusion of internet voting. Usage patterns of internet voting in Estonia between 2005 and 2015. Gov. Inf. Q. **33**(3), 453–459 (2016)

53. Vassil, K., Weber, T.: A bottleneck model of e-voting: why technology fails to boost turnout. New Media Soc. **13**(8), 1336–1354 (2011)

54. Vinkel, P., Krimmer, R.: The how and why to internet voting an attempt to explain E-Stonia. In: Krimmer, R., et al. (eds.) E-Vote-ID 2016. LNCS, vol. 10141, pp. 178–191. Springer, Cham (2017). https://doi.org/10.1007/978-3-319-52240-1_11

55. VVAA: Information and Communication Technologies for the Public Service: A Small States Focus. Commonwealth Secretariat, London (2008)

56. Webster, F.: Theories of the Information Society. Routledge, New York (2007)

57. Wilks-Heeg, S.: Treating voters as an afterthought? The legacies of a decade of electoral modernisation in the United Kingdom. Polit. Q. **80**(1), 101–110 (2009)

58. Xenakis, A., Macintosh, A.: A generic re-engineering methodology for the organized redesign of the electoral process to an e-electoral process. In: Krimmer, R. (ed.) 2nd International Workshop on Electronic Voting, EVOTE 2006, pp. 119–130. Gesellschaft für Informatik, Bregenz (2006)

59. Xenakis, A., Macintosh, A.: Levels of difficulty in introducing e-voting. In: Traunmüller, R. (ed.) EGOV 2004. LNCS, vol. 3183, pp. 116–121. Springer, Heidelberg (2004). https://doi.org/10.1007/978-3-540-30078-6_20

60. Xenakis, A., Macintosh, A.: Procedural security analysis of electronic voting. In: Proceedings of the 6th International Conference on Electronic Commerce, pp. 541–546. ACM, New York (2004)

61. Yildiz, M.: E-government research: reviewing the literature, limitations, and ways forward. Gov. Inf. Q. **24**(3), 646–665 (2007)

62. Council of Europe: 62. Code of Good Practices in Electoral Matters: Guidelines and Explanatory Report. CoE, Venice (2002)

63. World Bank: EU-8: Administrative Capacity in the New Member States: The Limits of Innovation? Poverty Reduction and Economic Management Unit, Washington (2006)

Implementing an Audio Side Channel for Paper Voting

Kristjan Krips[1], Jan Willemson[1,2(✉)], and Sebastian Värv[1]

[1] Cybernetica AS, Ülikooli 2, 51003 Tartu, Estonia
{krisjan.krips,jan.willemson,sebastian.varv}@cyber.ee
[2] Software Technology and Applications Competence Center,
Ülikooli 2, 51003 Tartu, Estonia

Abstract. In the ongoing debate between the proponents of electronic and paper voting, a frequently used argument is that electronic voting is susceptible to electronic attacks, and those are less detectable by a human than physical ones. This paper contributes to the research of electronic attacks against paper voting by building a proof-of-concept classifier for audio samples recorded while writing numbers. Such a classifier can be used to break the privacy, for example, in case of preferential voting ballot sheets, or voting systems where the voter must fill in the candidate number. We estimate the quality of the classifier and discuss its implications to the physical security measures of polling stations and ballot design.

1   Introduction

Voting is a form of public opinion polling used when a group of people needs to take a common decision. The size of the group may vary from just a few persons to whole societies, and the decisions may vary from selecting a beauty queen to determining who is going to rule the country for the next 5 years.

The bigger implications the decision has, the more critical role is played by the actual voting and vote counting processes. There are a number of requirements set to contemporary voting systems, and thick rule books describing how to enforce them.

Unfortunately, these rules can be contradictory. In order to gain public acceptance of an election result, all the processes should be fully auditable, ideally by everyone. On the other hand, to prevent coercion and vote-buying, the actual votes should remain secret, introducing an inherently non-auditable component into the system.

It is also the case that important elections tend to have a large voter set easily reaching millions of people. This has implications on the vote counting. A single person is unable to count millions of votes in a reasonable time frame, so this work has to be distributed between many people, not all of whom are equally careful or trustworthy. If a physical medium like paper is used for voting, there can also be ambiguous markings that need interpretation, and this interpretation

© Springer Nature Switzerland AG 2018
R. Krimmer et al. (Eds.): E-Vote-ID 2018, LNCS 11143, pp. 132–145, 2018.
https://doi.org/10.1007/978-3-030-00419-4_9

may depend on the interpreter. And last-but-not-least, organizing voting based on physical carriers is a huge logistical challenge, requiring all of these millions of people to go to polling stations and collecting the ballots later.

These problems have motivated research in alternative vote casting mechanisms, including electronic ones. Starting from T.A.Edison's "Electrographic Vote Recorder and Register"[1], various methods including voting machines and remote vote casting over Internet have been proposed and tried out.

While helping to ease some of the inherent difficulties of elections, electronic means can bring up new concerns. Humans can not control digital environments directly and need to rely on imperfect interfaces. Also, it is hard to be sure that a digital device acts according to its specification and does not include anything extra, like malware.

Another example of out-of-specification behaviour is the existence of side channels threatening vote privacy. Perhaps one of the most notorious examples of potential implications of such problems was observed in the Netherlands. As those events greatly inspired our current research, we will make a short recap here.

1.1   The Rise and Fall of Electronic Voting in the Netherlands

Netherlands has been a true pioneer of electronic voting. Legislation allowing machine voting was put in place already in 1965, and the first voting machines appeared in 1966 [8]. The first attempts to automate counting were done in late 1980s. From 1994, the government actively promoted the usage of electronic apparatus in voting [6]. By 2005, the Dutch market had been divided by two bigger suppliers of the voting machines – Nedap and Sdu [8]. There had been a few complaints e.g. favouring a candidate with number 31 due to his/her name being displayed on top of the second column of candidates [6], but in general the public trust in voting machines seems to have been rather high.

However, in 2006, a series of events took place that changed the situation drastically. First, during 2006 elections a fraud suspicion was raised in one of the districts where Nedap voting machines were used. After repeated shadow elections and several rounds in court, this led to a conviction [8].

As a reaction to this (and probably also earlier complaints), a civil activist and hacker Rop Gonggrijp initiated a movement called "Wij vertrouwen stemcomputers niet" ("We don't trust voting computers"). He got access to some of the Nedap machines, managed to reverse engineer the source code and demonstrated the ease of maliciously replacing the onboard chips [6].

The other major problem Gonggrijp and his collaborator Maurice Wessling discovered was the possibility to eavesdrop electromagnetic emanations (called a TEMPEST attack) which, under certain circumstances, revealed the voter's party preferences. More precisely, the name of one of the parties (Christen-Democratisch Appèl) contained a diacritic letter (è) and in order to display this, the voting machine screen had to be switched to a different mode. It was

---

[1] US patent no. 90,646, patented June 1st, 1869.

this switch that could be detected from a distance using rather standard radio equipment [5].

The fix for this problem was straightforward (just use e instead of è), but the authorities also looked at the Sdu machines and the electromagnetic emanation problem was much worse there. In the beginning of 2007, Sdu attempted to re-certify its machines, but they managed to deliver a device for testing that did not pass other requirements, so this attempt eventually failed. As a result, in October 2007, the existing regulation allowing voting machines was withdrawn [6]. The Netherlands has been using 19th century paper voting ever since.

1.2   Side Channel Attacks on Voting

As mentioned above, the TEMPEST exploit implemented by Gonggrijp and Wessling falls into the category of side channel attacks. These sorts of attacks are in general relatively difficult to prevent since, by definition, they make use of some out-of-system-model feature like power consumption, message timing, etc.

Electromagnetic emanation leakage is not the first side channel vulnerabil-ity considered for voting. Taking a photo of the ballot with a phone or some other device is a well-known privacy problem [2]. Moran and Naor note that in case Direct Recording Electronic (DRE) equipment posts encrypted votes on a bulletin board, posting timing can be used by a compromised DRE machine to reveal the voter preference [9].

An interesting side channel attack (called Three-Pattern) against the Three-Ballot optical scan voting system was described by the original author Ronald Rivest himself [11]. As the voter in this system has exponentially many choices for encoding her vote on the ballot, the coercer may convince her to do so in a predefined pattern, checking later from the public bulletin board that the pattern has been followed. This leakage is actually so severe that, according to Rivest, "...it makes ThreeBallot much less attractive than I had originally hoped for" [11].

Recently, Toreini et al. have improved paper fingerprinting techniques. Their approach allows to create short fingerprints of physical paper sheets using off-the shelf apparatus like overhead projector and photo camera with a sufficiently good resolution. As a result, this makes the vote privacy violation attack proposed by Calandrino et al. [3] more accessible to a moderately-resourced attacker. This example demonstrates clearly how advancement of technology also makes paper voting more insecure.

In this paper, we will be considering another type of emanation occurring during paper voting, namely the sound that the pen makes while marking the ballot.

The feasibility of extracting (capital) letters from the audio recording was studied by Yu et al. in 2016 [13]. Their results are encouraging, but also show significant challenges. If the training data from the attack subjects can be col-lected in advance and the position of the microphone can be well predicted, the letter recognition precision can achieve almost 65%. However, if the subjects' handwriting can not be studied beforehand, precision drops below 27%. The authors of [13] also extend their attack to recognising words from a predefined dictionary and achieve the best case accuracy of 50–60%.

We will concentrate our efforts on a smaller set of glyphs to recognise, namely Arabic numerals. We will study how well decimal digits can be recognised from the audio samples of writing them, and discuss the implications to voting privacy and ballot design.

The rest of the paper is organised as follows. In Sect. 2 we will discuss different types of ballot designs and their implications on the vulnerability to audio side channel attacks. Section 3 describes audio sample classification and Sect. 4 discusses its implications on security of various election settings. Finally, Sect. 5 draws some conclusions and sets directions for future work.

2   Types of Ballots

The primary sources of requirements for the ballot sheet design are local voting traditions and the implied legal requirements. Susceptibility to audio side channels has most likely not been taken into account as a concern. Hence we start our discussion by reviewing some of the typical ballot designs from this viewpoint.

A frequently used ballot type lists a number of candidates and requires marking one or several of them somehow (writing "X" marks next to one's preferences, crossing some candidates out, etc.). Even though audio side channels against such ballot designs are still possible (e.g., the attacker may draw conclusions based on the timings between writing several "X"-s), they require development effort that remains outside of the scope of the current paper.

Good detection accuracy can potentially be obtained for the ballots allowing write-ins, e.g. leaving an empty slot on the ballot sheet to allow voting for an unlisted candidate.[2] As the voters are not forced to write the names in capital letters, recognising each person's handwriting becomes a major problem, and without reliable personalised training data the results can be expected to be considerably worse than those of Yu et al. [13].

Still, we can consider a subset of the handwriting recognition problem. For example, in a referendum the participant might be asked to make a binary decision by writing either "Yes" or "No" to the referendum sheet. Such ballots have been previously used e.g. in Australian constitutional referendums and are currently used e.g. in Swiss referendums. We can see that the corresponding ballot design leaks information that can be classified as Yu et al. have already shown. Due to the uniqueness of letters and the lengths of the words it should be easy to distinguish between the two cases.

However, there is a specific type of write-ins that has not yet been considered, namely numbers. This is the most promising target of attack for an audio side channel, because the amount of decimal digits is limited to 10, and the variance

---

[2] This option has been used to cast protest votes. For example, in 1985, Donald Duck received 291 votes in Sweden. As a result, voting for non-existing candidates was prohibited in Sweden starting from 2006: https://abcnews.go.com/Entertainment/WolfFiles/story?id=91051&page=1.

of handwritten numbers between different individuals can be expected to be smaller compared to the variance of handwritten letters.

The most common types of ballots where the voter is expected to fill in some numbers come from preferential voting, e.g. single transferable vote (STV) systems (see an example ballot from the Tasmanian House of Representatives elections in Fig. 1). Similar kinds of ballots are used, for instance, in:

- Ireland for municipal, parliamentary and European Parliament elections,
- Malta for municipal, parliamentary and European Parliament elections,
- Northern Ireland for European Parliament elections,
- Scotland for municipal elections,
- Austria for European Parliament elections (preference number is optional),
- Australia for electing the Senat and for electing the House of Representatives.

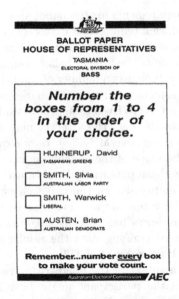

Fig. 1. An example of the Tasmanian election ballot. (Australian electoral systems, https://www.aph.gov.au/About_Parliament/Parliamentary_Departments/Parliamentary_Library/pubs/rp/RP0708/08rp05).

When implementing an audio side channel attack against a preferential ballot, we can largely expect to detect two kinds of patterns. First, when we hear the numbers written in the order 1-2-3-4-..., the voter is probably filling her preferences in the ascending order and finding the correct slots on the fly. Without looking at the timings between the numbers, this pattern does not reveal the voter preferences.

However, if the voter uses some other order of the numbers, she can be conjectured to fill the ballot from start till the end of the slot sequence, and her preferences leak. This may be expected to be the case with higher probability when the number of slots to fill is smaller.

There are also some countries (e.g. Estonia and Finland) where the voter is expected to write the candidate number on the ballot (see Fig. 2). In these cases the audio side channel has the potential of completely breaking the vote privacy.

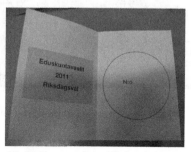

(a) Ballot used in Estonia for the municipal council elections in 2017 [1]

(b) Ballot used in Finland for the parliamentary elections in 2011. The same ballot design was also used in the 2015 elections.

Fig. 2. Examples of ballots that are designed to be filled with numbers.

The core contribution of this paper is studying the feasibility of identifying the digits by the sound of handwriting. We have created a proof-of-concept implementation that takes an audio sample, splits it into digits and then tries to recognize them. We also created a classifier which performs this task.

The following Section will describe our results in more detail.

3   Audio Sample Preprocessing and Classification

By looking at the waveforms of recordings that correspond to the writing of different digits, it can be observed that the representations of digits are more or less unique. Thus building a good automatic classifier should at least theoretically be possible.

To verify this hypothesis, we conducted several experiments. First, we collected a number of writing samples from volunteers (see Sect. 3.1 for more details).

Next we tried the standard step of converting the samples into the frequency domain by using fast Fourier transform (FFT). However, if we would only apply FFT, we would get the frequency distribution for the sample, but lose the time dimension. On the other hand, time dimension carries useful information about the digits following the movement of the pen or pencil on the paper. Therefore, we decided to transform the samples into spectrograms. Spectrograms are created by moving a window over the audio sample and applying FFT to the corresponding audio fragments. This gives a representation of the sample where one dimension represents frequency and the other represents time. An example of the result is shown in Fig. 3.

Fig. 3. Spectrogram representations of numbers five, seven and eight.

3.1 Recording and Preprocessing

We tested several microphones to find out which one is best suited for the task. The following devices were used: HP laptop, iPhone SE, Jabra Speak 410 and Rode VideoMic Pro. The first three devices had omnidirectional microphones, while Rode VideoMic Pro was a directional cardioid microphone. Comparison of the technical parameters of the microphones is given in Table 1.

Table 1. Comparison of tested recording devices. There was no technical specification available for the microphones in HP laptop and iPhone.

	Number of microphones	Type	Range	Sensitivity
HP laptop	2	Omni-directional	N/A	N/A
iPhone SE	3	Omni-directional	N/A	N/A
Jabra 410 Speak	1	Omni-directional	100 Hz–10 kHz	N/A
Rode VideoMic Pro	1	Directional	40 Hz–20 kHz	−38 dB re 1 V/Pa ± 2 dB @ 1 kHz

Testing showed that the laptop microphone was not able to capture handwriting as it could not distinguish the signal from background noise. Rode VideoMic Pro and the microphone of iPhone SE were able to capture the signal, but the quality was not as good as we got from Jabra Speak 410. It was a bit surprising that the more expensive Rode VideoMic Pro was not able to capture the signal as well as a common conference call device. Therefore, we decided to use Jabra Speak 410 for collecting the training data.

We prepared a sheet of square cells for collecting the samples in order to make the process as uniform as possible. The recording was performed in a closed office room which blocked most of the outside noise. Each volunteer was asked to fill in at least one sheet of ten rows, such that each row would contain all the digits from 0 to 9 once. In addition, the volunteers were asked to leave a small pause after writing each digit to make automatic labelling of the samples easier. The same room and the same table were used for all the samples. The locations of the microphone and the sheet were kept the same throughout the sample collection, with the microphone placed in about 15 cm from the edge of the sheet.

Once we had the samples, the next task was to label them to prepare training data for the automatic classifier. As the samples were written on the sheet in a predefined order, we were able to create a script to extract and label the samples. However, manual review of the samples was still necessary to ensure correct operation of the script.

Now that the labelled samples were ready, they had to be prepared for analysis. For that, we converted stereo recording to mono and normalized the tempo. We used WSOLA algorithm [12] to transform the samples such that all of them would have the length of 0.55 s. It is important to note that WSOLA does not change the pitch of the sound, otherwise the change of tempo could distort the representation of the digit.

3.2 Building the Classifier

We used the k-nearest neighbors algorithm (k-NN) [4] for the classification task. One of the reasons to prefer this method is its capability of producing good results with a small training set. The method works by calculating distance between all samples and then uses majority vote on k nearest samples to determine the class. This was also one of the reasons for normalizing the tempo of the samples as it allowed us to represent the samples as arrays of the same length and therefore align the corresponding frequencies. We pre-processed the data by creating a spectrogram representation from each sample and flattened the output (an array or arrays) to get a one-dimensional array.

We used scikit-learn [10] implementation of the k-NN method to build the model. To use it, the dataset was split into training and testing sets using the train_test_split function of scikit-learn. This method allowed us to make sure that the labels would be uniformly distributed in the output sets. The dataset was randomly split into training and test sets so that 10% of the samples were used for testing. As the splitting was done on the whole dataset, the ratio of training data to test data did not necessarily hold for the samples belonging to one individual. Thus, individuals might have been over- or under-represented in the training set and test set.

We tested multiple distance metrics to find the one that is most suitable for the representation of the audio data. The results showed that Canberra distance [7] gave significantly better results compared to other distance metrics.

Finally, we used cross-validation for parameter tuning in order to obtain the optimal value of k. We created a list of odd integers as the candidates, fitted a model for each value of k and used cross-validation to determine the k value which gave the best out-of-sample accuracy. In our case, the optimal value for k turned out to be 7.

3.3   Classification Results

We used cross-validation to measure the out-of-sample accuracy of the model. Cross-validation partitions the dataset into n equally sized non-overlapping sets, $n-1$ sets are used for training and the n-th set is used for validation. This process is repeated n times, so that each set is validated once. Overall result is calculated by averaging accuracy over all partitions.

Our dataset consisted of 1676 samples and contained recordings from 11 volunteers. Some of the volunteers contributed more than one data sheet and in one case only part of the data sheet recording was usable due to the corruption of data.

We used scikit-learn implementation of 10-fold cross-validation which uses stratified KFold partitioning strategy. This method provided that uniform number of labels was assigned into each subset. For the classification we used aforementioned k-NN classifier with hyperparameter $k = 7$ as it was previously found to be best suited for our dataset by producing best out-of-sample accuracy. The 10-fold cross validation with the given configuration produced an accuracy of 60.14%. The corresponding confusion matrix can be seen in Fig. 4.

We can see from the confusion matrix that the digits 8 and 9 have lower detection accuracy compared to others. One of the reasons for this might be the way how the implementation of scikit-learn breaks ties. Namely, in case of a tie the winner is picked according to the ordering of the classes. Thus, when there is a tie between, say, digits 3 and 8, the first one would win, causing 8 to be determined less.

The low accuracy of 8 and 9 might also be caused by their placement on the data sheet with respect to the microphone. The data sheet was in landscape mode during the recording and the microphone was placed close to the top middle part of the sheet. Therefore, the recorded signal of the digits that were written to the middle of the sheet should have slightly better quality compared to the digits on the sides of the sheet. This reasoning seems not to hold for 0 and 1, but this might be explained by their rather unique audio fingerprint.

Next, we ran a test to find the accuracy for the case when training data is available for the test subject. We took datasets from eleven volunteers and split them into test sets and training sets so that every person contributed 10% of their stratified data points to the test set and the remainder was used for training. Each person had 100 labelled data points and thus 1000 samples were used for training and 100 for testing. Results showed that by using such data on average 70.6% of digit predictions were accurate. This result loosely corresponds to the 65% outcome of the experiment by Yu *et al.* [13].

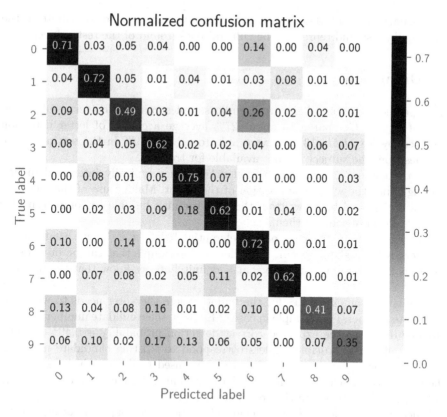

Fig. 4. A confusion matrix that was created from the output of cross-validation. The accuracy of cross-validation was 60.14%.

However, the more interesting question concerns usefulness of the classifier when the subject's training data is unavailable. We simulated this situation by selecting one data sheet recording from each of the eleven volunteers. Then we ran eleven tests so that in each test the datasets of ten volunteers was used for training and the data of the volunteer was used for testing the model. Again, training was performed with 1000 samples and the remaining 100 samples were used for validation. The results showed an average accuracy of 49%, with the minimal accuracy of 37% and maximum 65%, respectively. This accuracy can probably improved by collecting more training data.

We also observed an interesting phenomenon during our tests. There was one potential volunteer coming from a completely different cultural background, and the audio samples extracted from his recordings were classified with significantly lower probability.

Visual inspection of his handwriting revealed that this person had a completely different style of writing the numbers, most probably originating from the way numbers are taught in the schools of his country of origin. Thus, in order to achieve good detection accuracy, the volunteers who contribute to the training data should represent the cultural background of the test subjects.

4   Discussion

As expected, detecting digits from audio samples can give better results than that of letters. Compared to about 27% average accuracy of letter detection reported by Yu *et al.* [13], we were able to achieve 49% in the setting where samples from the subject are not available for training.

In the context of elections, the attacker is not typically interested in just one digit, but the whole composition of the ballot. Making use of the fact that several digits need to be written, the attacker may be able to compensate for poor detection of some of them.

For example, in the case of a preferential ballot it is known that all the numbers 1-2-3-... should occur, so if there is one sample that can be interpreted either as 2 or 6 and another one that is definitely 6, we know that the first one must be 2.

Similar reasoning applies for the ballots where the voter needs to write the candidate number. For example in case of Estonia, the candidate number consists of three digits, so the expected correct detection probability is $0.49^3 \approx 0.118$, but not all of the possible triplets correspond to existing candidate numbers. Note that the audio side channel can also be used to detect which candidates the voter *did not* select with high probability. This information may be of equal interest for the attacker in the coercion setting.

Success of the audio side channel attack in the setting of paper voting directly depends on the quality of the audio samples the attacker is able to capture. This quality in turn depends on several aspects: amount of background noise, quality of the microphone and the ability to place the microphone into a good location.

Adding more noise in the polling station does not work as a good countermeasure, since it may have a general irritating effect on the voters. In case the level of the background noise is low, our experiments show that already a mid-class microphone can get relatively good results.

Hence, the main success factor that both the attacker and defender can influence is the microphone placement.

We have conducted no research on the physical protection measures of polling stations, but we conjecture that these measures mostly do not take the threat of audio surveillance into account. There are several strategies the attacker may use to plant the microphones into the voting booths. He may try to access the booth tables in the storage before elections, or assume the role of a voter himself, entering the booth to both mark his own ballot and to leave a microphone there.

Assuming physical access to the voting booths, a similar attack of planting video recording equipment is conceivable. Contemporary cameras also have miniature size; however, they require a direct line of sight, restricting the choice of potential locations. We have not studied the effect of microphone placement extensively, but our testing shows that the signal one gets when attaching a microphone under a wooden table is actually pretty strong and clear.

The only reasonable countermeasure against audio side channel attacks is regular inspection of the voting booths during the elections to detect illegitimate recording equipment. In principle, changing the ballot designs to avoid write-ins could also help, but this may require changing the whole voting tradition and may hence not work in practice. Also, alternative designs (like marking some candidates with "X"-s) may be vulnerable to other side channel attacks of timing, triangulating the locations of the marks, etc. Studying such side channels is an interesting avenue for future research.

And last-but-not-least we would like to emphasize that the privacy-leaking side channel is inherently an issue of paper-based elections, and, to an extent, less so in case of remote electronic voting. Of course, one can imagine video recording equipment installed in someone's home, but such an attack would scale much worse than planting a microphone in a polling booth.

Thus, the main wide-scale privacy attack vector against Internet voting would still require using specially crafted malware.

Note that just an attack against vote privacy is not very interesting on its own, it becomes a real problem in conjunction with coercion. Coercion, in turn, implies the need to target specific voters.

The ease of installing malware on the computers of a particular set of target persons may depend on many aspects like physical security of their homes and general level of digital hygiene. However, we argue that determining the polling station where the target group goes voting and planting microphones there is an attack of lower technical complexity.

Planting the recording equipment can be performed by a corrupt voter (who may be the attacker himself or a voter bribed by the attacker). The attacker may then remain in the polling station observing the times when the voters enter the booth. The recording equipment, in turn, may save time stamps of the collected writing samples, and the time stamps can later be cross-referenced with the times recorded by the observing attacker. Alternatively, the recording equipment may have radio communication capability, reporting the recordings as soon as they have been detected.

Note that this attack requires significant human involvement as the attacker would need to visually identify the voters who enter the booth. However, this step can also be automated by using facial recognition software together with a corresponding personalized facial features database. At the time of this writing (summer 2018), such databases are probably not yet available for medium-level attackers, but they are being built by intelligence organizations based on vast amount of personal images available via social networks.[3] It is only a matter of time when such databases can be bought on black markets.

---

[3] https://www.forbes.com/sites/thomasbrewster/2018/04/16/huge-facebook-facial-recognition-database-built-by-ex-israeli-spies/.

We stress again that our final argument is made only about vote privacy violations via side channel leakages, and does not seek to compare security of paper and remote electronic voting otherwise.

5 Conclusions and Further Work

There are entire communities devoting their efforts to proving superiority of paper voting over its electronic counterpart (like https://www.verifiedvoting. org/ and http://handcountedpaperballots.org/). An important argument used in such efforts is that high-tech solutions are vulnerable to high-tech attacks, and the latter ones are not yet understood well enough to provide satisfactory mitigation measures.

What proponents of such arguments often do not mention is that high-tech methods can also be used against low-tech elections. The current paper stressed this point by presenting an audio side channel attack against the form of paper voting where the voter is expected to fill in the ballot by writing some numbers.

Success of such an attack in practice depends on many aspects like noisiness of the polling station and the ability to place microphones well enough to capture good-quality audio samples. However, we argue that the resulting leakage is considerably more severe than that of the TEMPEST attack by Gonggrijp and Wessling that forced all electronic voting initiatives in the Netherlands to halt in 2007. Our attack has the potential of revealing the exact voter preference, whereas the attack by Gonggrijp and Wessling only leaked whether the vote was given to one specific party (CDA) or not.

We are not claiming that all the paper voting should be discontinued, but we do advocate for balancing the criticism against electronic voting based on the problems that actually exist in the case of paper voting as well. Our research also implies that side channel attacks should be taken into account while designing the ballot sheets and planning physical protection measures in the polling stations.

This paper presented an attack on a rather specific form of paper voting. However, there are also many other designs of ballot sheets that deserve attention from the viewpoint of advanced technological attacks as well. This remains the subject for future research.

Acknowledgments. The research leading to these results has received funding from the Estonian Research Council under Institutional Research Grant IUT27-1 and the European Regional Development Fund through the Estonian Centre of Excellence in ICT Research (EXCITE) and the grant number EU48684. We would also like to thank all the volunteers contributing the writing samples used in this research, anonymous reviewers for their comments, and our shepherd Dr. Marco Prandini for helpful and thought-provoking discussions.

References

1. Kohaliku omavalitsuse volikogu valimiste käsiraamat (2017). https://www. valimised.ee/sites/default/files/uploads/kov2017/KOV2017_kasiraamat_web.pdf
2. Adida, B., Neff, C.A.: Ballot casting assurance. In: USENIX Electronic Voting Technology Workshop (2006)
3. Calandrino, J.A., Clarkson, W., Felten, E.W.: Some consequences of paper fingerprinting for elections. In: EVT/WOTE (2009)
4. Cover, T.M., Hart, P.J.: Nearest neighbor pattern classification. IEEE Trans. Inf. Theor. **13**(1), 21–27 (1976)
5. Gonggrijp, R., Hengeveld, W.J.: Studying the Nedap/Groenendaal ES3B voting computer: a computer security perspective. In: Proceedings of the USENIX Workshop on Accurate Electronic Voting Technology. USENIX Association, Berkeley (2007)
6. Jacobs, B., Pieters, W.: Electronic voting in the Netherlands: from early adoption to early abolishment. In: Aldini, A., Barthe, G., Gorrieri, R. (eds.) FOSAD 2007-2009. LNCS, vol. 5705, pp. 121–144. Springer, Heidelberg (2009). https://doi.org/10.1007/978-3-642-03829-7_4
7. Lance, G.N., Williams, W.T.: Computer programs for hierarchical polythetic classification (similarity analyses). Comput. J. **9**(1), 60–64 (1966)
8. Loeber, L.: E-voting in the Netherlands; from general acceptance to general doubt in two years. In: 3rd International Conference on Electronic Voting. LNI, GI-Edition, vol. 131, pp. 21–30 (2008)
9. Moran, T., Naor, M.: Receipt-free universally-verifiable voting with everlasting privacy. In: Dwork, C. (ed.) CRYPTO 2006. LNCS, vol. 4117, pp. 373–392. Springer, Heidelberg (2006). https://doi.org/10.1007/11818175_22
10. Pedregosa, F., et al.: Scikit-learn: machine learning in Python. J. Mach. Learn. Res. **12**, 2825–2830 (2011)
11. Rivest, R.L.: The ThreeBallot Voting System (2006). http://people.csail.mit.edu/rivest/Rivest-TheThreeBallotVotingSystem.pdf
12. Verhelst, W., Roelands, M.: An overlap-add technique based on waveform similarity (WSOLA) for high quality time-scale modification of speech. In: 1993 IEEE International Conference on Acoustics, Speech, and Signal Processing, vol. 2, pp. 554–557, April 1993
13. Yu, T., Jin, H., Nahrstedt, K.: Audio based eavesdropping of handwriting via mobile devices. In: Proceedings of the 2016 ACM International Joint Conference on Pervasive and Ubiquitous Computing, pp. 463–473. ACM (2016)

The E-voting Readiness Index
and the Netherlands

Leontine Loeber[(✉)]

University of East Anglia, Norwich, UK
Leontine_loeber@xs4all.nl

Abstract. In this paper the four dimensions of the E-voting Readiness Index are applied to the Netherlands. It examines how the Dutch systems should be scored when it comes to political willingness to introduce "e-voting", the legal system concerning elections, the existing technological level and the societal aspects concerning "e-voting". Special attention is given to the trust that voters stated to have in different voting technologies during the Dutch Parliamentary Election Study held during the 2017 Parliamentary Elections. In conclusion, even though the Netherlands scores relatively high on the technological dimension, the current state of the political, legal and societal dimensions do not point towards a likely adaptation of "e-voting" in the near future of the Netherlands.

Keywords: E-voting readiness index · Case study · Trust · "e-voting"
The Netherlands

1 Introduction

Although a majority of countries that hold elections seem to be using forms of technology within their election process, the use of technology to actually cast a vote is relatively low [1]. Casting a vote through technology in this context means voting through electronic means in a polling station or through the internet.[1] Even though a number of countries have considered introducing "e-voting", not many have done so, where as some countries have even stopped using "e-voting" [2–5]. So what determines if a country is likely to introduce "e-voting"? To examine this, Prosser and Krimmer introduced criteria to assess and compare different "e-voting" initiatives [6]. This model was further developed into the E-voting Readiness Index by Krimmer and Schuster [7]. Although the model is very useful [8], this has not lead to a substantial body of literature in which it is applied to different countries [9, 10]. To add to the existing literature, in this paper the index is applied to the Netherlands. This paper could then be used to compare this country to other countries for which the index is applied.

---

[1] In the literature sometimes the first form is described as "e-voting" and the second as "i-voting". In this paper the two forms together will be referred to as "e-voting".

© Springer Nature Switzerland AG 2018
R. Krimmer et al. (Eds.): E-Vote-ID 2018, LNCS 11143, pp. 146–159, 2018.
https://doi.org/10.1007/978-3-030-00419-4_10

2 The E-voting Readiness Index

As described by Prosser and Krimmer, the model focuses on all relevant areas to determine if a country is ready and likely to introduce "e-voting". The model differentiates between four separate dimensions: (i) Politics, (ii) Law, (iii) Technology, and (iv) Society. The model distinguishes between a project and a national level to prevent pilot experiences to be mistaken for national experiences [6].

For the Politics dimension, the kind of political system (constitutional monarchy, parliamentary democracy, etc.) should be taken into account, the method and frequency of elections as well as general statistics on elections (number of eligible voters, electoral districts, polling stations etc.). Another important aspect of this dimension is the attitude of the government and parliament toward "e-voting" and more in general toward "e-government". Other factors that are included in this dimension are the current stage in the policy making process with regards to "e-voting", the aim of the policy if in place and if an official organisation is planned for the implementation of "e-voting" [6].

Key element for the Law dimension is the kind of legal system that exists within a country. Most relevant is whether the electoral law provides a basis for technological solutions within the election process. This means that the existing legal principles for elections are important, possible ways "e-voting" could be implemented in the legal framework and the stage in which "e-voting" is in the current legislation-making process [6].

The third dimension, Technology looks at the status of registers in general and the register of citizens and of eligible voters in particular. Other important technological infrastructure questions are if a country has implemented a digital national ID card, digital signatures and if international "e-voting" standards are or will be adopted. This dimension also looks at the level of "e-government" services in general [6].

The last dimension looks at society. This dimension focuses on the level of political participation, the turnout for voting and the attitude of citizens towards new technologies and "e-voting" in particular. To make an assessment of this dimension, it is also important to know the penetration rate of mobile phones, personal computers and tablets and the Internet. An interesting factor is the actual use of Internet in society [6].

The model shows similarities with models developed to test the capacity of countries to adopt "e-government" [11]. In these models, key indicators are the country's political will, the availability and strength of their human capital, the ICT (telecommunications) infrastructure, and the presence of administrative priorities. The UN used these factors to present an "e-government" index, that that reflects the 'requisite conditions' that contribute to establishing an enabling environment for "e-government" [12].

3 Data

The data used to measure the societal dimension (described in paragraph 8) stems from the Dutch Parliamentary Election Survey 2017 (known in Dutch as the NKO 2017). The Dutch Parliamentary Election Study is conducted in two waves before and after elections for Parliament interviewing the same group of persons. For each Study, persons are randomly selected out of the all the voters that are eligible to vote in those Parliamentary elections. Selected persons are interviewed in person twice, a few weeks before the election and directly after the elections. These interviews are conducted at the homes of the participants. After the second interview, the participant is also asked to fill in a short written questionnaire. Also, for some questions drop-off forms are used. The Dutch Parliamentary Study contains nearly 700 questions on a wide range of subjects. During each study certain questions are added or removed, based on current events [13].

4   History of "E-voting" in the Netherlands

One of the reasons why it is interesting to apply the E-voting readiness index to the Dutch case is the history the Netherlands has had with "e-voting". The country introduced voting computers (DRE's) in the early 1960's and continued to use these until 2006. It also experimented with internet voting for voters living abroad and in 2005 the general wish of parliament was to introduce internet voting for all Dutch voters. In 2006 however, an action group successfully challenged the certification of the voting computers, claiming that they were not meeting the standards of transparency, verifiability and voter secrecy. The main problem that the action group had with the machines in use was the fact that they were "paperless", meaning that there was no way to check if the outcome of the election was indeed what the voters wanted. There is however no international legal obligation for governments to provide integer elections. They do have to ensure secrecy of the vote. Therefore, the action group also showed that it would be possible to breach the secrecy of the vote since the radiation (or Tempest) of the screens of the voting computers could be "read" with a handheld device. They thus challenged the use of the computers in court, leading to a withdrawal of the certification and a return to voting with paper ballots [2, 3]. At the same time, internet voting was considered for nationwide elections for the waterboards, a form of decentralized governments. Because of the discussion on the voting computers, a more substantial technical analysis of the intended system was performed, showing several weaknesses. This led to the decision not to use the internet voting system anymore [2, 14]. Since that time, several attempts by the central government, members of parliament and municipalities have been made to re-introduce forms of "e-voting", but so far none have been successful [14]. Given this history, application of the index could perhaps shed some light on the question why there has been no success yet and if the country is ready for re-introduction of "e-voting".

5   Political Dimension

5.1   Political System

The Netherlands is a constitutional monarchy. Legislative power is held by a bicameral Parliament. The First House (Eerste Kamer or Senate) consists of 75 members, who are elected for a four year term by the 12 Provincial Councils. The Second House (Tweede

Kamer or House of Representatives) consists of 150 members that are elected every four years on the basis of a proportional system. The Second House has greater legislative powers than the First House, but the First House still has veto power over every bill. The Head of State is the Monarch, whose function is largely ceremonial. Executive power is exercised by the government. Based on the election results of the elections for the Second House, a coalition is negotiated. The Prime Minister is usually the party leader of the biggest party that is a member of the coalition. Part of the coalition agreement is the division of posts in the Council of Ministers or the Cabinet. The Cabinet plans and implements the government's policy. The Ministers are responsible to the Parliament, both collectively and individually. If a Minister loses the trust of Parliament, he or she will usually resign and a new Minister is appointed. The government however can also choose to disband the Second House and call for new elections.

The local Government in the Netherlands consists of 12 provinces and around 400 municipalities. They are governed by a locally elected provincial or municipal council. Elections for these councils are held every four years, in different years for provinces and municipalities. Dutch citizens also elect the Dutch members of the European Parliament, every 5 years.

5.2   Politics and "E-voting"

The political dimension of "e-voting" in the Netherlands can be characterized as one of extremes. As stated before, in 2005 practically the whole Parliament was in favour of introducing internet voting for all Dutch voters. After the problems with the voting computers in 2006, the political will to use technology in the voting process seems to have disappeared overnight. However, this didn't last long as soon after certain parties with Parliament already expressed to be in favour of re-introducing voting computers and even internet voting [14]. In the coalition agreement of the last government, specific mention was made of the use of technology in the voting process. Although a lot of debates have been held since 2006 and now on this topic in Parliament, there has not been a majority that managed to introduce new forms of technology in elections. The latest government has not mentioned "e-voting" in the coalition agreement.

However, when it comes to "e-voting" it is not just the national political dimension that should be considered. In the Netherlands, the municipalities are very involved when it comes to organizing elections, since they are given their own tasks in the Election Law. Because the municipalities are the bodies that actually have to find people that are willing to be poll workers and are also responsible for ensuring that voters can go to suitable polling stations that are also accessible for voters with a handicap, the most pressure to re-introduce "e-voting" seems to come from politicians and majors on the local level.

Interestingly, it is not always clear why politicians push for "e-voting". Turnout is really high in the Netherlands, compared to other countries. Without mandatory voting, in parliamentary elections on average 80% of the eligible voters will vote. As mentioned before, there might be a need for certain specific groups, such as visual impaired voters. However, no real study has been made on the size of this group or on other ways to improve the voting process for these voters. The most mentioned reason therefore remains the wish for speedy results after the polls close. Problematic is that in the debates in parliament, there is not always a clear distinction between "e-voting" and "e-counting", so is it hard to tell if there would be a political will for "e-counting" of paper ballots.

The liberal parties do generally push for "e-voting" for voters living abroad, since they tend to receive the most votes from this group of voters. Steps have been made to improve the voting process for voters living abroad, but is it likely that the introduction of "e-voting (or in this case i-voting") would increase the participation rate of voters living abroad.

5.3   Politics and "E-government"

Also on other areas of "e-government", the current government seems to approach the topic with more hesitation than previous governments. The approach of the last two governments was to not only introduce new forms of "e-government", especially with regard to communication between government and citizens through digital channels, but also to make it obligatory for citizens to use these channels (for example for filing taxes). In a vision paper presented in 2013 to the Parliament, the then Dutch government set the following goals. The provision of on-line services by the government must be improved. By 2017 at the latest citizens and businesses should be able to do any and all business they have to do with government bodies on-line. Examples are applying for a permit or lodging an objection. Off-line alternatives remain available. The government comprises all the central and local government bodies (municipalities, provinces and regional water authorities). The objective is to enable citizens to contact the government faster and more easily and to make it possible for them to do business at the time and place that suits them best. Another principle laid out in this vision paper is the strengthening of the position of citizens as a countervailing power to an increasingly interconnected "e-government". By means of digital tools, citizens should be allowed to verify how they are registered, which organisations are using their data, and to correct their personal data if it is incorrect.

From the previous, it is clear that the previous government was striving for a system where most citizens would only interact with the government via digital ways. This has led to critique from different independent bodies in the Netherlands, most notably from the National Ombudsman. Also, one of the government's independent scientific councils published a study which made it clear that there is a significant part of the Dutch population which is not capable to meet the demands that result from mandatory digital communication with governmental agencies [15]. Most notably from the study was that these citizens are not necessarily older, less technologically advanced citizens as was always assumed, but also younger, highly educated people. This has led to a reconsideration of the mandatory prescription of digital communication.

5.4   Political Dimension Conclusion

Overall, on the political dimension the Netherlands clearly scores lower on the Index than before 2006. However, the number of debates since then that were held on this topic do indicate that there is still a political will to re-introduce "e-voting", even if this will is less unanimous than it used to be.

6 Law Dimension

The Election Law of the Netherlands doesn't contain any articles on "e-voting". The articles that used to make it possible to use voting computers were removed after the events of 2006. The law is also written in a very technological dependent manner because the process of paper ballot voting is prescribed in great detail at the highest level of legislation. This means that it would not be easy to amend the legislation to include forms of "e-voting" without have to redraft the entire law or give a lot of discretionary room to the government in lower legislation. Given the discussions after 2006 and the problems that were discovered by the parliamentary committees [16, 17], it is unlikely that Parliament wouldn't want to be closely involved in case of re-introduction of "e-voting". However, since the Netherlands does have previous experience with "e-voting" and how to translate this into legislation, there is still existing knowledge that could be used if a re-introduction of "e-voting" would be considered. Overall, the score on the Law dimension would currently not be very high, but on this dimension it could be foreseen that it would be fairly easy to change this.

7 Technological Dimension

As stated in paragraph 5, the current government is taking a slightly more cautious approach to "e-government" then the previous ones. However, in the Netherlands there already exists a pretty good technological support system for any form of "e-voting". This technological infrastructure is good; all areas of the country have excellent power supply and coverage of internet and wifi is almost perfect. There is a national register of all citizens that is used to automatically produce a register of eligible voters. Everybody older than 14 has to have an ID card. Although the ID cards currently are not suitable for digital identification purposes, a bill is just been introduced in the legislative process to change this. If the bill is passed, all ID cards will be usable for online identification. Besides this form of identification, there is a system with a digital ID that citizens currently use to log in to governmental services. It also functions as a digital signature for different areas, such as tax returns. The government is working on improving the digital signature system by allowing private companies such as banks to expand their own online log-in systems for usage in communication between citizens and governmental organizations. The Netherlands has not played a very active role in the development of the new guidelines on "e-voting" of the Council of Europe, but because of the previous use of "e-voting", there is awareness of these types of standards.

Overall, the technological dimension should not be considered to be an obstacle in any way for a re-introduction of "e-voting" in the Netherlands.

8 Societal Dimension

8.1 Internet Penetration and Mobile Phone Use

When it comes to internet penetration and mobile phone use, the Netherlands scores very high. The Netherlands is among the top EU 28 countries with the highest level of internet access at home. In 2017, 98% of Dutch households had internet access against a European average of 87%. In terms of high-speed broadband connectivity as well, the Netherlands ranks at the top. Nearly all Dutch households have a broadband connection at home.[2] In 2017, the Netherlands scored highest together with Sweden within Europe in terms of internet use on mobile devices, outside home or work, namely 87%. On average, 65% of the EU population aged 16 to 74 used the internet on their mobile devices. The use has grown rapidly in the Netherlands; in 2012, only 55% of the Dutch were mobile internet users. In 2017, 84% of people in the Netherlands used a smartphone outside their home or work. On average, in the EU, only 63% of people use a smartphone. Smartphone penetration was much lower in the Netherlands two years earlier in 2015, when 71% of the Dutch people used a smartphone. Laptops, notebooks and tablets were used by 54% of the Dutch population in 2017.

When looking at the amount of internet usage in the Netherlands, this is also very high. This graph shows the daily internet usage rate (for personal reasons) of online users in the Netherlands in 2017, sorted by age group. During the survey period, it was found that 99% of internet users between the ages of 25 and 34 were accessing the internet every day, but also that even within the group that used the internet the least, people of 55 and older, 88% uses the internet daily (Fig. 1).

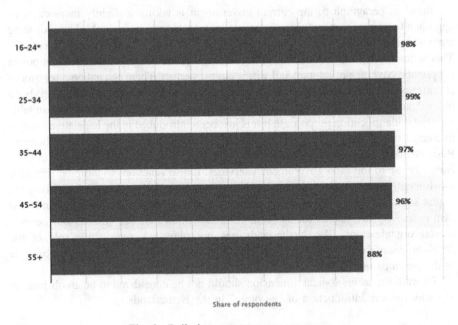

Fig. 1. Daily internet usage per age group

[2] This is based on an analysis of Eurostat figures by Statistics Netherlands (CBS).

Studies also show that the use of internet by Dutch citizens is varied. In 2016 85% reported that they use online banking. 76% of citizens use internet for interaction with public authorities, for example for online self-service. Finally, 74% uses internet for online shopping.

8.2   Attitudes Toward Elections

Dutch citizens are active when it comes to participation in elections. Turnout for parliamentary elections is usually between 75 and 80%. Even though the turnout rate for the other types of elections (European Parliament, municipal and provincial) is significantly lower, there seems to be no real indication of the trend of decreasing turnout that can be witnessed in many other European countries.

Dutch voters also express a very high level of trust in the integrity of the election process. As Fig. 2 shows, from the data of the Dutch Parliamentary Election Study 2017 it becomes clear that most voters feel that the election process is either fair or pretty fair.

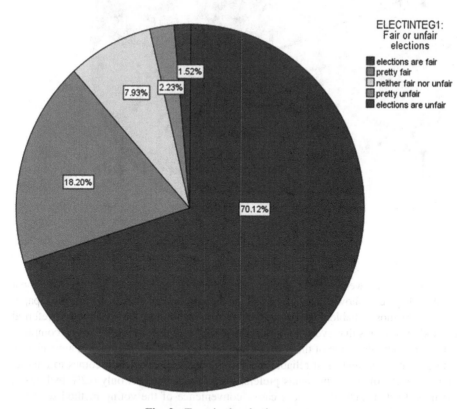

Fig. 2. Trust in the election process

8.3 Attitudes Towards "E-voting"

To test the attitudes within Dutch society with regard to "e-voting", two questions were asked in the Dutch Parliamentary Election Study 2017. First people were asked which voting method they would prefer. Figure 2 shows that a small majority prefers to use paper ballots. This is somewhat remarkable because in similar studies done in 2006 and 2010 the majority still preferred the voting computer [18].

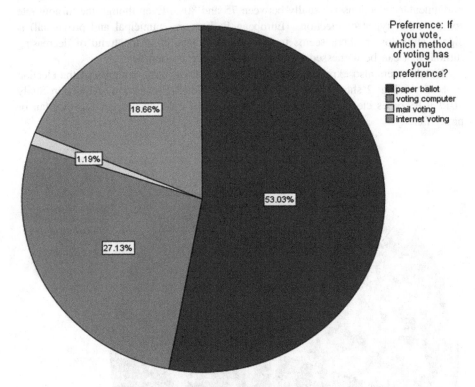

Fig. 3. Preferred voting method

Next, people were asked which voting method they would consider the most reliable. Figure 3 shows that almost 2/3 of the respondent feel that voting by paper ballot is the most reliable. Compared to the results mentioned above about the preferred method, this means that even though people do not feel that voting by voting computer is the most reliable, some of them would still prefer this. This difference in appreciation between preferred and most reliable method is even greater when it comes to internet voting; 18.1% of the respondents prefers this method, whereas only 6.2% feel this is the most trusted method. In these cases, convenience of the voting method seems to prevail over the question of trust.

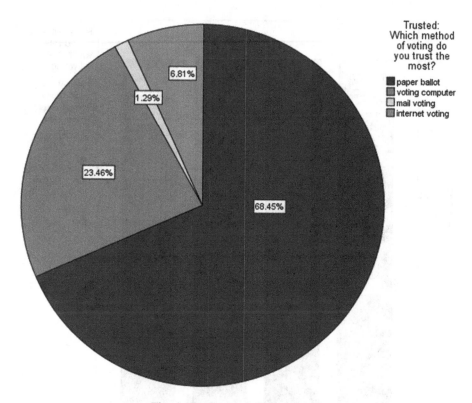

Fig. 4. Most trusted voting method

Often in debates concerning "e-voting", it is claimed that this is a more modern way of voting and that younger, newer voters expect to be voting by means of technology. Therefore it is interesting to see if there is a difference in appreciation of voting methods between different age groups. In Fig. 4 the results are shown. For the Netherlands, the argument that younger voters would prefer more technologically advanced voting methods could not be used, based on these findings. Especially the younger voters have a relatively high preference for voting through ballot paper and mail. It is the older voters that express a preference for voting computers. Due to the history of "e-voting" described above, where the Dutch voters used voting computers on a large scale between 1970 and 2006, this result might be easily explained. The older voters have use voting computers for most of their elections and are therefore less experienced with paper ballot voting then younger voters. The voters between 25 and 34 express the highest preference for internet voting of all the age groups.

Finally, the role of age with regard to the trust in voting methods was examined.

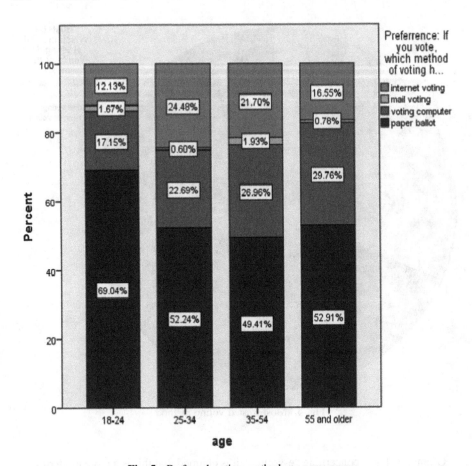

Fig. 5. Preferred voting method per age group

Figure 5 shows the results. Again, it should be noted that the youngest voters, those between 18 and 24 express the highest levels of trust in voting methods that are often described as being 'old fashioned' such as ballot papers and voting by mail. Compared to the other age groups these very young voters express the least trust in voting through voting computers or internet. The relative high level of trust in voting by mail expressed by this group is remarkable since they probably have the least day to day experience with the use of regular mail. As with the preferred method of voting, the voters between 25 and 34 express the highest level of trust in voting methods that use technology, such as voting computers and internet voting (Fig. 6).

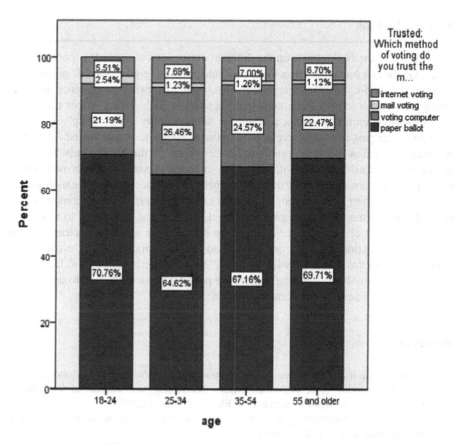

Fig. 6. Most trusted voting method per age group

8.4   Societal Dimension Conclusions

It is slightly difficult to determine how the Netherlands should be scored on the Index when it comes to the societal dimension. On the one hand, the country has a very high level of use of technological devices in daily life. Most people use smartphones and internet every day for a lot of different transactions. Also, participation in elections is high as well as the trust in the election process. However, the current attitudes of the voters towards new forms of use of technology in the voting process (voting computers and internet voting) show a preference for and a higher level of trust in paper ballot voting and even mail voting. Since it is especially the younger voters who express these attitudes, it seems unlikely that there will be a big push from society in the coming years to re-introduce "e-voting".

9 Conclusions

The position of the Netherlands on the different dimensions of the Index score a mixed image. On the one hand, there is a lot of movement on the "e-government" domain that could be useful for "e-voting" services. Also, there is previous experience with "e-voting" and a wish coming from municipalities to return to "e-voting". Even though the legal provisions currently do not account for the possibility of "e-voting", they have done so in the past and those previous provisions could be re-introduced. The technological dimension shows no problems for "e-voting" in the Netherlands. However, the societal dimension is more difficult. The attitudes of voters towards new voting technologies do not match with their willingness to embrace modern technologies in other aspects of their lives. As long as the trust of Dutch voters in voting computers and internet voting remains at the current low level, it might not be feasible to reconsider the abandonment of "e-voting". Finally, there seems to be a lack of a clear problem within Dutch elections that can only be solved by (re-)introduction of "e-voting". In light of the problems that arose with "e-voting" in 2006, there will be most likely need to be a pressing need for "e-voting" before the political and societal will to use it again could lead to a change in the current situation.

References

1. Loeber, L.: The use of technology in the election process: who governs? (forthcoming)
2. Loeber, L.: E-voting in the Netherlands; from general acceptance to general doubt in two years. In: 3rd International Conference on Electronic Voting (2008)
3. Oostveen, A.-M.: Outsourcing democracy: losing control of e-Voting in the Netherlands. Policy Internet 2(4), 201–220 (2010)
4. Jacobs, B., Pieters, W.: Electronic voting in the Netherlands: from early adoption to early abolishment. In: Aldini, A., Barthe, G., Gorrieri, R. (eds.) FOSAD 2007-2009. LNCS, vol. 5705, pp. 121–144. Springer, Heidelberg (2009). https://doi.org/10.1007/978-3-642-03829-7_4
5. Barrat, J., Vegas, C.: Overview of current state of E-voting worldwide. In: Real-World Electronic Voting, pp. 67–92. Auerbach Publications (2016)
6. Prosser, A., Krimmer, R.: The dimensions of electronic voting technology, law, politics and society. In: Electronic Voting in Europe Technology, Law, Politics and Society, pp. 21–28 (2004)
7. Krimmer, R., Schuster, R.: The E-voting readiness index. In: 3rd International Conference on Electronic Voting (2008)
8. Herawan, L., Sensuse, D.I., Rahayu, P.: CSF for Implementation E-voting model: a systematic review
9. Emaase, P.M., Miriti, E.: E-voting readiness in Kenya: a case study of Nairobi county
10. Hapsara, M.: E-voting Indonesia: framing the research. In: 2014 9th Iberian Conference on Information Systems and Technologies (CISTI). IEEE (2014)
11. Kumar, V., Mukerji, B., Irfan, B., Ajax, P.: Factors for successful E-government adoption: a conceptual framework. Electron. J. e-Gov. 5(1), 63–77 (2007)
12. United Nations Report: UN E-Government Survey 2008: From E-Government to Connected Governance (2008). UN White paper, http://unpan1.un.org/intradoc/groups/public/documents/UN/UNPAN028607.pdf. ISBN 978-92-1-123174-8

13. Schmeets, H., Van der Bie, R. (eds.) Het nationaal kiezersonderzoek 2006. Opzet, uitvoering en resultaten. Centraal Bureau voor de Statistiek, Voorburg (2008)
14. Loeber, L.: E-voting in the Netherlands; past, current, future. In: Proceedings of the 6th International Conference on Electronic Voting (EVOTE). TUT Press, Tallinn (2014)
15. Wetenschappelijke Raad voor het Regeringsbeleid. "Weten is nog geen doen. Een realistisch perspectief op zelfredzaamheid." (2017)
16. Hermans, L., et al.: Voting machines, an orphaned subject. Report by the Advisory Committee regarding the decision making process for voting machines, 17 April 2007
17. Korthals Altes, F., et al.: Voting with confidence. Report by the Election Process Advisory Commission, 27 September 2007
18. Loeber, L.: Voter trust in the Netherlands between 2006 and 2010. In: CeDEM11 Proceedings of the International Conference for E-Democracy and Open Government, pp. 323–334 (2011)

Winning the Election, but Losing the Litigation: A Prognosis of Nigerian Judicial Attitudes Toward Evidence Produced from 'E-Accreditation Machines'

Felix Oludare Omosele[⊠] [iD]

Leuphana Universitaet, Lüneburg, Germany
felix.omosele@gmail.com

Abstract. There is already a developed body of literature on electronic accreditation in the context of elections, but discourse on the evidence-related consequences of this e- accreditation is sparse.

In other words, scholarship's searchlight on the admissibility and weight of "computer evidence from e-accreditation machines (CEEM)" in electoral litigation needs to be brighter than ever. This legal inquiry is important as elections are sometimes won or lost in courts and on the basis of such electronically-obtained electoral data. This gap will be filled by the present paper.

Using Nigeria as a case study, this paper undertook a doctrinal analysis of its appellate courts' opinions on "electronic accreditation". The analysis shows that the admissibility of CEEM often turns on the age-long hearsay rule; however, considering the unique nature of CEEM, this paper argues for a revised attitude towards the hearsay rule.

In ascribing weight to the admitted CEEM, this paper proposes a standard that is based on the Relative Plausibility Theory; this standard will ensure that parties' evidence is fairly evaluated and that winners are not made into losers in the courts.

Keywords: E-registration · E-accreditation · Evidential weight
Computer evidence · Hearsay · Nigeria

1 Introduction

One of the consequences of globalization is that international norms and standards are now being prescribed for sectors that have historically had a nationalistic outlook. This holds true for the electoral systems of most sovereign nations, particularly those from developing democracies in sub-Saharan Africa. Thus, the concept of electoral integrity is quickly influencing the electoral processes of these democracies.

The importance of electoral integrity has received some attention in the literature. According to Norris [1], properly conducted elections help to elect public office holders and confer legitimacy upon elected authorities. Furthermore, while there are divergent theories of democracy, there appears to be a consensus that flawed elections are

© Springer Nature Switzerland AG 2018
R. Krimmer et al. (Eds.): E-Vote-ID 2018, LNCS 11143, pp. 160–173, 2018.
https://doi.org/10.1007/978-3-030-00419-4_11

injurious to the sustainment of democratic values [1]. The need for improved election administration, preservation of the integrity of elections, and the enfranchisement of the visually impaired necessitated the development and usage of electronic voting machines [2].

In recent times, developing democracies- like those of Nigeria[1]- have started utilizing some basic forms of voting technology[2] (i.e., e-identification) and this development has given rise to several statutory, evidential, and technical considerations. Therefore, the present use of these voting technologies, including the foreseeable deployment of EVM, and the impacts of evidence derived from these technologies in electoral litigations justify a critical analysis of some fundamental legal challenges.

Furthermore, though the literature (see e.g. [3–5]) has highlighted the constant conflict between e-voting codes and higher-order statutes[3], the discourse has, however, not adequately captured the hearsay and other evidential implications of these voting technologies and their outputs in electoral litigation. This paper will fill this gap by drawing on lessons from the few decided Nigerian judicial precedents that border on the application of e-accreditation rules in the electoral context.

Perhaps the most recurrent issue with the use of "Computer Evidence from Electronic-accreditation Machines" (CEEM)[4] in electoral litigation in Nigeria is the hearsay[5] challenge. This paper will review the statutory and judicial attitudes toward this challenge for e-accreditation. It will therefrom argue that a relaxed attitude toward hearsay with respect to CEEM is commendable and that judges should be more concerned with ascertaining the weight ascribable to CEEM.

Building up from there, the paper will discuss how courts can ascribe weight to the admitted "hearsay" CEEM. This discussion will be normative and based on the underlying principles of the Relative Plausibility Theory (RPT) [6]. The paper will contend that this normative standard, if followed, will ensure that the evidential goals of factual accuracy and fair allocation of risk of errors in trials are achieved (see the arguments of Pardo on this in Sect. 2.1).

---

[1] Nigeria's choice is strategic. Nigeria represents a group of countries with manual voting systems augmented by the most basic form of voting technology. Therefore, an incisive analysis of the evidential challenges of "evidence from e-accreditation machines" in these countries will provide their judicial systems with a good head-start for when and if they transit to full-blown electronic voting.

[2] At present, Nigeria utilizes voting technology for the purposes of voters' registration and accreditation. These technologies are in the form of a "direct data capture (DDC)" device for voters' registration and an "electronic card reader device" for the purpose of voters' accreditation.

[3] For example, conflict between e-accreditation rules on the one hand and constitutionally guaranteed rights or rights enshrined in the Electoral Act on the other hand.

[4] This species of evidence will hereinafter be simply referred to as "CEEM" in this paper.

[5] The "hearsay rule" is a long-standing rule in the law of evidence. Subject to established exceptions, it states that only the maker of a statement is permitted to tender such statement in proof of the truth thereof. The general rule is stated in section 38 of the Nigerian Evidence Act.

This paper will proceed as follows. Section 2 will provide an overview of the theoretical and conceptual framework that will be adopted in the paper. A doctrinal analysis[6] of judicial decisions will be undertaken in Sect. 3 to highlight the potential consequence of e-accreditation rules on extant electoral statutory provisions. In Sect. 4, the hearsay challenge to the admissibility of CEEM will be discussed and a normative framework for evaluating the weight of CEEM will be proffered. The concluding section will proffer some recommendations.

2 Theoretical and Conceptual Framework

2.1 Theoretical Framework

Pardo [7] argued that a successful evidentiary theory must accord with two basic epistemological foundations: factual accuracy and allocation of the risk of factual errors. "Factual accuracy" means that a theory must be able to account for a sufficient level of accuracy in its outcomes, whereas the "allocation of risk of errors" relates to an equal treatment of the parties when called upon to persuade the court as to their claims [7]. In other words, a sound theory of evidence must be founded on the necessary foundation of being accurate and fair. One such theory is the RPT.

The Relative Plausibility Theory[7] (in the form developed by Professor Allen) explains that evidence is the result of the interaction of the intelligence and knowledge of the fact finder coupled with the sum of the observations captured during a trial [6]. As such, this paper will be guided by the RPT because it satisfies both of the necessary conditions: it strives for accuracy and allocates the risk of factual errors.

The theory is made up of two sub-theories, namely the structural theory of juridical proof and the theory of juridical evidence. We shall now proceed to examine each of the sub-theories.

2.1.1 Structural Theory of Juridical Proof

This sub-theory deals with the formal structure of the proof process itself. It relates to what is to be proved (e.g., the elements of a civil cause) and the requisite standard of proof (e.g., the preponderance of evidence in a civil cause) [6].

Therefore, for the structural theory, "what is to be proven" is a story or set of stories that must be "told" as being more plausible than its competitors. Here, the task of the fact finder (a jury or a trial judge) is to determine the relative plausibility of the parties' stories and then allocate whatever ambiguities exist equally across the parties.

2.1.2 Theory of Juridical Evidence

This sub-theory of the RPT recognizes that there are three broad types of evidence: oral evidence, physical evidence, and miscellaneous trial observations. It defines evidence

---

[6] The Doctrinal Method was adopted because it allows this researcher to interpretatively analyze judicial reasoning in electoral litigations.

[7] Hereinafter referred to as the "RPT."

as not being a set of things but the process by which fact-finders come to conclusions about the past [6].

However, as a departure from the conventional theory of evidence, this sub-theory ascribes much value to the fact-finder's experiences at the moment of the decision, experiences which should affect the materials (oral and physical evidence), and other observations generated at trial [6]. In essence, the theory predicts that judicial decision makers' reasoning should be explanation-based and that rules should only be used to justify the outcome reached.

2.2 Conceptual Framework

A conceptualization of the key terms in the research question now follows.

2.2.1 Computer Evidence

In this paper, the term "evidence"- except where otherwise stated- is used in the loose sense, i.e., the term corresponds more to "data" or "records" that are capable of being legally admitted in proof of some facts. Therefore, "computer evidence" refers to "electronically stored information" (ESI) that is capable of being offered in court as proof of some facts- as opposed to an "electronically generated record" that is solely the creation of a computer and is therefore not subject to the hearsay rule [8].

In its broader sense, however, "evidence," in line with the RPT, will be seen as a process by which fact-finders come to conclusions about the past [6]. It will thus include not only physical evidence (e.g., reports of electronically-stored accredited voters), but also oral evidence and miscellaneous observations generated at trial. This conceptualization will guide this paper's central argument that triers of facts should play greater roles in interpreting hearsay and evaluating the weight ascribable thereto.

2.2.2 Electronic Accreditation Machines and E-accreditation

The conceptualization of electronic accreditation machines (EAM) in this research is limited to machines that are used for electronic voter registration prior to Election Day and voters' accreditation on Election Day. Therefore, e-accreditation is the use of electronic means to register and accredit voters but not using those means for actual voting purposes.

Thus, while the "Council of Europe Legal Standards for e-voting", defines e-voting as "the use of electronic means to cast and/or count the vote" [9], this paper's conceptualization embraces only "e-accreditation". In this regard, the paper's findings and recommendations are confined to e-accreditation and EAM.

However, e-accreditation, as conceptualized here, will exclude the use of the electronic machines in "uncontrolled environments" (e.g., voters' registration and accreditation over the internet) and will be limited to their usage in "controlled environments" (e.g., approved polling stations). See generally the discussion on the definition of e-voting in [3].

2.2.3 "Computer Evidence from E-Accreditation Machines" (CEEM)

CEEM, as conceptualized in this research, relates to computer evidence from EAM.

3 Judicial Opinions from Nigeria

In Nigeria, the decision of the Supreme Court in the case of *Nyesom & Others v. Peterside & Others* [10] brought to the fore the issue of how e-accreditation and its legal regime sometimes result in an "overreaching" of other higher-order statutes, like the Electoral Act.

To this end, this section will analyze how Nigerian appellate courts have interpreted these statutes and have successfully "isolated" the overreaching effect of any applicable e-accreditation rules.

3.1 Voting Technology, Electoral Rules, and Frictions with Higher-Order Statutes in Nigeria

Prior to the analysis of these judicial decisions, it will be worthwhile to briefly dis-cuss the relevant Nigerian standards and rules governing electoral e-registration, e-accreditation, and their admissibility in election petitions.

3.1.1 E-registration and Accreditation

Despite the fact that "electoral legislation" falls under the "concurrent list" in the second schedule of the Nigerian Constitution [11], the Constitutional structure, nonetheless, gives the National Assembly a pre-eminent position in electoral legislation.

Therefore, though the States' Legislative Houses can "… [make] laws with respect to election to a local government council…" Part II, paragraph 11 of the second schedule still subject their powers to that of the National Assembly. Therefore, the National Assembly can "make laws for the Federation with respect to the registration of voters and the procedure regulating elections *(even)* to a local government council…" [11].

Thus, the Electoral Act, a federal legislation, has been, unsurprisingly, at the center of most notable election petition holdings in Nigeria. With the establishment of the Independent National Electoral Commissions (INEC) by section 153(1)f of the Con-stitution [11] and the delegation of subsidiary rule-making to it in the Electoral Act [12], the coast was clear for the INEC to issue the much litigated '2015 Election Guidelines'.

While the e-registration of voters prior to Election Day- is clearly stipulated by INEC on its website [13], paragraphs 8–15 of the Electoral Guidelines provided the standards to be observed by electoral officers for the e-accreditation of voters on Election Day [14].

3.1.2 Higher-Order Statutory Provisions Regulating Admissibility of Electronic Evidence and E-accreditation

Sections 84(1) and (2) of the Evidence Act of 2011 [15] innovatively provide for the recognition of electronic evidence (and by implication, CEEM) and lay down condi-tions for the admissibility of computer-generated documentary statements. These conditions, if met, will provide proof of the chain of custody and reliability of the CEEM prior to being tendered in evidence. The section provides thus:

(1) In any proceeding a statement contained in a document produced by a computer shall be admissible as evidence of any fact stated in it of which direct oral evidence would be admissible. *if it is shown that the conditions in subsection (2) of this section are satisfied in relation to the statement and computer in question.*

(2) The conditions referred to in subsection (1) of this section are-

(a) that the document containing the statement was produced by the computer during a period over *which the computer was used regularly to store or process information* for the purposes of any activities regularly carried on over that period...;
...

(c) that throughout the material part of that period *the computer was operating properly* or, if not, that in any respect in which it was not operating properly or was out of operation during that part of that period was not such as to affect the production of the document or the accuracy of its contents; ...

If applied to this research focus, the "document" referred to in section 84(1) will be the "Card Readers' Voters Accreditation Report," whereas the "computer" will be the "card reader" device itself.

Therefore, to authenticate any form of electronic evidence under the Act, the state of the electronic device at the time of storing/producing the data is as important as the eventual evidence (data) produced. Thus, to prove that the conditions stated in section 84(2) have been complied with, the proponent of the electronic evidence is required by section 84(4)b to produce a certificate signed by a person occupying "...a responsible position in relation to the operation of the relevant device..." [15].

3.1.3 Conformity of E-accreditation Rules to Extant Constitutional and Statutory Provisions

Section 52(2) of the Electoral Act provides that electronic voting is prohibited for the time being in Nigeria [12] but voter registration and accreditation via electronic devices is permitted by paragraph 8b of the 2015 Electoral Guidelines [14].

However, prior to the 2015 general elections, while the principal legislation- the Electoral Act- stipulated that voters' accreditation on voting day was to be determined using a manual voters' register, the Electoral guidelines provided for the determination of the same using an electronic card reader device. Unsurprisingly, the situation amounted to a "waiting time bomb" for electoral management and was only resolved by the intervention of the judiciary in a host of cases.

For example, in the Supreme Court case of *Nyesom & Others v. Peterside & Others*, the petitioners[8] at the Governorship Election Tribunal[9] filed a petition seeking for declaratory reliefs that would ensure that the announcement of the Respondents as the winner of the Governorship Election in River State[10] was vacated.

---

[8] On appeal at both the Court of Appeal and the Supreme Court of Nigeria, the nomenclature of the petitioners later changed to "Respondents."

[9] Section 285(2) of the 1999 Constitution of Nigeria (as amended) established the "Governorship and Legislative Houses Election Tribunal" and granted it the original jurisdiction to hear challenges to the Governorship and State Legislative Houses elections.

[10] This is one of the 36 States in the Federal Republic of Nigeria.

After victories for the petitioners at both the Tribunal and the Court of Appeal (C. A.), the Respondents (Appellant at the Supreme Court) contested, at pages 42–43 of the report, the authenticity of data from the electronic card reader device. They argued that the examination alone of the card reader device- without an added examination of the paper-based voters' register- cannot provide proof of accreditation or over-voting for an election [10]. The Court, at page 63, agreed, holding that:

> [T]he Tribunal and the Lower Court were unduly swayed by the INEC [Independent National Electoral Commission] directives on the use of the card readers. As held by this court, the INEC directives, Guidelines and Manual cannot be elevated above the provisions of the Electoral Act *so as to eliminate manual accreditation of voters*. This will remain so *until INEC takes steps to have the necessary amendments made to bring the usage of the Card Reader within the ambit of the substantive Electoral* Act [10].

In essence, the Supreme Court found that the provisions of the e-accreditation rules (i.e., those contained in the electoral guidelines) issued by the INEC conflicted with those of the Electoral Act and hence declared that the former were inapplicable.

However, this decision was made at the time when the relevant provisions of the Electoral Act[11] provided only for the manual accreditation of voters. In other words, while the electronic card readers introduced by INEC were applauded by the National Assembly, the same body failed to amend the Electoral Act to legalize said "card readers" as the ultimate determinant of voters' accreditation, thus creating a legislative faux pas[12] with respect to Nigerian voting laws.

Therefore, the Supreme Court literally interpreted the extant electoral law, which does not grant any overriding importance to e-accreditation nor provides for it to be the decisive factor concerning the authentication of voters' identities. As succinctly expressed by Justice Nweze, this is the only logical approach since:

> [A]ny attempt to invest it (the Card Reader Machine procedure) with such overarching pre-eminence or superiority over the Voters' Register is like converting an auxiliary procedure-into the dominant method procedure – of proof, that is, proof of accreditation. This is a logical impossibility [16].

Against the background of the foregoing, it will be interesting to predict that further constitutional and statutory concerns might still attend the use of these "e-accreditation machines," even upon the successful amendment of the Electoral Act. However, a Justice of the Supreme Court, Rhodes-Vivour J.S.C, appeared not to foresee any danger. In a dictum, at pages 86–87, his Lordship opined that:

> [The Card Reader] was introduced to improve the accreditation process. The card reader does not violate any law. It makes election credible and transparent when it works properly. *It follows naturally that once the National Assembly amends the Electoral Act to provide for card readers, then card readers would be very relevant for nullifying elections* [17].

---

[11] Electoral Act 2010 (as amended), s 49(1) & (2) ("Any person intending to vote with this voter's card, shall present himself to a Presiding Officer at the Polling Unit… (The Officer) shall, on being satisfied that the name of the person is on the *Register of Voters*, issue him a ballot paper and indicate on the Register that the person has voted.") (emphasis added)

[12] "Faux pas"- "words or behaviour that are a social mistake or not polite" https://dictionary. cambridge.org/de/worterbuch/englisch/faux-pas Accessed 6th December, 2017.

Despite the above optimism, this researcher would rather prefer to tread with caution, particularly regarding the idea of relying solely on CEEM for the nullification of elections. The growing incidence of electoral fraud and allegations of electronic hacking[13] call for some circumspection, particularly for nascent democracies in developing countries; however, this subject is beyond the scope of the present study.

On a final note, it should be noted that the Nigerian Senate- with subsequent harmonization also done by the House of Representatives- has heeded the advice of the judiciary and amended the Electoral Act to give statutory recognition to card readers and other technological devices for accreditation purposes. The amendment to section 49 of the Electoral Act now "[m]andates presiding officers to use the Smart Card Reader… to record, verify, confirm or authenticate…the number of accredited voters in the polling unit…" [18].

4 The Hearsay Challenge to the Admissibility of CEEM and Standards in Evaluating Admitted Evidence

Pendleton [16] states that the admissibility framework for computer-generated evidence consists of a four-part analytical framework that includes: the consideration of whether the computer evidence has been authenticated; whether it is hearsay or not; whether it is relevant and not unfairly prejudicial; and whether it is not a privileged communication. With respect to CEEM, issues relating particularly to the "hearsay" component have created some problems that are worth reviewing for the Nigerian Courts.

Furthermore, closely related to the hearsay-admissibility challenge of CEEM is that of the weight ascribable to this species of evidence. Therefore, this section will examine the judicial stance on the hearsay effect of CEEM and also proffer standards for ascribing weight thereto.

4.1 Hearsay Challenge

With respect to admissibility, the holy grail of the appellate courts in Nigeria appears to be that such CEEM must be tendered in court by their makers. Without prejudice to other factors for admissibility (i.e., relevance, best evidence, etc.), this singular factor ("rule against hearsay with respect to electronic evidence") has been decisive for the outcomes of most electoral petitions involving electronic card readers.

In the case of *Emmanuel & Others v. Umana & Others* [17], the Supreme Court was asked to determine, among other things, the question of the propriety of the C.A.'s reliance on legally inadmissible documentary evidence, the makers of which did not testify before the Court of first instance- i.e., the Elections Tribunal.

The case arose out of a contested governorship election held in Akwa Ibom State. At the conclusion of the poll, the INEC declared the Respondent (Appellant at both the

---

[13] The 2016 general election in the USA is a notable example. The crisis of confidence in electronic voting can be seen in the unending allegations of interference levelled against the Russians and has highlighted the need to improve the security of elections.

C.A. and the Supreme Court) the winner, upon which the petitioners (Respondents at both the C.A. and the Supreme Court) petitioned to the Governorship Elections Tribunal for the nullification of the election. The Tribunal nullified the elections in 18 Local Government Areas (LGAs) but upheld them in the remaining 13 LGAs.

On further appeal against this decision to the C.A., the Appellant's fate was worsened. The C.A. ordered the nullification of the results in the entire State, after which the Appellant further appealed to the Supreme Court. The apex Court, at page 64, agreed with the Appellant that the C.A.:

> "[W]as in error…in relying on…all the documents that the Court[CA] relied upon including but not limited to exhibits… 317[Card Reader Report of Accredited Voters]… when the makers thereof did not testify before the Court…" [17].

In its holdings, the Court merely enforced the unambiguous provisions of the Evidence Act that prohibit legally inadmissible hearsay documents, except in the situations provided for in sections 40–54 of the Evidence Act [15]. Therefore, since the maker of the "Card Reader Report" did not testify, the statutory presumptions of regularity in section 146(i.e. Presumption as to genuineness of certified copies of documents made by public officers); section 148(e) (i.e. Presumption as to genuineness of document directed to be kept by a person by any law); and section 168(1) (i.e. Presumptions of regularity in favor of official act) [15] will hold in favor of INEC.

These presumptions will thus validate INEC's proffered figure of 1, 222, 836 manually accredited voters[14] (which was recorded in the paper voters' register), as opposed to the figure of 438, 127 accredited voters (which the Petitioners alleged were captured by the electronic card reader device and documented in the tendered "Card Reader Report").

Consequently, to rebut the said presumption of regularity, the proponent of a CEEM- which will adversely affect the results declared by INEC- must ensure that its maker testifies and tenders the CEEM and the Certificate required by section 84(4) of the Evidence Act. The maker does not, however, need to be an expert in computer forensics and it suffices if he/she merely occupies a responsible position with respect to the electronic device/computer.

Odukoya [20] has noted that politicians often employ the power of incumbency to perpetuate themselves in governance. In view of the undermining effect such actions has on the independence of the electoral commission and the judiciary, there is the need for the relaxation of the hearsay rule in electoral litigation. Such an exception to the rigidity of the hearsay rule will ensure that potential evidence for an election challenger is available, irrespective of the antics[15] of the ruling-incumbent party.

This initiative has been adopted by some legal systems. For example, hearsay evidence is no longer inadmissible in the United Kingdom (UK) solely upon the

---

[14] The petitioner had, relying on the card readers, sought the voiding of the election based on the allegation that the figure was over-bloated and that only 438, 127 voters were accredited.

[15] These antics sometimes result in the strange unavailability of key electoral officers whose testimony could have strengthened the case of the petitioners. Furthermore, where the independence of the judiciary is compromised, the issuance of a "Subpoena ad testificandum" on a key witness might serve no practical purpose.

ground that it is hearsay; it is now possible for a party wishing to adduce hearsay evidence that does not fall under any recognized exemption to merely give notice of such to the other party [21]. This implies that the law of evidence in the UK rule takes a flexible attitude towards the admissibility of all evidence and focuses more on evaluating the weight to be attached to such admitted evidence. In such jurisdictions, it can be inferred that CEEM will also not be disallowed merely because the maker was not called as a witness.

Also, in Nigeria, the Evidence Act appears to provide a unique way of ameliorating the "rigidness" of the Hearsay Rule through s. 52 of the Act. That section provides that records in electronic form made by public officers[16]- like INEC officials- are admissible as exceptions to the hearsay rule.

Notwithstanding this provision, the Supreme Court has held in the Nyesom's case (see page 56) that section 52 does not exempt public records (e.g., a certified "Card Reader Report") from the hearsay rule [10]. In other words, the community reading of ss. 52, 104, and 105 of the Evidence Act only makes the exception in s 52 apply to "proof of contents" of such public documents and not to the "proof of the truth of those contents."

In summation, the approach adopted by the UK rules of evidence[17] on hearsay challenges is largely commendable because it is preferable for the ordinarily "inadmissible" hearsay CEEM to be admitted and the court left with the tasked of evaluating its probative-ness and weight.

4.2 Standards in Evaluating the Weight of Admitted CEEM

According to the jurisprudence of the Nigerian courts, cross-examination is one of the measures that judges can rely on in deciding the weight ascribable to any piece of evidence, including electronic evidence/CEEM. In a host of cases, the Courts have reiterated this principle. In Emmanuel's case (see page 66), the principle was eloquently stated thus:

> What is more, there is, even, authority for the view that as "cross examination plays a vital role in the truth –searching process of evidence procured by examination-in chief it relates to authenticity or veracity of the witness, a Court of law is entitled not to place probative value on evidence which does not pass the test of cross-examination [17].

In addition to the "test of cross-examination," the Court, in Nyesom's case (see page 56) has also held that it will:

> "... [Have regard] inter alia, to all the circumstances from which any inference can reasonably be drawn to the accuracy or otherwise of the statement [rendered admissible by the Evidence Act]." [10].

---

[16] Specifically, records that are regarded as "certified public documents" under Nigerian laws.

[17] The Nigerian rules of evidence can also adopt this initiative, for example, by admitting a "Card Readers' Report" tendered by a non-maker public officer while preserving the courts' right to ascribe relevant weight thereto.

Thus, the Court also laid down the "test of circumstantial inference" as another important guide in evaluating the weight to be attached to an admitted CEEM. Therefore, under the present state of the law in Nigeria, the weight ascribable to a CEEM can pale if the testifying witness's veracity (in relation to the CEEM) is punctured. The same result will occur if there are negating circumstances that will erode the accuracy of the CEEM.

Some basic clarifications, however, need to be made on the standard being proposed. To effectively evaluate admitted "hearsay" CEEM based on the theoretical underpinnings of the RPT, the following is noteworthy:

i. The standard does not seek to replace the operation of the rules of evidence and proof, but rather to complement them.
ii. Therefore, the rules of evaluating evidential weight should be capable of being broadly defined to encompass the drawing of circumstantial inference from all species of evidence.[18]
iii. Appellate courts must be empowered by the rules of court to overturn perverse findings of facts by trial courts.

4.2.1 Structural Sub-theory of the RPT and Election Petitions' Claims

Against the background of our discussion in Sect. 2, the Courts must evaluate the weight ascribable to CEEM in such a way that the facts are accurately determined and the risks of errors fairly distributed between the parties. Considering, however, the presumption of regularity that holds in favor of the Nigerian electoral body and the complexities of electronic evidence, it is important to propose a standard that will treat the testimonies of the petitioners and the respondents fairly.

It is this purpose that the RPT serves. If applied to this research need, the structural sub-theory of the RPT entails that the parties to an electoral petition are to come up with stories that either buttress their own claim to electoral victory or negate that of their challenger in the said election.

For example, a petitioner relying on Section s.138(1)c of the Electoral Act that "… the respondent was not duly elected by majority of lawful votes cast at the election" [12] might come up with stories/claims like: there was unauthorized human access to the electronic card readers before, during, or after the accreditation; the card readers malfunctioned at any time during the accreditation process, etc.[19] In other words, the reasoning behind such claims, if successfully established, is to leave the courts with only lawful votes, votes that will ensure that the petitioner is clearly decided as the winner of the election.

The fact that the Nigerian National Assembly recently gave legislative backing to the use of e-accreditation [18] makes it tempting to agree with Justice Rhodes-Vivour

---

[18] For example, section 34 of the Nigerian Evidence Act makes provision for the role of "circumstantial inference" in evaluating the weight ascribable to any admitted evidence.

[19] See generally: the USA Case of *Americans for Safe Access* v. *County of Alameda*, 174 Cal.App.4th 1287, 1291 (2009), where the Court listed the relevant documents that must be produced to authenticate the accuracy of votes produced from a DRE voting machine.

that card readers might eventually- though arguably- be relevant in nullifying elections and the Nigerian Courts need to be prepared for the type of stories enumerated above.

However, the structural sub-theory of the RPT does not explain how the fact-finder will be assisted in determining the most plausible of the offered stories. This task is left to the "theory of juridical evidence." to which we shall now turn.

4.2.2   Theory of Juridical Evidence and Weight of CEEM in Election Petitions

If applied to the present research need, this sub-theory of the RPT implies that the trial court is expected to evaluate the effect of the proffered CEEM on the parties' claims by utilizing the tripartite evidential tools (oral, physical, and miscellaneous trial observations). While undertaking these tasks, the trial courts and appellate courts are to be guided by the principles of "coherence"[20] and "rationality"[21] to prevent arbitrary judicial decision-making.

Therefore, in proving his case, a petitioner whose witness, for example, has provided a coherent explanation of incidences of malfunctioning "electronic card reader devices" during accreditation deserves equal weight as an expert witness who testified as to the technical details of such malfunctions. In other words, this sub-theory predicts that extant evidentiary rules might not always be sufficient to explain legal evidence and calls for a more inclusive approach.

Using the earlier analogy of a petition founded on not being "elected by majority of lawful votes cast," a judge is expected to bring his intelligence and knowledge to bear in evaluating the substantiating CEEM. In other words, the evidence supportive of the "allegation of unauthorized human access to the electronic card readers" will only be highly weighted if:

  i. the tendering witness was coherent and rational in the explanations that he proffered before the trial court;
 ii. the evidence passed the test of cross-examination;
iii. the tendered evidence is consistent with the judge's miscellaneous observations during trial and prior background knowledge on the nature of such evidence;
 iv. and despite the evidence being ordinarily "hearsay," it complies with (i)-(iii) in such a way that it appears circumstantially superior to the corresponding evidence from the opposing party.

5   Recommendations and Policy Implications

The possible transition of developing democracies (like Nigeria) to full-blown e-voting requires some circumspection. Recognizing the tendencies of some of these developing countries to adopt electoral initiatives from advanced democracies hook, line, and

---

[20] Since the RPT requires the party to bring up their own stories, we will only be concerned with how "coherence" helps the fact-finders to determine the best of the offered stories.

[21] According to Prof. Allen, it might be difficult to give "rationality" a fixed definition; however, it entails that the explanation is consistent, uniform, coherent, simple and economic.

sinker, policy formulators for such countries must -at present- be prepared to combine the positive aspect of e-accreditation with that of manual procedures.

To this end, there is a need for the continuous training of judges, electoral staff, and other stakeholders on the peculiarities of e-accreditation. The current training modules utilized by bodies like the BRIDGE[22] magnanimously recognized that there are "... powerful people used to working with laws and getting their own way with government employees..." [22]. However, to address this shortcoming in electoral litigations, the relative plausibility and inclusionary approach to evaluating CEEM- proposed in this paper- needs to be reflected. This will ensure that the need of justice is served to all parties in an electoral litigation.

6 Conclusion

The dynamics of the modern world demand a dynamic legal system. This paper has sought to broaden the discussion of e-accreditation to include a new frontier- an evidential standard for the admissibility and weight of "hearsay" CEEM.

Recognizing the need to ensure that all parties to an electoral litigation have equal access to evidence, the paper has argued for a relaxed attitude towards the interpretation of hearsay conditions. By relying on advances being made in this regard in some advanced democracies, the paper contends that Nigerian courts cannot afford to be unnecessarily bogged down by the formalities of rules of evidence and procedure. If laws are made for men and not vice versa, then our attitude to admissible hearsay CEEM, particularly in the context of developing democracies, requires urgent reforms.

It is hoped that the proposed standard will be inclusive and fair to all the parties in a post-election litigation. If this happens, then a culture of trust in electronic accreditation will be engendered and electronic accreditation machines will foster strong democratic institutions.

Acknowledgements. The author is grateful to the DAAD for providing the funding with which this research work was carried out. Special appreciation also goes to Prof. Dr. Tim W. Dornis and Prof. Dr. Axel Halfmeier of the Leuphana Law School for their valuable advice on its original draft. For finding time to shepherd the paper to completion, the author is also indebted to Prof. Jordi Barrat. However, any error(s) discovered in the paper remains that of the author.

References

1. Norris, P.: Why Electoral Integrity Matters. Cambridge University Press, Cambridge (2014)
2. Caltech/MIT Voting Technology Project: Voting - What Is, What Could Be (2001). https://vote.caltech.edu/reports/1. Accessed 01 July 2018
3. Maurer, A.D.: E-voting: what do judges say? In: Maurer, A.D., Barrat, J. (eds.) E-Voting Case Law: A Comparative Analysis. Routledge (2016)

---

[22] BRIDGE is an acronym for "Building Resources in Democracy, Governance and Elections".

4. Saphire, R.B., Moke, P.: Litigating Bush v. Gore in the states: dual voting systems and the fourteenth amendment. 51 VILL. L. 229, 232–233 (2006)
5. Schwartz, P.M.: Voting technology and democracy. 77 N.Y.U. L.Q. Rev. 625, 631–640 (2002)
6. Allen, R.J.: Factual ambiguity and a theory of evidence. 88 Northwestern U. Law Rev. 604, 604–634 (1993–1994)
7. Pardo, M.S.: The nature and purpose of evidence theory. 66 Vanderbilt Law Rev. 547, 556 (2013)
8. Moore, J.L.: Time for an upgrade: amending the federal rules of evidence to address the challenges of electronically stored information in civil litigation. Jurimetrics **50**(2), 147, 167 (2010)
9. Council of Europe. https://www.coe.int/en/web/electoral-assistance/-/council-of-europe-adopts-new-recommendation-on-standards-for-e-voting. Accessed 01 Aug 2017
10. Nyesom & Others v. Peterside & Others (2016) LPELR-40036(SC)
11. Federal Ministry of Justice. http://www.justice.gov.ng/index.php/laws/constitution. Accessed 04 July 2018
12. ACE Electoral Knowledge Network. Nigeria Electoral Act 2010. http://aceproject.org/ero-en/regions/africa/NG/nigeria-electoral-act-2010/view. Accessed 29 July 2018
13. Independent National Electoral Commission: Voter Registration. http://www.inecnigeria.org/?page_id=5198. Accessed 04 July 2018
14. Independent National Electoral Commission: Approved Guidelines for 2015 Elections. http://www.inecnigeria.org/?page_id=3463. Accessed 29 July 2018
15. Federal Republic of Nigeria National Assembly: Evidence Act (2011). https://nass.gov.ng/document/download/5945. Accessed 29 July 2018
16. Okereke v. Umahi & Others (2016) LPELR-40035, 37-38 (SC)
17. Emmanuel v. Umana & others (2016), LPELR-40037 (SC)
18. Policy and Legal Advocacy Center: Factsheet on the Electoral Act Amendment Bill. https://placng.org/wp/category/publications/. Accessed 29 July 2018
19. Bench and Bar of Minnesota: Admissibility of Electronic Evidence: A New Evidentiary Frontier. http://mnbenchbar.com/2013/10/admissibility-of-electronic-evidence/. Assessed 29 July 2018
20. Independent National Electoral Commission: Conference Papers. http://www.inecnigeria.org/wp-content/uploads/2015/07/Conference-Paper-by-Adelaja-Odukoya.pdf. Assessed 04 July 2018
21. Nicoll, C.: Should computers be trusted? Hearsay and authentication with special reference to electronic commerce. J. Bus. L. **332**, 341 (1999)
22. BRIDGE. http://www.bridge-project.org/en/curriculum/979-modules/1002-electoral-dispute-resolution-synopsis.html/. Accessed 28 July 2018

Risk-Limiting Audits by Stratified Union-Intersection Tests of Elections (SUITE)

Kellie Ottoboni[1]([✉]) [iD], Philip B. Stark[1]([✉]) [iD], Mark Lindeman[2] [iD],
and Neal McBurnett[3] [iD]

[1] Department of Statistics, University of California, Berkeley, CA, USA
kellieotto@berkeley.edu, stark@stat.berkeley.edu
[2] Verified Voting Foundation, Philadelphia, PA, USA
[3] Boulder, CO, USA

Abstract. Risk-limiting audits (RLAs) offer a statistical guarantee: if a full manual tally of the paper ballots would show that the reported election outcome is wrong, an RLA has a known minimum chance of leading to a full manual tally. RLAs generally rely on random samples. Stratified sampling—partitioning the population of ballots into disjoint strata and sampling independently from the strata—may simplify logistics or increase efficiency compared to simpler sampling designs, but makes risk calculations harder. We present SUITE, a new method for conducting RLAs using stratified samples. SUITE considers all possible partitions of outcome-changing error across strata. For each partition, it combines P-values from stratum-level tests into a combined P-value; there is no restriction on the tests used in different strata. SUITE maximizes the combined P-value over all partitions of outcome-changing error. The audit can stop if that maximum is less than the risk limit. Voting systems in some Colorado counties (comprising 98.2% of voters) allow auditors to check how the system interpreted each ballot, which allows *ballot-level comparison* RLAs. Other counties use *ballot polling*, which is less efficient. Extant approaches to conducting an RLA of a statewide contest would require major changes to Colorado's procedures and software, or would sacrifice the efficiency of ballot-level comparison. SUITE does not. It divides ballots into two strata: those cast in counties that can conduct ballot-level comparisons, and the rest. Stratum-level P-values are found by methods derived here. The resulting audit is substantially more efficient than statewide ballot polling. SUITE is useful in any state with a mix of voting systems or that uses stratified sampling for other reasons. We provide an open-source reference implementation and exemplar calculations in Jupyter notebooks.

Keywords: Stratified sampling · Nonparametric tests
Fisher's combining function · Sequential hypothesis tests
Colorado risk-limiting audits
Maximizing P-values over nuisance parameters
Union-intersection test · Intersection-union test

© Springer Nature Switzerland AG 2018
R. Krimmer et al. (Eds.): E-Vote-ID 2018, LNCS 11143, pp. 174–188, 2018.
https://doi.org/10.1007/978-3-030-00419-4_12

1   Introduction

A risk-limiting audit (RLA) of an election contest is a procedure that has a known minimum chance of leading to a full manual tally of the ballots if the electoral outcome according to that tally would differ from the reported outcome. *Outcome* means the winner(s) (or, for instance, whether there is a runoff)—not the numerical vote totals. RLAs require a durable, voter-verifiable record of voter intent, such as paper ballots, and they assume that this audit trail is sufficiently complete and accurate that a full hand tally would show the true electoral outcome. That assumption is not automatically satisfied: a *compliance audit* [16] is required to check whether the paper trail is trustworthy.

Current methods for risk-limiting audits are generally *sequential hypothesis testing procedures*: they examine more ballots, or batches of ballots, until either (i) there is strong statistical evidence that a full hand tabulation would confirm the outcome, or (ii) the audit has led to a full hand tabulation, the result of which should become the official result.

RLAs have been conducted in California, Colorado, Ohio, and Denmark, and are required by law in Colorado (CRS 1-7-515) and Rhode Island (SB 413A and HB 5704A).

The most efficient and transparent sampling design for risk-limiting audits selects individual ballots uniformly at random, with or without replacement [13]. Risk calculations for such samples can be made simple without sacrificing rigor [6,14]. However, to audit contests that cross jurisdictional boundaries then requires coordinating sampling in different counties, and may require different counties to use the lowest common denominator method for assessing risk from the sample, which would not take full advantage of the capabilities of some voting systems. For instance, any system that uses paper ballots as the official record can conduct *ballot-polling audits*, while *ballot-level comparison audits* require systems to generate *cast vote records* that can be checked manually against a human reading of the paper [5,6]. (These terms are described in Sect. 3.)

Stratified RLAs have been considered previously, primarily to conform with legacy audit laws under which counties draw audit samples independently of each other, but also to allow auditors to start the audit before all vote-by-mail or provisional ballots have been tallied, by sampling independently from ballots cast in person, by mail, and provisionally, as soon as subtotals for each group are available [4,9]. However, extant methods address only a single approach to auditing, batch-level comparisons, and only a particular test statistic.

Here, we introduce SUITE, a more general approach to conducting RLAs using stratified samples. SUITE is a twist on *intersection-union* tests [7], which represent the null hypothesis as the intersection of a number of simpler hypotheses, and the alternative hypothesis as a union of their alternatives. In contrast, here, the null is the union of simpler hypotheses, and the alternative is the intersection of their alternatives. The approach involves finding the maximum *P*-value over a vector of nuisance parameters that describe the simple hypotheses: all allocations of tabulation error across strata for which a full count would find a different electoral outcome than was reported. (A *nuisance parameter* is a property of the population that is not of direct interest, but that affects the probability distribution of the data. *Overstatement* is error that made the margin of one or more winners over one or more losers appear larger than it really was. The total overstatement across strata determines whether the reported outcome is correct; the overstatements in individual strata are nuisance parameters that affect the distribution of the audit sample.)

The basic building block for the method is testing whether the overstatement error in a single stratum is greater than or equal to a quota. Fisher's combining function is used to merge P-values for tests in different strata into a single P-value for the hypothesis that the overstatement in every stratum is greater than or equal to its quota. If that hypothesis can be rejected for *all* stratum-level quotas that could change the outcome—that is, if the maximum combined P-value is sufficiently small—the audit can stop.

It is not actually necessary to consider all possible quotas: the P-value involves a sum of monotonic functions, which allows us to find upper and lower bounds everywhere using only values on a discrete grid. We present a numerical procedure, implemented in Python, to find bounds on the maximum P-value when there are two strata. The procedure can be generalized to more than two strata.

Section 2 presents the new approach to stratified auditing. Section 3 illustrates the method by solving a problem pertinent to Colorado: combining ballot polling in one stratum with ballot-level comparisons in another. This requires straightforward modifications to the mathematics behind ballot polling and ballot-level comparison to allow the overstatement to be compared to specified thresholds other than the overall contest margin; those modifications are described in Sects. 3.1 and 3.2. Section 4 gives numerical examples of simulated audits, using parameters intended to reflect how the procedure would work in Colorado. We provide example software implementing the risk calculations for our recommended approach in Python Jupyter notebooks.[1] Section 5 gives recommendations and considerations for implementation.

2   Stratified Audits

Stratified sampling involves partitioning a population into non-overlapping groups and drawing independent random samples from those groups. [4,9] developed RLAs based on comparing stratified samples of batches of ballots to hand counts of the votes in those batches: batch-level comparison RLAs, using a particular test statistic. The method we develop here is more general and more flexible: it can be used with any test statistic, and test statistics in different strata need not be the same—which is key to combining audits of ballots cast using diverse voting technologies.

Here and below, we consider auditing a single plurality contest at a time, although the same sample can be used to audit more than one contest (and

---

[1] See https://github.com/pbstark/CORLA18.

super-majority contests), and there are ways of combining audits of different contests into a single process [10,14]. We use terminology drawn from a number of papers, notably [6].

An *overstatement error* is an error that caused the margin between *any* reported winner and *any* reported loser to appear larger than it really was. An *understatement error* is an error that caused the margin between *every* reported winner and *every* reported loser to appear to be smaller than it really was. Overstatements cast doubt on outcomes; understatements do not, even though they are tabulation errors.

We use w to denote a reported winner and ℓ to denote a reported loser. The total number of reported votes for candidate w is V_w and the total for candidate ℓ is V_ℓ. Thus $V_w > V_\ell$, since w is reported to have gotten more votes than ℓ.

Let $V_{w\ell} \equiv V_w - V_\ell > 0$ denote the contest-wide margin (in votes) of w over ℓ. We have S strata. Let $V_{w\ell,s}$ denote the margin (in votes) of reported winner w over reported loser ℓ in stratum s. Note that $V_{w\ell,s}$ might be negative in one stratum, but $\sum_{s=1}^{S} V_{w\ell,s} = V_{w\ell} > 0$. Let $A_{w\ell}$ denote the margin (in votes) of reported winner w over reported loser ℓ that a full hand count would show: the *actual* margin, in contrast to the *reported* margin $V_{w\ell}$. Reported winner w really beat reported loser ℓ if and only if $A_{w\ell} > 0$. Define $A_{w\ell,s}$ to be the actual margin (in votes) of w over ℓ in stratum s.

Let $\omega_{w\ell,s} \equiv V_{w\ell,s} - A_{w\ell,s}$ be the *overstatement* of the margin of w over ℓ in stratum s. Reported winner w really beat reported loser ℓ if and only if $\omega_{w\ell} \equiv \sum_s \omega_{w\ell,s} < V_{w\ell}$.

An RLA is a test of the hypothesis that the outcome is wrong, that is, that w did not really beat ℓ: $\sum_s \omega_{w\ell,s} \geq V_{w\ell}$. The null is true if and only if there exists *some* S-tuple of real numbers $(\lambda_s)_{s=1}^{S}$ with $\sum_s \lambda_s = 1$ such that $\omega_{w\ell,s} \geq \lambda_s V_{w\ell}$ for all s.[2] Thus if we can reject the conjunction hypothesis $\cap_s \{\omega_{w\ell,s} \geq \lambda_s V_{w\ell}\}$ at significance level α for all (λ_s) such that $\sum_s \lambda_s = 1$, we can stop the audit, and the risk limit will be α.

2.1 Fisher's Combination Method

Fix $\lambda \equiv (\lambda_s)_{s=1}^{S}$, with $\sum_s \lambda_s = 1$. To test the conjunction hypothesis that stratum null hypotheses are true, that is, that $\omega_{w\ell,s} \geq \lambda_s V_{w\ell}$ for all s, we use Fisher's combining function. Let $p_s(\lambda_s)$ be the P-value of the hypothesis $\omega_{w\ell,s} \geq \lambda_s V_{w\ell}$. If the null hypothesis is true, then

$$\chi(\lambda) = -2 \sum_{s=1}^{S} \ln p_s(\lambda_s) \tag{1}$$

has a probability distribution that is dominated by the chi-square distribution with $2S$ degrees of freedom.[3] Fisher's combined statistic will tend to be small

---

[2] "If" is straightforward. For "only if," suppose $\omega_{w\ell} \geq V_{w\ell}$. Set $\lambda_s = \frac{\omega_{w\ell,s}}{\sum_t \omega_{w\ell,t}}$. Then $\sum_s \lambda_s = 1$, and $\omega_{w\ell,s} = \lambda_s \omega_{w\ell} \geq \lambda_s V_{w\ell}$ for all s.

[3] If the stratum-level tests had continuously distributed P-values, the distribution would be exactly chi-square with $2S$ degrees of freedom, but if any of the P-values

when all stratum-level null hypotheses are true. If any is false, then as the sample size increases, Fisher's combined statistic will tend to grow.

If, for all λ with $\sum_s \lambda_s = 1$, we can reject the conjunction hypothesis at level α (i.e., if the minimum value of Fisher's combined statistic over all λ is larger than the $1 - \alpha$ quantile of the chi-square distribution with $2S$ degrees of freedom), the audit can stop.

If the audit is allowed to "escalate" in steps, increasing the sample size sequentially, then either the tests used in the separate strata have to be sequential tests, or multiplicity needs to be taken into account, for instance by adjusting the risk limit at each step. Otherwise, the overall procedure can have a risk limit that is much larger than α. For examples of controlling for multiplicity when using non-sequential testing procedures in an RLA, see [9,11].

The stratum-level P-value $p_s(\lambda)$ could be a P-value for the hypothesis $\omega_{w\ell,s} \geq \lambda_s V_{w\ell}$ from any test procedure. We assume, however, that p_s is based on a one-sided test, and that the tests for different values of λ "nest" in the sense that if $a > b$, then $p_s(a) > p_s(b)$. This monotonicity is a reasonable requirement because the evidence that the overstatement is greater than a should be weaker than the evidence that the overstatement is greater than b, if $a > b$. In particular, this monotonicity holds for the tests proposed in Sects. 3.1 and 3.2.

One could use a function other than Fisher's to combine the stratum-level P-values into a P-value for the conjunction hypothesis, provided it satisfies these properties (see [7]):

- the function is non-increasing in each argument and symmetric with respect to rearrangements of the arguments
- the combining function attains its supremum when one of the arguments approaches zero
- for every level α, the critical value of the combining function is finite and strictly smaller than the function's supremum.

For instance, one could use Liptak's function, $T = \sum_i \Phi^{-1}(1 - p_i)$, or Tippett's function, $T = \max_i (1 - p_i)$.

Fisher's function is convenient for this application because the tests in different strata are independent, so the chi-squared distribution dominates the distribution of $\chi(\cdot)$ when the null hypothesis is true. If tests in different strata were correlated, the null distribution of the combination function would need to be calibrated by simulation; some other combining function might have better properties than Fisher's [7].

2.2   Maximizing Fisher's Combined P-value for $S = 2$

We now specialize to $S = 2$ strata. The set of $\lambda = (\lambda_1, \lambda_2)$ such that $\sum_s \lambda_s = 1$ is then a one-dimensional family: if $\lambda_1 = \lambda$, then $\lambda_2 = 1 - \lambda$. For a given set of data,

---

has atoms when the null hypothesis is true, it is in general stochastically smaller. This follows from a coupling argument along the lines of Theorem 4.12.3 in [3].

finding the maximum P-value over all λ is thus a one-dimensional optimization problem. We provide two software solutions to the problem.

The first approach approximates the maximum via a grid search, refining the grid once the maximum has been bracketed. This is not guaranteed to find the global maximum exactly, although it can approximate the maximum as closely as one desires by refining the mesh, since the objective function is continuous.

The second, more rigorous approach uses bounds on Fisher's combining function χ for all λ. (A lower bound on χ implies an upper bound on the P-value: if, for all λ, the lower bound is larger than the $1-\alpha$ quantile of the chi-squared distribution with 4 degrees of freedom, the maximum P-value is no larger than α.)

Some values of λ can be ruled out *a priori*, because (for instance) $\omega_{w\ell,s} \leq V_{w\ell,s} + N_s$, where N_s is the number of ballots cast in stratum s, and thus

$$1 - \frac{V_{w\ell,2} + N_2}{V_{w\ell}} \leq \lambda \leq \frac{V_{w\ell,1} + N_1}{V_{w\ell}}. \tag{2}$$

Let λ_- and λ_+ be lower and upper bounds on λ.

Recall that $p_s(\cdot)$ are monotonically increasing functions, so, as a function of λ, $p_1(\lambda)$ increases monotonically and $p_2(1-\lambda)$ decreases monotonically. Suppose $[a,b] \subset [\lambda_-, \lambda_+]$. Then for all $\lambda \in [a,b)$, $-2\ln p_1(\lambda) \geq -2\ln p_1(b)$ and $-2\ln p_2(1-\lambda) \geq -2\ln p_2(1-a)$. Thus

$$\chi(\lambda) = -2(\ln p_1(\lambda) + \ln p_2(1-\lambda)) \geq -2(\ln p_1(b) + \ln p_2(1-a)) \equiv \chi_-[a,b). \tag{3}$$

This gives a lower bound for χ on the interval $[a,b)$; the corresponding upper bound is $\chi(\lambda) \leq -2(\ln p_1(a) + \ln p_2(1-b)) \equiv \chi_+[a,b)$. Partitioning $[\lambda_-, \lambda_+]$ into a collection of intervals $[a_k, a_{k+1})$ and finding $\chi_-[a_k, a_{k+1})$ and $\chi_+[a_k, a_{k+1})$ for each yields piecewise-constant lower and upper bounds for $\chi(\lambda)$.

If, for all $\lambda \in [\lambda_-, \lambda_+]$, the lower bound on χ is larger than the $1-\alpha$ quantile of the chi-square distribution with 4 degrees of freedom, the audit can stop. On the other hand, if for some $\lambda \in [\lambda_-, \lambda_+]$, the upper bound is less than the $1-\alpha$ quantile of the chi-square distribution with 4 degrees of freedom, or if $\chi(a_k)$ is less than this quantile at any grid point $\{a_k\}$, the sample size in one or both strata needs to increase. If the lower bound is less than the $1-\alpha$ quantile on some interval, but $\chi(a_k)$ is above this quantile at every grid point $\{a_k\}$, then one should improve the lower bound by refining the grid and/or by increasing the sample size in one or both strata.

3   Auditing Cross-jurisdictional Contests

As mentioned above, stratified sampling can simplify audit logistics by allowing jurisdictions to sample ballots independently of each other, or by allowing a single jurisdiction to sample independently from different collections of ballots (e.g., vote-by-mail versus cast in person). SUITE allows stratified samples to be combined into an RLA of contests that include ballots from more than one stratum.

We present an example where SUITE is helpful for a different reason: it enables an RLA to take advantage of differences among voting systems to reduce audit sample sizes, which solves a current problem in Colorado.

CRS 1-7-515 requires Colorado to conduct risk-limiting audits beginning in 2017. The first risk-limiting election audits under this statute were conducted in November, 2017; the second were conducted in July, 2018.[4] Counties cannot audit contests that cross jurisdictional boundaries (*cross-jurisdictional* contests, such as gubernatorial contests and most federal contests) on their own: margins and risk limits apply to entire contests, not to the portion of a contest included in a county. Colorado has not yet conducted an RLA of a cross-jurisdictional contest, although it has performed RLA-like procedures on individual jurisdictions' portions of some cross-jurisdictional contests. To audit statewide elections and contests that cross county lines, Colorado will need to implement new approaches and make some changes to its auditing software, RLATool.

Colorado's voting systems are heterogeneous. Some counties (containing about 98% of active voters, as of this writing) have voting systems that export cast vote records (CVRs) in a way that the paper ballot corresponding to each CVR can be identified uniquely and retrieved. We call counties with such voting systems *CVR counties*. In CVR counties, auditors can manually check the accuracy of the voting system's interpretation of individual ballots. In other counties (*legacy* or *no-CVR* counties) there is no way to check the accuracy of the system's interpretation of voter intent for individual ballots.

Contests entirely contained in CVR counties can be audited using *ballot-level comparison audits* [6], which compare CVRs to the auditors' interpretation of voter intent directly from paper ballots. Ballot-level comparison audits are currently the most efficient approach to risk-limiting audits in that they require examining fewer ballots than other methods do, when the outcome of the contest under audit is in fact correct. Contests involving no-CVR counties can be audited using *ballot-polling audits* [5,6], which generally require examining more ballots than ballot-level comparison audits to attain the same risk limit.

Colorado's challenge is to audit contests that include ballots cast in both CVR counties and no-CVR counties. There is no literature on how to combine ballot polling with ballot-level comparisons to audit cross-jurisdictional contests that include voters in CVR counties and voters in no-CVR counties.[5]

Colorado could simply revert to ballot-polling audits for cross-jurisdictional contests that include votes in no-CVR counties, but that would entail a loss of efficiency. Alternatively, Colorado could use batch-level comparison audits, with single-ballot batches in CVR counties and larger batches in no-CVR counties.[6] The statistical theory for such audits has been worked out (see, e.g., [9,10,12,14]

---

[4] See https://www.sos.state.co.us/pubs/elections/RLA/2017RLABackground.html.

[5] See [8] for a different (Bayesian) approach to auditing contests that include both CVR counties and no-CVR counties. In general, Bayesian audits are not risk-limiting.

[6] Since so few ballots are cast in no-CVR counties, cruder approaches might work, for instance, pretending that no-CVR counties had CVRs, but treating any ballot sampled from a no-CVR county as if it had a 2-vote overstatement error. See [1].

and Appendix A, below); indeed, this is the method that was used in several of California's pilot audits, including the audit in Orange County, California. However, batch-level comparison audits were found to be less efficient than ballot-polling audits in these pilots [2].

Moreover, to use batch-level comparison audits in Colorado would require major changes to RLATool, for reporting batch-level contest results prior to the audit, for drawing the sample, for reporting audit findings, and for determining when the audit can stop. The changes would include modifying data structures, data uploads, random sampling procedures, and the county user interface. No-CVR counties would also have to revise their audit procedures. Among other things, they would need to report vote subtotals for physically identifiable groups of ballots before the audit starts. No-CVR counties with voting systems that can only report subtotals by precinct might have to make major changes to how they handle ballots, for instance, sorting all ballots by precinct. These are large changes.

We show here that SUITE makes possible a "hybrid" RLA that keeps the advantages of ballot-level comparison audits in CVR counties but does not require major changes to how no-CVR counties audit, nor major changes to RLATool. The key is to use stratified sampling with two strata: ballots cast in CVR counties and those cast in no-CVR counties.

In order to use Eq. 1, we must develop stratum-level tests for the overstatement error that are appropriate for the corresponding voting system. Sections 3.1 and 3.2 describe these tests for overstatement in the CVR and no-CVR strata, respectively.

3.1   Comparison Audits of Overstatement Quotas

To use comparison auditing in the approach to stratification described above requires extending previous work to test whether the overstatement error is greater than or equal to $\lambda_s V_{w\ell}$, rather than simply $V_{w\ell}$. Appendix A derives this generalization for arbitrary batch sizes, including batches consisting of one ballot. The derivation considers only a single contest, but the MACRO test statistic [10,14] automatically extends the result to auditing any number of contests simultaneously. The derivation is for plurality contests, including "vote-for-k" plurality contests. Majority and super-majority contests are a minor modification [9].[7]

3.2   Ballot-Polling Audits of Overstatement Quotas

To use the new stratification method with ballot polling requires a different approach than [5] took: their approach tests whether w got a larger *share* of the

---

[7] So are some forms of preferential and approval voting, such as Borda count, and proportional representation contests, such as D'Hondt [15]. For a derivation of ballot-level comparison risk-limiting audits for super-majority contests, see https://github.com/pbstark/S157F17/blob/master/audit.ipynb. (Last visited 14 May 2018.) Changes for IRV/STV are more complicated.

votes than ℓ, but we need to test whether the margin *in votes* in the stratum is greater than or equal to a threshold (namely, $\lambda_s V_{w\ell}$). This introduces a nuisance parameter, the number of ballots with votes for either w or ℓ. We address this by maximizing the probability ratio in Wald's Sequential Probability Ratio Test [17] over all possible values of the nuisance parameter. Appendix B develops the test.

4   Numerical Examples

Jupyter notebooks containing calculations for hybrid stratified audits intended to be relevant for Colorado are available at https://www.github.com/pbstark/CORLA18.

hybrid-audit-example-1 contains two hypothetical examples. The first has 110,000 cast ballots, of which 9.1% were in no-CVR counties. The diluted margin (the margin in votes, divided by the total number of ballots cast) is 1.8%. In 94% of 10,000 simulations in which the reported results were correct, drawing 700 ballots from the CVR stratum and 500 ballots from the no-CVR stratum (1,200 ballots in all) allowed SUITE to confirm the outcome at 10% risk. For the remaining 6%, further expansion of the audits would have been necessary.

If it were possible to conduct a ballot-level comparison audit for the entire contest, an RLA with risk limit 10% could terminate after examining 263 ballots if it found no errors. A ballot-polling audit of the entire contest would have been expected to examine about 14,000 ballots, more than 10% of ballots cast. The hybrid audit is less efficient than a ballot-level comparison audit, but far more efficient than a ballot-polling audit.

The second contest has 2 million cast ballots, of which 5% were cast in no-CVR counties. The diluted margin is about 20%. The workload for SUITE at 5% risk is quite low: In 100% of 10,000 simulations in which the reported results were correct, auditing 43 ballots from the CVR stratum and 15 ballots from the no-CVR stratum would have confirmed the outcome. If it were possible to conduct a ballot-level comparison audit for the entire contest, an RLA at risk limit 5% could terminate after examining 31 ballots if it found no errors. The additional work for the hybrid stratified audit is disproportionately in the no-CVR counties.

A second notebook, hybrid-audit-example-2, illustrates the workflow for SUITE for an election with 2 million ballots cast. The reported margin is just over 1%, but the reported winner and reported loser are actually tied in both strata. The risk limit is 5%. For a sample of 500 ballots from the CVR stratum and 1000 ballots from the no-CVR stratum, the maximum combined P-value is over 25%, so the audit cannot stop there.

A third notebook, fisher_combined_pvalue, illustrates the numerical methods used to check whether the maximum combined P-value is below the risk limit. It includes code for the tests in the two strata, for the lower and upper bounds λ_- and λ_+ for λ, for evaluating Fisher's combining function on a grid, and for computing bounds on the P-value via Eq. 3.

5 Discussion

We present SUITE, a new class of procedures for RLAs based on stratified random sampling. SUITE is agnostic about the capability of voting equipment in different strata, unlike previous methods, which require batch-level comparisons in every stratum. SUITE allows arbitrary tests to be used in different strata; if those tests are sequentially valid, then the overall RLA is sequential. (Otherwise, multiplicity adjustments might be needed if one wants an audit that escalates in stages. See [9,11] for two approaches.)

Like other RLA methods, SUITE poses auditing as a hypothesis test. The null hypothesis is a union over all partitions of outcome-changing error across strata. The hypothesis is rejected if the maximum P-value over all such partitions is sufficiently small. Each possible partition yields an intersection hypothesis, tested by combining P-values from different strata using Fisher's combining function (or a suitable replacement).

Among other things, the new approach solves a current problem in Colorado: how to conduct RLAs of contests that cross jurisdictional lines, such as statewide contests and many federal contests.

We give numerical examples in Jupyter notebooks that can be modified to estimate the workload for different contest sizes, margins, and risk limits. In our numerical experiments, the new method requires auditing far fewer ballots than previous approaches would.

Acknowledgements. We are grateful to Ronald L. Rivest and Steven N. Evans for helpful conversations and suggestions.

A   Comparison Tests for an Overstatement Quota

A.1   Notation

- W: the set of reported winners of the contest
- $\mathcal{L}$: the set of reported losers of the contest
- N_s ballots were cast in stratum s. (The contest might not appear on all N_s ballots.)
- P "batches" of ballots are in stratum s. A batch contains one or more ballots. Every ballot in stratum s is in exactly one batch.
- n_p: number of ballots in batch p. $N_s = \sum_{p=1}^{P} n_p$.
- $v_{pi} \in \{0,1\}$: reported votes for candidate i in batch p
- $a_{pi} \in \{0,1\}$: actual votes for candidate i in batch p. If the contest does not appear on any ballot in batch p, then $a_{pi} = 0$.
- $V_{w\ell,s} \equiv \sum_{p=1}^{P}(v_{pw} - v_{p\ell})$: Reported margin in stratum s of reported winner $w \in W$ over reported loser $\ell \in \mathcal{L}$, in votes.
- $V_{w\ell}$: overall reported margin in votes of reported winner $w \in W$ over reported loser $\ell \in \mathcal{L}$ for the entire contest (not just stratum s)
- $V \equiv \min_{w \in W, \ell \in \mathcal{L}} V_{w\ell}$: smallest reported overall margin in votes between any reported winner and reported loser

- $A_{w\ell,s} \equiv \sum_{p=1}^{P}(a_{pw} - a_{p\ell})$: actual margin in votes in the stratum of reported winner $w \in \mathcal{W}$ over reported loser $\ell \in \mathcal{L}$
- $A_{w\ell}$: actual margin in votes of reported winner $w \in \mathcal{W}$ over reported loser $\ell \in \mathcal{L}$ for the entire contest (not just in stratum s)

A.2   Reduction to Maximum Relative Overstatement

If the contest is entirely contained in stratum s, then the reported winners of the contest are the actual winners if

$$\min_{w \in \mathcal{W}, \ell \in \mathcal{L}} A_{w\ell,s} > 0.$$

Here, we address the case that the contest may include a portion outside the stratum. To combine independent samples in different strata, it is convenient to be able to test whether the net overstatement error in a stratum is greater than or equal to a given threshold.

Instead of testing that condition directly, we will test a condition that is sufficient but not necessary for the inequality to hold, to get a computationally simple test that is still conservative (i.e., the level is not larger than its nominal value).

For every winner, loser pair (w, ℓ), we want to test whether the overstatement error is greater than or equal to some threshold, generally one tied to the reported margin between w and ℓ. For instance, for a hybrid stratified audit, we set the threshold to be $\lambda_s V_{w\ell}$.

We want to test whether

$$\sum_{p=1}^{P}(v_{pw} - a_{pw} - v_{p\ell} + a_{p\ell})/V_{w\ell} \geq \lambda_s.$$

The maximum of sums is not larger than the sum of the maxima; that is,

$$\max_{w \in \mathcal{W}, \ell \in \mathcal{L}} \sum_{p=1}^{P}(v_{pw} - a_{pw} - v_{p\ell} + a_{p\ell})/V_{w\ell} \leq \sum_{p=1}^{P} \max_{w \in \mathcal{W}, \ell \in \mathcal{L}}(v_{pw} - a_{pw} - v_{p\ell} + a_{p\ell})/V_{w\ell}.$$

Define

$$e_p \equiv \max_{w \in \mathcal{W}\ell \in \mathcal{L}}(v_{pw} - a_{pw} - v_{p\ell} + a_{p\ell})/V_{w\ell}.$$

Then no reported margin is overstated by a fraction λ_s or more if

$$E \equiv \sum_{p=1}^{P} e_p < \lambda_s.$$

Thus if we can reject the hypothesis $E \geq \lambda_s$, we can conclude that no pairwise margin was overstated by as much as a fraction λ_s.

Testing whether $E \geq \lambda_s$ would require a very large sample if we knew nothing at all about e_p without auditing batch p: a single large value of e_p could make

E arbitrarily large. But there is an *a priori* upper bound for e_p. Whatever the reported votes v_{pi} are in batch p, we can find the potential values of the actual votes a_{pi} that would make the error e_p largest, because a_{pi} must be between 0 and n_p, the number of ballots in batch p:

$$\frac{v_{pw} - a_{pw} - v_{p\ell} + a_{p\ell}}{V_{w\ell}} \leq \frac{v_{pw} - 0 - v_{p\ell} + n_p}{V_{w\ell}}.$$

Hence,

$$e_p \leq \max_{w \in W, \ell \in L} \frac{v_{pw} - v_{p\ell} + n_p}{V_{w\ell}} \equiv u_p. \tag{4}$$

Knowing that $e_p \leq u_p$ might let us conclude reliably that $E < \lambda_s$ by examining only a small number of batches—depending on the values $\{u_p\}_{p=1}^P$ and on the values of $\{e_p\}$ for the audited batches.

To make inferences about E, it is helpful to work with the *taint* $t_p \equiv \frac{e_p}{u_p} \leq 1$. Define $U \equiv \sum_{p=1}^P u_p$. Suppose we draw batches at random with replacement, with probability u_p/U of drawing batch p in each draw, $p = 1, \ldots, P$. (Since $u_p \geq 0$, these are all positive numbers, and they sum to 1, so they define a probability distribution on the P batches.)

Let T_j be the value of t_p for the batch p selected in the jth draw. Then $\{T_j\}_{j=1}^n$ are IID, $\mathbb{P}\{T_j \leq 1\} = 1$, and

$$\mathbb{E}T_1 = \sum_{p=1}^P \frac{u_p}{U} t_p = \frac{1}{U} \sum_{p=1}^P u_p \frac{e_p}{u_p} = \frac{1}{U} \sum_{p=1}^P e_p = E/U.$$

Thus $E = U\mathbb{E}T_1$. So, if we have strong evidence that $\mathbb{E}T_1 < \lambda_s/U$, we have strong evidence that $E < \lambda_s$.

This approach can be simplified even further by noting that u_p has a simple upper bound that does not depend on v_{pi}. At worst, the reported result for batch p shows n_p votes for the "least-winning" apparent winner of the contest with the smallest margin, but a hand interpretation would show that all n_p ballots in the batch had votes for the runner-up in that contest. Since $V_{w\ell} \geq V \equiv \min_{w \in W, \ell \in L} V_{w\ell}$ and $0 \leq v_{pi} \leq n_p$,

$$u_p = \max_{w \in W, \ell \in L} \frac{v_{pw} - v_{p\ell} + n_p}{V_{w\ell}} \leq \max_{w \in W, \ell \in L} \frac{n_p - 0 + n_p}{V_{w\ell}} \leq \frac{2n_p}{V}.$$

Thus if we use $2n_p/V$ in lieu of u_p, we still get conservative results. (We also need to re-define U to be the sum of those upper bounds.) An intermediate, still conservative approach would be to use this upper bound for batches that consist of a single ballot, but use the sharper bound (4) when $n_p > 1$. Regardless, for the new definition of u_p and U, $\{T_j\}_{j=1}^n$ are IID, $\mathbb{P}\{T_j \leq 1\} = 1$, and

$$\mathbb{E}T_1 = \sum_{p=1}^P \frac{u_p}{U} t_p = \frac{1}{U} \sum_{p=1}^P u_p \frac{e_p}{u_p} = \frac{1}{U} \sum_{p=1}^P e_p = E/U.$$

So, if we have evidence that $\mathbb{E}T_1 < \lambda_s/U$, we have evidence that $E < \lambda_s$.

A.3   Testing $\mathbb{E}T_1 \geq \lambda_s/U$

A variety of methods are available to test whether $\mathbb{E}T_1 < \lambda_s/U$. One particularly elegant sequential method is based on Wald's Sequential Probability Ratio Test (SPRT) [17]. Harold Kaplan pointed out this method on a website that no longer exists. A derivation of this *Kaplan-Wald* method is in Appendix A of [15]; to apply the method here, take $t = \lambda_s$ in their Eq. 18. A different sequential method, the *Kaplan-Markov* method (also due to Harold Kaplan), is given in [12].

B   Ballot-Polling Tests for an Overstatement Quota

In this section, we derive a ballot-polling test of the hypothesis that the margin (in votes) in a single stratum is greater than or equal to a threshold c.

B.1   Wald's SPRT with a Nuisance Parameter

Consider a single stratum s containing N_s ballots, of which $N_{w,s}$ have a vote for w but not for ℓ, $N_{\ell,s}$ have a vote for ℓ but not for w, and $N_{u,s} = N_s - N_{w,s} - N_{\ell,s}$ have votes for both w and ℓ or neither w nor ℓ, including undervotes and invalid ballots. Ballots are drawn sequentially without replacement, with equal probability of selecting each as-yet-unselected ballot in each draw.

We want to test the compound hypothesis that $N_{w,s} - N_{\ell,s} \leq c$ against the alternative that $N_{w,s} = V_{w,s}$, $N_{\ell,s} = V_{\ell,s}$, and $N_{u,s} = V_{u,s}$, with $V_{w,s} - V_{\ell,s} > c$.

The values $V_{w,s}$, $V_{\ell,s}$, and $V_{u,s}$ are the reported results for stratum s (or values related to those reported results; see [5]). In this problem, $N_{u,s}$ (equivalently, $N_{w,s} + N_{\ell,s}$) is a nuisance parameter: we care about $N_{w,s} - N_{\ell,s}$.

Let X_k be w, ℓ, or u according to whether the ballot selected on the kth draw shows a vote for w but not ℓ, ℓ but not w, or something else. Let $W_n \equiv \sum_{k=1}^{n} 1_{X_k = w}$; and define L_n and U_n analogously.

The probability of a given data sequence $X_1, \ldots, X_n$ under the alternative hypothesis is

$$\frac{\prod_{i=0}^{W_n-1}(V_{w,s} - i) \ \prod_{i=0}^{L_n-1}(V_{\ell,s} - i) \ \prod_{i=0}^{U_n-1}(V_{u,s} - i)}{\prod_{i=0}^{n-1}(N_s - i)}.$$

If $L_n \geq W_n - cn/N_s$, the data obviously do not provide evidence against the null, so we suppose that $L_n < W_n - cn/N_s$, in which case, the element of the null that will maximize the probability of the observed data has $N_{w,s} - c = N_{\ell,s}$. Under the null hypothesis, the probability of $X_1, \ldots, X_n$ is

$$\frac{\prod_{i=0}^{W_n-1}(N_{w,s} - i) \ \prod_{i=0}^{L_n-1}(N_{w,s} - c - i)\prod_{i=0}^{U_n-1}(N_{u,s} - i)}{\prod_{i=0}^{n}(N_s - i)},$$

for some value $N_{w,s}$ and the corresponding $N_{u,s} = N_s - 2N_{w,s} + c$. How large can that probability be under the null? The probability under the null is maximized by any integer $x \in \{\max(W_n, L_n + c), \ldots, (N - U_n)/2\}$ that maximizes

$$\prod_{i=0}^{W_n-1} (x - i) \ \prod_{i=0}^{L_n-1} (x - c - i) \ \prod_{i=0}^{U_n-1} (N_s - 2x + c - i).$$

The logarithm is monotonic, so any maximizer x^* also maximizes

$$f(x) = \sum_{i=0}^{W_n-1} \ln(x - i) + \sum_{i=0}^{L_n-1} \ln(x - c - i) + \sum_{i=0}^{U_n-1} \ln(N_s - 2x + c - i).$$

The first two terms on the right increase monotonically with x and the last term decreases monotonically with x. This yields bounds without having to evaluate f everywhere. Suppose $y < z$. Then for all integer x between y and z,

$$f(x) \le \sum_{i=0}^{W_n-1} \ln(z - i) + \sum_{i=0}^{L_n-1} \ln(z - c - i) + \sum_{i=0}^{U_n-1} \ln(N_s - 2y + c - i).$$

The optimization problem can be solved using a branch and bound approach. For instance, start by evaluating

$$f^+(x) \equiv \sum_{i=0}^{W_n-1} \ln(x - i) + \sum_{i=0}^{L_n-1} \ln(x - c - i)$$

and

$$f^-(x) \equiv \sum_{i=0}^{U_n-1} \ln(N_s - 2x + c - i)$$

at $\max(W_n, L_n + c)$, $(N_s - U_n)/2$, and their midpoint, to get the values of $f = f^+ + f^-$ at those three points, along with upper bounds on f on the ranges between them. At stage j, we have evaluated f, f^+, and f^- at j points $x_1 < x_2 < \ldots < x_j$, and we have upper bounds on f on the $j - 1$ ranges $R_m = \{x_m, x_m + 1, \ldots, x_{m+1}\}$ between those points. Let U_m be the upper bound on $f(x)$ for $x \in R_m$. Suppose that for some h, $f(x_h) = \max_{m=1}^j U_m$. Then $x^* = x_h$ is a global maximizer of f. If there is some $U_m > \max_i f(x_i)$, then subdivide the range with the largest U_m, calculate f, f^+, and f^- at the new point, and repeat. This algorithm must terminate by identifying a global maximizer x^* after a finite number of steps.

A conservative P-value for the null hypothesis after n items have been drawn is thus

$$P_n = \frac{\prod_{i=0}^{W_n-1}(x^* - i) \ \prod_{i=0}^{L_n-1}(x^* - c - i) \ \prod_{i=0}^{U_n-1}(N_s - 2x^* + c - i)}{\prod_{i=0}^{W_n-1}(V_{w,s} - i) \ \prod_{i=0}^{L_n-1}(V_{\ell,s} - i) \ \prod_{i=0}^{U_n-1}(V_{u,s} - i)}.$$

Because the test is built on Wald's SPRT, the sample can expand sequentially and (if the null hypothesis is true) the chance that $P_n < p$ is never larger than p. That is, $\Pr\{\inf_n P_n < p\} \le p$ if the null is true.

A Jupyter notebook implementing this approach is given in https://github. com/pbstark/CORLA18.

References

1. Bañuelos, J., Stark, P.: Limiting risk by turning manifest phantoms into evil zombies. Technical report, arXiv.org (2012). http://arxiv.org/abs/1207.3413. Accessed 17 July 2012
2. California Secretary of State: California Secretary of State Post-Election Risk-Limiting Audit Pilot Program 2011–2013: Final Report to the United States Election Assistance Commission (2014). http://votingsystems.cdn.sos.ca.gov/oversight/risk-pilot/final-report-073014.pdf Accessed 6 May 2018
3. Grimmett, G.R., Stirzaker, D.R.: Probability and Random Processes. Oxford University Press, Oxford, August 2001. www.amazon.ca/exec/obidos/redirect?tag=citeulike09-20&path=ASIN/0198572220
4. Higgins, M., Rivest, R., Stark, P.: Sharper p-values for stratified post-election audits. Stat. Polit. Policy 2(1) (2011). http://www.bepress.com/spp/vol2/iss1/7
5. Lindeman, M., Stark, P., Yates, V.: BRAVO: ballot-polling risk-limiting audits to verify outcomes. In: Proceedings of the 2011 Electronic Voting Technology Workshop/Workshop on Trustworthy Elections (EVT/WOTE 2011). USENIX (2012)
6. Lindeman, M., Stark, P.B.: A gentle introduction to risk-limiting audits. IEEE Secur. Priv. 10, 42–49 (2012)
7. Pesarin, F., Salmaso, L.: Permutation Tests for Complex Data: Theory, Applications, and Software. Wiley, West Sussex (2010)
8. Rivest, R.L.: Bayesian tabulation audits: explained and extended, 1 January 2018. https://arxiv.org/abs/1801.00528
9. Stark, P.: Conservative statistical post-election audits. Ann. Appl. Stat. 2, 550–581 (2008). http://arxiv.org/abs/0807.4005
10. Stark, P.: Auditing a collection of races simultaneously. Technical report. arXiv.org (2009). http://arxiv.org/abs/0905.1422v1
11. Stark, P.: CAST: canvass audits by sampling and testing. IEEE Trans. Inf. Forensics Secur. Spec. Issue Electron. Voting 4, 708–717 (2009)
12. Stark, P.: Risk-limiting post-election audits: P-values from common probability inequalities. IEEE Trans. Inf. Forensics Secur. 4, 1005–1014 (2009)
13. Stark, P.: Risk-limiting vote-tabulation audits: the importance of cluster size. Chance 23(3), 9–12 (2010)
14. Stark, P.: Super-simple simultaneous single-ballot risk-limiting audits. In: Proceedings of the 2010 Electronic Voting Technology Workshop/Workshop on Trustworthy Elections (EVT/WOTE 2010). USENIX (2010). http://www.usenix.org/events/evtwote10/tech/full_papers/Stark.pdf
15. Stark, P.B., Teague, V.: Verifiable European elections: risk-limiting audits for D'Hondt and its relatives. JETS: USENIX J. Election Technol. Syst. 3(1) (2014). https://www.usenix.org/jets/issues/0301/stark
16. Stark, P.B., Wagner, D.A.: Evidence-based elections. IEEE Secur. Priv. 10, 33–41 (2012)
17. Wald, A.: Sequential tests of statistical hypotheses. Ann. Math. Stat. 16, 117–186 (1945)

Rounding Considered Harmful

Carsten Schürmann[(✉)]

DemTech, IT University of Copenhagen, Copenhagen, Denmark
carsten@itu.dk

Abstract. Party-list proportional representation methods aim to allocate seats proportionally to the votes cast for each party. In general, exact proportionality is not possible as it would require a fractional allocation of seats. Therefore several methods have been devised to compute seat allocations that differ in the way they try to achieve proportionality. Examples of such methods include the d'Hondt and Sainte-Laguë methods that allocate seats according to fractional values. These methods are used in many countries. Numerically, these fractions appear harmless, however they are not. Computers do not work with infinite precision floating point numbers, implementations tend to round the fractions to several digits, which can, with a certain probability, lead to incorrect seat allocations.

1 Introduction

Denmark's electoral law requires a combination of d'Hondt and Sainte-Laguë methods to compute the seat allocation of parliament after a parliamentary election. These methods aim at producing a seat allocation that is proportional and reflects the vote. The methods are deceptively simple as they consist of computing a table of quotients and the selection of the largest those quotients, each of which corresponds to a seat.

However, whenever quotients are computed, one has to be careful with bad numeric effects. Floating point numbers are not represented with infinite precision, and often the digits after the comma are rounded off. In this paper we ask the question if it safe to round quotients, and if rounding can have an effect in real elections. The answer is that it is not safe to round and that rounding can change the outcome of the election (with a certain probability).

For conducting this work, we have been granted access the source code of Denmark's Seat allocation System (DSAS). While inspecting the software, we observed that DSAS rounds quotients to the next whole number before storing then in the table, and then uses randomness to draw lots to break ties. In the

---

C. Schürmann—This paper was made possible by grant NPRP 097-988-1-178, Automated verification of properties of concurrent, distributed and parallel specifications with applications to computer security, from the Qatar National Research Fund (a member of the Qatar Foundation). The statements made herein are solely the responsibility of the author.

R. Krimmer et al. (Eds.): E-Vote-ID 2018, LNCS 11143, pp. 189–202, 2018.
https://doi.org/10.1007/978-3-030-00419-4_13

analysis described in this paper, we show that this is highly problematic and that situation can arise where DSAS computes the wrong result. We also conduct a Monte-Carlo experiment to provide some statistical evidence, how likely the error scenario actually is in practice, at least for the Danish case. We estimate that one out of every 66 Danish elections is effected and that DSAS computes the wrong seat allocation in average for one out of 132 elections. The version of DSAS under consideration in this paper was used only since 2007. Seat allocation for elections before 2007 were computed with another system. We have not conducted any further statistical analysis for other countries.

We have written this paper out of concern that similar programming mistakes may be hiding in seat allocations programs used by other countries.

This paper is organized as follows. In Sect. 2 we describe abstractly the d'Hondt method, variants of which are used in dozens countries around the world. In Sect. 3, we describe the effects of rounding and define the probability of how prematurely rounding quotients can effect the result of the seat allocation algorithm. In Sect. 4 we then look at real election data from the Danish 2007 parliament election, and argue, that the effects of rounding are likely and serious. We also provide evidence that the Danish Seat Allocation System, at least in the version examined, rounds quotients to the next whole number and breaks ties by drawing lots. In Sect. 5 we describe briefly how we disclosed the findings to the Ministry, before we we assess results and describe how a fix for the rounding problem in Sect. 6.

Related Work: The subject of this paper touches on several different areas: Party-list proportional representation methods are social choice functions, and their properties have been studied in political science and social choice [1,5]. The d'Hondt was originally invented by Thomas Jefferson in 1791, and then introduced to Europe by Victor d'Hondt in 1878. The method was designed to be executed by hand. Nowadays, social choice functions such as d'Hondt, single transferable vote (STV) and others are implemented as computer programs. Programming mistakes are common place unless one uses formal methods to verify the implementation of tie breaking rules, which not many implementors do. One of the few works in this area is by Goré and Lebedeva [4], which focuses on verifying implementations of STV and the respective tie-breaking rules. Their reasoning techniques applied to d'Hondt (assuming it is correctly specified) would then automatically recognize programming mistakes such as those that we discuss in this paper. Lastly, even if premature rounding is used in the implementation of d'Hondt and Sainte-Laguë methods, variants of risk-limiting auditing tailored for d'Hondt elections [7] can be used to identify statistically, if seats have been erroneously assigned to the wrong party.

2   The d'Hondt Method

The d'Hondt and Sainte-Laguë methods are a part-list proportional representation methods used for seat allocation in more than 50 countries including

Denmark, Germany, and Switzerland. In the following, we focus on d'Hondt. It is defined as follows. Let $t_1 \ldots t_n$ represent the vote totals of an election with n parties. The total number of votes cast is therefore $\sum_{1 \leq i \leq n} t_i$, and the goal of the d'Hondt method is to assign the m seats in such a way that they are proportionally allocated in the number of votes obtained by each party: As there are no fractional seats, we cannot expect d'Hondt or any other voting rule for this matter to produce the perfectly proportional seat allocation. The underlying idea of d'Hondt is this: If a party were to pay for a seat with votes then d'Hondt rule allocates the number of seats to each party to maximize the highest (average) price per seat.

Example 1. Let A and B be two parties with 10000 and 15000 votes, respectively, and five seats to be allocated.

	A's bid	B's bid	Allocation
(1)	10,000 for 1 seat	15,000 for 1 seat	B
(2)	10,000 for 1 seat	15,000 for 1 seat	B, A
(3)	10,000 for 1 seat	7,500 for 2 seats	B, A, B
(4)	5,000 for 2 seats	7,500 for 2 seats	B, A, B, A
(5)	5,000 for 2 seats	5,000 for 3 seats	B, A, B, A, B

The algorithm starts with highest price, here 15,000 votes, and reduces the price until all seats are sold! In line (1), the first seat goes to party B, because B is bidding 15,000. In line (2), A obtains the second seat, because at this stage the price is 10,000. B cannot bid, because B has spent all of its money. In line (3), the average price for a seat has dropped to 7,500, which allows B to argue that it should be entitled to a second seat. (B has already spent 15,000 and $2 \times 7{,}500 = 15{,}000$). After 5 rounds, all seats are sold.

The d'Hondt rule results in a simple algorithm that consists of two steps.

1. Construct a table, one column per party, where the first row are initialized with the vote totals $t_1 \ldots t_n$. All other rows are identified by a divisor, and the row is computed from the first row by dividing t_i by this divisor. The entries in the table are also called *quotients*. In the simplest case, the divisors range over $1, 2, 3, \ldots$, but other choices of divisors are used in practice as well, as we will see in Sect. 4.
2. To allocate s seats, traverse the table and mark the s highest quotients. The number of markings in each column correspond to the seats assigned for the respective party.

The intended meaning of the table is that the field located at row i and row j is the bidding price for party i for j seats. Note, that if a quotient is marked in a table, all the quotients above (in the same column) are also marked.

Example 2. Back to the example above. The table in this case has the following form. The markings are indicated as check marks.

Divisor	Party A	Party B
1	10000 ✓	15000 ✓
2	5000 ✓	7500 ✓
3	3333.$\bar{3}$	5000 ✓
4	2500	3750
5	2000	3000

3 To Round or Not to Round?

Although computing the table is not difficult there are some decision designs that have to be taken when implementing it. The most important perhaps is if and how to round quotients that are not whole numbers. The quotient in Row 3, Party A, for example, is a number with infinitely many digits after the comma. Would it be ok to round these quotients to the nearest whole number? By rounding to the next whole number we mean that if the digits after the "," < 0.5 the number will be rounded down and if ≥ 0.5 it will be rounded up. One may expect the answer is yes, after all, the differences between the tallies of a typical national election are usually quite large, so what could go wrong? Rounding must be considered problematic, if it affects the result of seat allocation, which means that the margin between two quotients in the d'Hondt table are sufficiently close, and this means introducing a tie that has to be resolved by a tie-breaking rule.

Example 3. Consider, for example, a multi-member constituency where three parties A, B and C with tallies 999, 500, 1501, respectively, compete for four constituency seats. Selecting the four highest quotients from the table below

Tallies	A	B	C
	999	500	1501
Divisor 1	999	500	1501
Divisor 2	499.5	250	750.5
Divisor 3	333	166.$\bar{6}$	500.$\bar{3}$

results in the following correct election result: one seat is allocated to A, three seats are allocated to C. In the case with rounding to the next whole number, the table has the following form:

Tallies	A	B	C
	999	500	1501
Divisor 1	999	500	1501
Divisor 2	500	250	750
Divisor 3	333	167	500

The algorithm allocates the first three seats to C, A, and C, and the last seat is drawn by lot, and as each party has a quotient of 500, the probability that the correct result is drawn is only $1/3$.

If we were to allocate five seats instead of four, the correct result implies that the fifth seat belongs to B, because $500 > 499.5$. In the rounded version, however, we would have to draw two seats of the set of three, which means here again, the probability that the correct result is only $1/3$.

In real elections there are several factors that impact the margins of the quotient registered in the table: (1) In some countries, d'Hondt is applied not only to the nation-wide totals, but often also on the constituency level, where the tallies are much smaller, which means the likelihood that two quotient are close increases. (2) The choice of divisors varies form country to country. In some countries, for example in Denmark, under certain but rare circumstances, the divisors $1, 4, 7 \ldots$ are being used to construct the d'Hondt table, which means that for large divisors, the quotients, can become quiet close. (3) The size of the elected body plays a big role in how small the margins are between any to quotients in the table.

We distinguish to kinds of errors due to rounding, depending on if they affect allocated seats alone, or allocated and non-allocated seats. The former is called *Incorrect Allocation Order* is relatively harmless, because it does not affect the overall election result, but only the evidence of how the election result was determined. In some countries already this might be considered an infringement of the law. Things become much more worrisome, when rounding creates an artificial tie situation affecting the last seat(s) to be awarded. In this case, the drawing of the lots may in fact the overall election result. This error is called *Incorrect Seat Allocation*.

To make our analysis precise, we need to distinguish between two n-way tie situations: We say an n-way tie between n quotients is *genuine*, if the quotients (before rounding) are all equal. In the case that the quotients (before rounding) are not equal, but they are equal after rounding, we speak of a *false n-way tie* situation. A genuine tie must be broken by drawing lots, whereas a false tie must not. For the following two definitions, we assume a false tie situation.

Error 1: Incorrect Allocation Order. In the case that the number of seats to be allocated exceeds the number of k quotients rounded to the same number, drawing lots may affect the order in which the seats are allocated, but it does not effect the overall election result. For a false tie, the probability p of allocating seats in the wrong order is

$$p = \frac{1}{k!}.$$

Error 2: Incorrect Seat Allocation. In the case that the number of quotients rounded to the same number exceeds the number of seats to be allocated, lots will have to be drawn, which means that seats may be allocated in error with non-negligible probability. More precisely, if there is a false tie between n rounded quotients and only $k(< n)$ seats are left to be allocated, the probability p that the result of seat allocation is correct result is precisely

$$p = \frac{1}{\binom{n}{k}}.$$

4   Case Study Denmark

In order to learn if this a real or just an academic problem, we describe a case study that we conducted in Denmark. We discuss the Danish legal framework in Sect. 4.1, empirical evidence that Errors 1 and 2 could have actually been encountered in Sect. 4.2, and a discussion of the implementation of Denmark's seat allocation system, in Sect. 4.3 where we demonstrate that the system actually rounds quotients.

4.1   Legal Framework

Danish election law[1] defines the rules for how mandates are to be distributed. The law distinguishes two kinds of seats, constituency seats *kredsmandater* and compensatory seats *tillægsmandater*. In this report, we focus mostly only compensatory seats, but our findings also apply to the calculation of constituency seats. We quote the relevant sections from the Danish Parliamentary Elections Act [3].

Allocation of Constituency Seats

§76. (1) The votes cast for each party in all nomination districts in a multi-member constituency shall be summed up. The votes cast for each individual candidate shall equally be summed up.

(2) Each number of votes appearing as a result of the summation, cf. subsection (1), shall be divided by 1 - 2 - 3 and so on until such number of divisions equivalent to the maximum number of seats expected to be allocated to the party or to the independent candidate has been performed. The party or the independent candidate having the highest resulting quotients shall be given the first seat in the multi-member constituency. The second highest quotient entails the second seat and so on and so forth, until all constituency seats in the multi-member constituency have been distributed among the parties and the independent candidates. If two or more quotients are of equal size, lots shall be drawn.

---

[1] LBK nr 416 af 12/05/2016.

Allocation of Compensatory Seats to Parties by Region

§78.(1) For each of the parties which are allocated compensatory seats according to section 77, the number of votes cast for the party in each of the three regions shall be computed.

(2) Each of these votes shall be divided by the figures 1 - 3 - 5 - 7 and so on. Next, a number of the largest quotients equivalent to the number of constituency seats obtained by the party in the region according to section 76 shall be omitted.

(3) The region and the party which subsequently has the largest quotient shall have the first compensatory seat. The region and the party which has the second largest quotient shall have the next compensatory seat and so on and so forth. Where a region or a party has obtained the number of compensatory seats it should have, cf. sections 10 and 77, the region or the party shall not be considered any further. The allocation continues for the other regions and the other parties until all compensatory seats have been distributed. If a party which has not received votes in all three regions cannot be allocated the compensatory seats to which the party is entitled by this distribution, these seats shall be allocated in advance to the party in the regions where votes have been cast in its favor.

This law text describes the social choice function to compute the seat allocation for the 135 constituency seats and 40 compensatory seats in the Danish Parliament, called *Folketinget*. We focus our attention on the allocation of compensatory seats, because the divisors become larger and the quotients smaller than those when allocating constituency seats. Denmark is divided into three regions, *Hovedstaden*, *Sjælland-Syddanmark*, and *Midtjylland-Nordjylland*.

The technique described in the law is a variant of d'Hondt, as described in Sect. 2 (see §10 (2), *den største brøks metode*). Constituency seats are assigned using divisors $1, 2, 3, \ldots$, and compensatory seats are allocated in a second step using divisors $1, 3, 5 \ldots$ In the case of a tie, lots shall be drawn. We want to emphasize, that neither the published versions of the largest remainder methods, nor the Danish election law permits that rounded versions of the quotients may be considered. This interpretations has been confirmed by the Danish Ministry.

4.2 Empirical Analysis

For our empirical analysis, the interesting step is 3. where the quotients are computed. Consider the seat allocation of compensatory seats 20 and 21 during Denmark's parliamentary election in 2007, as depicted in Fig. 1, which has been taken from [2, p. 17]. This election is relatively recent and it was chosen, because it demonstrates that Error 1 and 2 do actually arise in real elections. Both seats were awarded with a rounded quotient of 11,097. The seat 20 was awarded to *Det Konservative Folkeparti*, because

$$\frac{122063}{11} = 11,096.6363636$$

and seat 21 was awarded to *Venstre* because

$$\frac{366186}{33} = 11,096.5454545.$$

In Fig. 1, we have marked the important entries using boxes to help the reader identify these more easily.

If we were to use instead a seat allocation algorithm that rounds all quotients to the nearest whole number, these two quotients would round to 11,097 and

Tabel 7: Tillægsmandaternes fordeling på partier og landsdele den 13. november 2007

	A. Socialdemo-kratiet	B. Det Radikale Venstre	C. Det Konserva-tive Folkeparti	F. SF - Sociali-stisk Folke-parti	O. Dansk Folke-parti	V. Venstre, Dan-marks Libera-le Parti	Y. Ny Alliance	Ø. Enhedslisten
	(1)	(2)	(3)	(4)	(5)	(6)	(7)	(8)
Hovedstaden	**251.473**	**73.582**	**122.063**	**159.548**	**126.959**	**201.890**	**40.241**	**40.948**
1. kvot. ved divisor 1	-	-	-	-	-	-	2)40.241	-
2. kvot. ved divisor 3	-	-	-	-	-	-	14)13.414	12)13.649
3. kvot. ved divisor 5	-	10)14.716	-	-	-	-	8.048	8.190
4. kvot. ved divisor 7	-	10.512	5)17.438	-	-	-	5.749	5.850
5. kvot. ved divisor 9	-	8.176	13)13.563	-	-	-	4.471	4.550
6. kvot. ved divisor 11	-	6.689	20)11.097	-	17)11.542	-	3.658	3.723
7. kvot. ved divisor 13	-	5.660	9.389	-	9.766	-	3.095	3.150
8. kvot. ved divisor 15	-	4.905	8.138	26)10.637	8.464	-	2.683	2.730
9. kvot. ved divisor 17	-	4.328	7.180	9.385	7.468	-	2.367	2.409
10. kvot. ved divisor 19	-	3.873	6.424	8.397	6.682	27)10.626	2.118	2.155
11. kvot. ved divisor 21	-	3.504	5.813	7.598	6.046	9.614	1.916	1.950
12. kvot. ved divisor 23	23)10.934	3.199	5.307	6.937	5.520	8.778	1.750	1.780
Tillægsmandater	1	1	1	1	1	1	2	1
Sjælland-Syddanmark	**319.232**	**51.476**		**161.312**	**203.745**	**366.186**	**30.358**	**17.388**
1. kvot. ved divisor 1	-	1)51.476	-	-	-	-	3)30.358	6)17.388
2. kvot. ved divisor 3	-	8)17.159	-	-	-	-	34)10.119	5.796
3. kvot. ved divisor 5	-	33)10.295	-	-	-	-	6.072	3.478
4. kvot. ved divisor 7	-	7.354	-	-	-	-	4.337	2.484
5. kvot. ved divisor 9	-	5.720	11)13.653	-	-	-	3.373	1.932
6. kvot. ved divisor 11	-	4.680	19)11.170	-	-	-	2.760	1.581
7. kvot. ved divisor 13	-	3.960	9.452	-	-	-	2.335	1.338
8. kvot. ved divisor 15	-	3.432	8.192	24)10.754	-	-	2.024	1.159
9. kvot. ved divisor 17	-	3.028	7.228	9.489	-	-	1.786	1.023
10. kvot. ved divisor 19	-	2.709	6.467	8.490	25)10.723	-	1.598	915
11. kvot. ved divisor 21	-	2.451	5.851	7.682	39)9.702	-	1.446	828
12. kvot. ved divisor 23	-	2.238	5.342	7.014	8.858	-	1.320	756
13. kvot. ved divisor 25	-	2.059	4.915	6.452	8.150	-	1.214	696
14. kvot. ved divisor 27	-	1.907	4.551	5.975	7.546	-	1.124	644
15. kvot. ved divisor 29	-	1.775	4.237	5.562	7.026	-	1.047	600
16. kvot. ved divisor 31	32)10.298	1.661	3.964	5.204	6.572	-	979	561
17. kvot. ved divisor 33	9.674	1.560	3.723	4.888	6.174	21)11.097	920	527
18. kvot. ved divisor 35	9.121	1.471	3.511	4.609	5.821	28)10.462	867	497
19. kvot. ved divisor 37	8.628	1.391	3.321	4.360	5.507	38)9.897	820	470
Tillægsmandater	1	3	2	1	2	3	2	1
Midtjylland-Nordjylland	**310.332**	**52.103**	**114.468**	**130.115**	**148.828**	**340.396**	**26.696**	**16.646**
1. kvot. ved divisor 1	-	-	-	-	-	-	4)26.696	9)16.646
2. kvot. ved divisor 3	-	7)17.368	-	-	-	-	8.899	5.549
3. kvot. ved divisor 5	-	29)10.421	-	-	-	-	5.339	3.329
4. kvot. ved divisor 7	-	7.443	-	-	-	-	3.814	2.378
5. kvot. ved divisor 9	-	5.789	15)12.719	-	-	-	2.966	1.850
6. kvot. ved divisor 11	-	4.737	30)10.406	16)11.829	-	-	2.427	1.513
7. kvot. ved divisor 13	-	4.008	8.805	36)10.009	18)11.448	-	2.054	1.280
8. kvot. ved divisor 15	-	3.474	7.631	8.674	37)9.922	-	1.780	1.110
9. kvot. ved divisor 17	-	3.065	6.733	7.654	8.755	-	1.570	979
10. kvot. ved divisor 19	-	2.742	6.025	6.848	7.833	-	1.405	876
11. kvot. ved divisor 21	-	2.481	5.451	6.196	7.087	-	1.271	793
12. kvot. ved divisor 23	-	2.265	4.977	5.657	6.471	-	1.161	724
13. kvot. ved divisor 25	-	2.084	4.579	5.205	5.953	-	1.068	666
14. kvot. ved divisor 27	-	1.930	4.240	4.819	5.512	-	989	617
15. kvot. ved divisor 29	-	1.797	3.947	4.487	5.132	-	921	574
16. kvot. ved divisor 31	35)10.011	1.681	3.693	4.197	4.801	22)10.981	861	537
17. kvot. ved divisor 33	40)9.404	1.579	3.469	3.943	4.510	31)10.315	809	504
Tillægsmandater	2	2	2	2	2	2	1	1

Fig. 1. Compensatory seat allocation.

consequently seat 20 and seat 21 can only be allocated by drawing lots. In this situation, the following two outcomes are equally likely.

1. Seat 20 will be allocated to *Det Konservative Folkeparti* and seat 21 to *Venstre*.
2. Seat 20 will be allocated to *Venstre* and seat 21 to *Det Konservative Folkeparti.*

Both outcomes are correct, as we have discussed in Sect. 2, however Denmark's law does regard—strictly speaking—only the first outcome as correct and the second outcome as an instance of Error 1. Evidently, the order in which the seats were assigned was correct, perhaps because it was computed with an earlier version of seat allocation system and not the one we will discuss below.

Regarding Error 2, we notice that the last compensatory seat (Seat 40) was awarded with a quotient of exactly 9404 to the *Socialdemokratiet*. The next highest quotient in Fig. 1 is 9,389 but what cannot be seen in the table is that there are actually two entries: One for region *Hovedstaden*, *Det Konservative Folkeparti*, divisor 13,

$$\frac{122063}{13} = 9389.46153846$$

and the other for region *Sjælland-Syddanmark*, *Venstre*, divisor 39

$$\frac{366186}{39} = 9389.38461538.$$

This means that in the hypothetical situation where the Danish Parliament had 41 compensatory seats, a rounding seat allocation system might have assigned the 41st seat to the wrong party with a probability of 50%, i.e. to *Venstre* instead of *Det Konservative Folkeparti.*

The remaining question is, of course, how big of a problem Error 1 and Error 2 in practice really are. A statistical analysis proves difficult, in part because of the many random variables that need to be considered. Therefore we resort to a Monte-Carlo experiment and develop an election simulator to compute the probabilities of false n-way ties. In our experiment, where we work with 8 parties with tallies chosen at random between 20,000 and 400,000 votes, a situation, which pretty accurately describes the parameters of a Danish election. We then run the simulator 1,000,000 times where we compute a d'Hondt table with 50 rows (which corresponds to a highest divisor of 101).

Error 1: The following table depicts the expected value of n-way ties occurring in a single d'Hondt table.

$n =$	1	2	3	4
E(false n-way tie)	173.17545	0.904989	0.0048	0.000022

This means that in 9 of 10 d'Hondt tables, there will be in average one false 2-way tie that is decided by drawing lots. However, our experiment also shows that the risk of an Error 1 in the cases of false 3- and 4-way ties are extremely rare. Recall, that Error 1 will not change the election result but only the order in which seats are assigned.

Error 2: In the same statistical experiment, we look at the 175th seat being chosen. The following table depicts the number of false n-way ties observed.

$n =$	1	2	3	4
# observations	984,089	15,766	144	1

This means, that the probability of a false 2-way tie situation is roughly 1.5%, which means that in one out of 66 elections, the last seat will be awarded with drawing lots.

In summary, rounding while computing the d'Hondt and Sainte-Laguë tables should be considered harmful. We have demonstrated that there is a non-negligible chance that seats are being allocated in the wrong order and/or to the wrong party.

4.3   Implementation

The software for Denmark's Seat Allocation System (DSAS) has been implemented by Statistics Denmark (*Danmarks Statistik*), in a programming language called PL/SQL (part of the official ORACLE database distribution) used to program stored procedures. DSAS implements the problematic rounding version of the seat allocation algorithm outlined in the previous section. In a nutshell, the implementation rounds to the nearest number and then generate randomly the digits after the comma as a tie breaker. For the above example, instead of computing the quotients precisely, DSAS rounds and randomly generates after comma digits.

Fraction	Correct result	DSAS result
$\frac{122063}{11}$	$11,096.6363636$	$11,096 + r_1$
$\frac{366186}{33}$	$11,096.5454545$	$11,096 + r_2$

where $r_1, r_2 \in [0, 1)$ randomly chosen.

The problematic code can be found in the file `packages.sql`, dated 16. September 2013, 16:12. The three procedures that support our claim regarding the allocation of compensatory seats are depicted in Fig. 2 that describes how quotients for compensatory seats are computed, Fig. 3 that illustrates how the quotients are introduced into the main table, and Fig. 4 that demonstrates how the quotients are ordered for further computation. The program for allocating the constituency seats is very similar, suffers from the same rounding problem, and can be found elsewhere in this file.

```
23158    for I in 1 .. V_antal_divisioner loop
23159      if I = 1 then
23160        V_divisor := 1;
23161      else
23162        V_divisor := V_divisor + 2;
23163      end if;
23164
23165      select Obj_tillaegsmandater_landsdele
                        (Landsdel_id, Parti_id, Antal_stemmer,
                         Antal_kredsmandater, Kvotient_nr, Kvotient, Random_nr)
23166        bulk collect into Temptab
23167        from (select Landsdel_id,
23168                     Parti_id,
23169                     Antal_stemmer,
23170                     Antal_kredsmandater,
23171                     V_divisor Kvotient_nr,
23172                     round (Antal_stemmer / V_divisor) Kvotient,
23173                     dbms_random.Normal Random_nr
23174                from table (P_col_tillaegsman_landsdele));
23175
23176      Insert_tillaeg_landsdel_kvot (Temptab,
23177                                     P_log_bruger_in,
23178                                     P_term_bruger_in,
23179                                     P_valg_id_in,
23180                                     P_valgfase_in,
23181                                     P_debug_in,
23182                                     P_log_id_in);
23183    end loop;
```

Fig. 2. Procedure `Tillaeg_landsdel_dankvot_ins`

Tillaeg_landsdel_dankvot_ins. In Fig. 2, the loop starting in line 23158 ranges over all possible divisors, starting from 1 until the maximal number stored in variable V_antal_divisioner. The body of the loop consists of two steps. In the first step, a temporary table TempTab is defined that stores all possible quotients (in no particular order). In lines 23165–23174 it is determined what precisely is stored in TempTab. The two critical lines here are 23172 and 23173. In the former DSAS uses SQL's rounding function to compute round (Antal_stemmer/V_divisor), which computes the quotient rounded to the nearest whole number. The string Kvotient tells the ORACLE database engine to name the column Kvotient. In the latter DSAS stores a random value using Oracle's random generator in a column called Random_nr as a tie breaker. How precisely Oracle's random generator was seeded, could not be determined. As we will see below, if two quotients are compared and if the Kvotient part is equal, the Random_nr will determine which of the two is ranked higher. In the second step, after computing all quotients, DSAS calls a function to copy the quotients from TempTab into the right table using a stored procedure called

```
23384   procedure Insert_tillaeg_landsdel_kvot (
...
23404      insert into Tillaeg_man_land_kvotienter (Landsdel_id,
23405                                               Parti_id,
23406                                               Antal_kredsmandater,
23407                                               Tmk_land_kvotientnr,
23408                                               Tmk_land_kvotient,
23409                                               Tmk_random_nr,
23410                                               Valgfase_kode,
23411                                               Tmk_koersel_id,
23412                                               Valg_id)
23413      select Landsdel_id,
23414             Parti_id,
23415             Antal_kredsmandater,
23416             Kvotient_nr,
23417             Kvotient,
23418             Random_nr,
23419             P_valgfase,
23420             P_log_id_in,
23421             P_valg_id_in
23422          from table (P_col_tillaegsman_landsdele);
```

Fig. 3. Procedure Insert_tillaeg_landsdel_kvot

Insert_tillaeg_landsdel_kvot (see line 23176), which we discuss next. Note that the first argument to this method is TempTab.

Insert_tillaeg_landsdel_kvot. Figure 3 depicts a procedure that simply reads all tuples from the table referred to by first argument, i.e. TempTab. The destination table is Tillaeg_man_land_kvotienter, where the attributes for the table are renamed to Tmk_land_kvotient (line 23408) and Tmk_random_nr (line 23409), respectively.

The tuples in the table Tillaeg_man_land_kvotienter are stored in no particular order.

Tillaeg_landsdel_hentpotkvot. A fragment of the procedure that accesses and sorts the table Tillaeg_man_land_kvotienter is depicted in Fig. 4. It illustrate how the quotients and random numbers are used for further computation (which we will not discuss here).

All tuples from table Tillaeg_man_land_kvotienter are ordered lexicographically, first by the rounded quotient Tmk_land_kvotient (line 23617) and the random number Tmk_random_nr (line 23618), both in descending order.

```
23583    select Obj_tillaeg_ldel_til_kvvalg (Tmk_land_id, Landsdel_id,
                                Parti_id, Antal_kredsmandater, Kvotient, Random_nr)
23584      bulk collect into P_col_tillaeg_ldel_til_kvvalg
23585      from (select   Tmk_land_id,
23586                     Landsdel_id,
23587                     Parti_id,
23588                     Antal_kredsmandater,
23589                     Tmk_land_kvotient Kvotient,
23590                     Tmk_random_nr Random_nr
23591              from (select Tmk_land_id,
23592                           Landsdel_id,
23593                           Parti_id,
23594                           Antal_kredsmandater,
23595                           Tmk_land_kvotient,
23596                           Tmk_random_nr,
23597                           row_number ()
23598                           over (partition by Landsdel_id, Parti_id
23599                                 order by Tmk_land_kvotient desc)
23600                             Nr_starttillaeg
23601                    from (select Tmk_land_id,
23602                                 Landsdel_id,
23603                                 Parti_id,
23604                                 Antal_kredsmandater,
23605                                 Tmk_land_kvotient,
23606                                 Tmk_random_nr
23607                          from (select Tmk_land_id,
23608                                       Landsdel_id,
23609                                       Parti_id,
23610                                       Antal_kredsmandater,
23611                                       Tmk_land_kvotient,
23612                                       Tmk_random_nr
23613                                from Tillaeg_man_land_kvotienter
23614                                where    Valg_id = P_valg_id_in
23615                                   and Valgfase_kode = P_valgfase_in)))
23616                where Nr_starttillaeg > Antal_kredsmandater
23617          order by Tmk_land_kvotient desc,
23618                   Tmk_random_nr desc);
```

Fig. 4. Procedure `Tillaeg_landsdel_hentpotkvot`

5 Responsible Disclosure

Denmark has been using a computer program to compute the seat allocations of the Danish Parliament since for at least two decades [6]. The new version of DSAS (studied in this paper) was introduced only after 2007. We identified the rounding problem in DSAS in 2016 and informed the Ministry immediately about our findings. To the best of our knowledge the software as been updated, and the rounding problem has been addressed and fixed.

6 Conclusion

We have shown, that countries that use d'Hondt or Sainte-Laguë methods for computing the final seat allocation of parliament should be aware that round-ing quotients in the table may lead to Error 1, *Incorrect Allocation Order*, or even worse, Error 2, *Incorrect Seat Allocation*. We have shown that erroneously rounding can impact an election outcome and that this observation is not just hypothetical, but can with a non-zero probability actually impact real elections. We have also shown that accidental rounding is difficult to detect, after all, on the face of it, how much damage could rounding actually do?

Social choice experts agree that rounding quotients when implementing d'Hondt or Sainte-Laguë methods is a mistake. However, it the election law and relevant election regulations that define the exact rules. The law defines the requirements for seat allocation systems, and if the law requires to round two digits then so be it. The Danish law does is not specific when it comes to rounding, and therefore, it should be the mathematical definition of the voting method that prevails.

Therefore, to implement a d'Hondt or Sainte-Laguë voting rule correctly is easy: One must not store the quotient but instead store both numerator (the `Antal_stemmer`) and denominator (the `V_divisor`) in two different fields. Using the following simple rule of arithmetic assuming $b, d \neq 0$

$$\frac{a}{b} < \frac{c}{d} \quad \text{if and only if} \quad a \cdot d < c \cdot b,$$

it is possible to implement the seat allocation for both constituency and compensatory seats without fractions and rounding guaranteeing that the correct seat allocation is computed.

Acknowledgments. The author would like to thank the Danish Ministry for Economic Affairs and the Interior and Statistics Denmark for their support and cooperation. The author would also like to thank Prof. Jørgen Elklit for comments on earlier drafts of this paper.

References

1. Benoit, K.: Which electoral formula is the most proportional? A new look with new evidence. Polit. Anal. **8**(4), 381–388 (2000)
2. Statistik, D.: Folketingsvalget den 13. Statistiske Efterretninger, 27 November 2007
3. Folketing (parliamentary) elections act. Online Report (2014). (Translated: Consolidated Act No. 369 of 10 April 2014)
4. Goré, R., Lebedeva, E.: Simulating STV hand-counting by computers considered harmful: A.C.T. In: Proceedings of Electronic Voting - First International Joint Conference, E-Vote-ID 2016, Bregenz, Austria, 18–21 October 2016, pp. 144–163 (2016)
5. Lijphart, A., Grofman, B.: Degrees of proportionality of proportional representation formulas. In: Electoral Laws and Their Political Consequences, pp. 170–179. Agathon Press (2003)
6. Pedersen, R.: Unix-veteran kender valgresultatet før alle andre. Computerworld, 13 November 2007
7. Stark, P.B., Teague, V.: Verifiable european elections: Risk-limiting audits for D'Hondt and its relatives. USENIX Journal of Election Technology and Systems (JETS) **1**, 18–39 (2014)

Author Index

Blom, Michelle 1, 17
Budd, Brian 67

Cardillo, Anthony 35

Dubuis, Eric 84
Duenas-Cid, David 117

Essex, Aleksander 35

Gabel, Chelsea 67
Ghale, Milad K. 51
Goodman, Nicole 67
Goré, Rajeev 51

Haenni, Rolf 84

Jamroga, Wojciech 100

Knapik, Michal 100
Koenig, Reto E. 84
Koitmae, Arne 117
Krimmer, Robert 117
Krips, Kristjan 132

Krivonosova, Iuliia 117
Kurpiewski, Damian 100

Lindeman, Mark 174
Locher, Philipp 84
Loeber, Leontine 146

McBurnett, Neal 174

Omosele, Felix Oludare 160
Ottoboni, Kellie 174

Pattinson, Dirk 51

Schürmann, Carsten 189
Stark, Philip B. 174
Stuckey, Peter J. 1, 17

Teague, Vanessa J. 1, 17
Tiwari, Mukesh 51

Värv, Sebastian 132
Vinkel, Priit 117

Willemson, Jan 132

Author Index

Printed in the United States
By Bookmasters